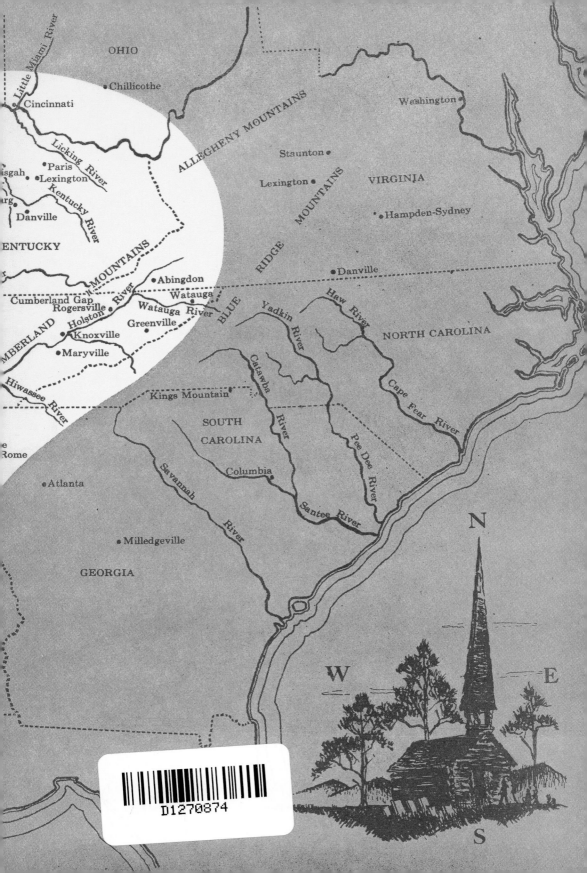

OHIO

Little Miami River

• Chillicothe

• Cincinnati

Licking River

isgah
• Paris
• Lexington

arg.
Kentucky River

• Danville

ENTUCKY

MOUNTAINS

ALLEGHENY MOUNTAINS

Washington •

Staunton •

Lexington •

VIRGINIA

• Hampden-Sydney

MOUNTAINS

RIDGE

Danville •

• Abingdon

Cumberland Gap

Rogersville • • Watauga

River

Watauga River

Holston

Greenville •

BLUE

Yadkin River

Haw River

NORTH CAROLINA

MBERLAND

• Knoxville

• Maryville

Hiwassee River

Kings Mountain

Catawba

River

SOUTH
CAROLINA

Pee Dee River

Cape Fear River

e
Rome

• Atlanta

Columbia •

Santee River

Savannah

River

• Milledgeville

GEORGIA

N

W

E

S

The close of the American Revolution found the Presbyterian Church the best organized and strongest Protestant group in America. It was a frontier church and a missionary church. Across the Appalachians lay a vast new land to be won from the wilderness. The Scotch-Irish pioneers led the way. In this new frontier that stretched from the mountains to the basin of the wide Mississippi, the Presbyterians were to be divided by problems arising from new conditions, and were to lose the following of the masses to the more emotional denominations. Although they would not change their methods to win the rude West for their cause, the influence of their churches, their schools, and their standard of conduct led the region from a raw wilderness to a stable and ordered society.

This book is a fully documented account of the events of this era—of the Great Revival, of missionary work among the Indians, of the development of education, and of the church's stand on the slavery question. The ministers, churches, and religious life of the period are depicted in detail. In the appendix is printed the actual minutes of the session of the first Presbyterian church in Mississippi.

A valuable contribution to the history of America, a challenge to today's church members in the face of a changing environment, this volume paints a vivid picture of the struggles of religion in the Old Southwest.

THE PRESBYTERIAN CHURCH IN
THE OLD SOUTHWEST
1778-1838

THE AUTHOR

WALTER BROWNLOW POSEY is a historian noted
for his keen interest in the early days of the
lower Mississippi Valley region. His earlier
study, *The Development of Methodism in the
Old Southwest, 1783–1824,* is a notable contribution to our knowledge of this important phase
of American history.

Dr. Posey began his teaching career twenty-nine
years ago at Cumberland University. He is now
head of the department of history at Agnes
Scott College and professor of history at Emory
University, Atlanta, Georgia. Dr. Posey has
taught at Vanderbilt University, Tulane University, the University of Alabama, the University of Hawaii, and the Shrivenham American
University of England. Dr. Posey holds the
Ph.B. degree from the University of Chicago
and M.A. and Ph.D. degrees from Vanderbilt
University.

THE
PRESBYTERIAN CHURCH
IN THE
OLD SOUTHWEST

1778-1838

by

WALTER BROWNLOW POSEY

JOHN KNOX PRESS
RICHMOND, VIRGINIA
1952

PRINTED IN THE UNITED STATES OF AMERICA
2025-(20)—4866

To

MARGARET AND BLYTHE

PREFACE

The generous reception given to an early book of mine, *The Development of Methodism in the Old Southwest, 1783-1824,* has encouraged me to write this companion volume on the early Presbyterian Church in the same area. This volume restates the importance and influence of a church as a strong social factor in the development of a new land. The reader will readily agree that there is a common denominator in these studies, even though the statements consist of different terms. A further expansion of the investigation, of course, will include the Baptist Church. Research on this denomination has already been completed, and it is my plan to tell at a later date the contribution of the third democratic church to the development of the area under investigation.

In several respects the Presbyterian Church was admirably equipped to provide a satisfactory religious life for the frontier people, but it failed, if judged by numbers alone, in comparison with the more popular Methodist and Baptist churches. On the other hand, Presbyterian interest in education created a literate church membership that stood for religion, virtue, and knowledge—intrinsic values with which the church enriched the rough and ready frontiersmen and thereby gave tone and stability to Western life.

Much of the material used in the writing of this book is widely scattered in many small libraries, but the bulk of the valuable history of local churches is concentrated in the excellent collections of the Historical Foundation of the Presbyterian and Reformed Churches, Montreat, North Carolina, and in the Presbyterian Historical Society, Philadelphia. A research grant from Vanderbilt University and a Carnegie grant-in-aid have provided financial assistance for the writing of this study. I am further indebted to the University Center in Georgia for a generous research grant which aided in the publication.

Three chapters have been published previously in the *Journal of Southern History,* the *Journal of Mississippi History,* and the *Journal of the Presbyterian Historical Society*. To the editors of these journals appreciative acknowledgment is made for the permission of republication. I am under a debt of gratitude to two of my colleagues at Agnes Scott College, George P. Hayes and Paul L. Garber, who read and corrected the manuscript. From its inception to its close my wife, Margaret Grisham Posey, has been my constant guide, helpful critic, and valuable aid. Complete fairness would demand the inclusion of her name on the title page.

WALTER BROWNLOW POSEY

CONTENTS

I. The Presbyterians Reach Tennessee and Kentucky   11

II. The Presbyterians and the Camp Meetings . . . 22

III. A Sequel to the Revivals 30

IV. The Presbyterian Minister 39

V. Presbyterian Interest in Education 49

VI. The Presbyterian Church Among the Indians . . 61

VII. The Slavery Question 73

VIII. The Negro Slave in the Presbyterian Church . . 83

IX. The Church Elevates Western Morals 93

X. The Local Church: Its Physical Structure and Social Services 102

XI. Expansion and Division 111

XII. In Retrospect 124

Appendix. The First Session Book of the Oldest Presbyterian Church in Mississippi 127

Notes 139

Index 187

I

THE PRESBYTERIANS
REACH TENNESSEE AND KENTUCKY

IN ORDER TO PROMOTE loyalty in rebellious Ireland, Elizabeth of England conceived the idea of planting colonies of Protestants in that country. This plan was brought to fruition by James I, who settled Ulster chiefly with Scotch Lowlanders, many Englishmen, and a small number of Highlanders. Between the inauguration of the Ulster Plantation and the persecution of the Ulstermen by Charles I and Charles II, there had emerged "a type of man who was high-principled and narrow, strong and violent, as tenacious of his own rights as he was blind often to the rights of others, acquisitive yet self-sacrificing, but most of all fearless, confident of his own power, determined to have and to hold." [1] Twice expatriated, first from Scotland and later from Ireland, these strong and determined people found in America the land of hope.

In a large measure Presbyterianism in the Old Southwest owes its origin to the Scotch-Irish, whose first settlement in America was planted on the eastern shore of Maryland sometime after 1649,[2] when Lord Baltimore made an attractive offer to adventurers and planters who would bring in settlers. Small groups of Scotch-Irish arrived in Maryland, East Jersey, and the Carolinas during the quarter of a century between the Restoration and the Revolution in England.[3] The French Huguenots had established a distinctively Presbyterian church in South Carolina by 1686; by 1710 there were five Presbyterian churches in the colony.[4] With the aid of some New England Puritans, a presbytery was organized in 1722 or 1723. In the same decade several settlements of Scotch-Irish were made near Philadelphia,[5] and in another ten years they had begun moving southward into the Shenandoah Valley of Virginia and the Yadkin Valley of North Carolina. Here these folk met other Scottish people who, leaving Charleston and pushing south and west, were in quest of good lands.[6] Stubbornly determined to achieve their goals, they

11

rapidly seized unoccupied lands and refused to pay quitrents.[7] Forming settlements in all of the thirteen colonies, they numbered by the opening of the American Revolution five hundred communities— approximately half of which were in the Southern colonies.[8] At the end of the war, when the opportunity arrived to share in winning a permanent freedom from economic, political, and religious restriction, "the Presbyterians and Congregationalists combined had the ecclesiastical control of the American colonies." [9]

Towering above his Presbyterian contemporaries stood Francis Makemie, the first Presbyterian appointed in the regular form as a minister to the American colonies. Born of Scottish parents in Ulster and educated in Glasgow, he was ordained by the Presbytery of Laggan in Ireland and sent to America in 1683. Quickly he organized churches in Maryland and Virginia. Preaching over a territory from South Carolina to New York, he suffered many hardships. In 1704 he returned to Scotland and Ireland to beg help for the work in America. By this time he was the acknowledged leader of a small group of Presbyterian and Puritan ministers [10] who met in Philadelphia in 1705 or 1706 and organized the first presbytery in America.[11] Almost immediately the presbytery took note of the westward movement of population and adopted in 1707 a resolution to supply "desolate places" with ministers.[12]

The first Presbyterian minister to settle in the western portion of Virginia was John Craig, a native of Ireland, who had been educated at the University of Edinburgh. In 1740 Craig began a long pastorate in Augusta County near the present town of Staunton.[13] Here in a region threatened by Indian raids Craig encouraged his people to attend church with their guns at their sides and sentries on watch.[14] In 1746 John Blair, a Scot born in Ireland, moved from Pennsylvania to Rockbridge County, Virginia, where he organized the congregations of Timber Ridge, New Providence, and New Monmouth. Seven years later John Brown, a Scot from North Ireland and a graduate of Princeton College, succeeded to the pastorates at Timber Ridge and New Providence.[15] A large number of people signing a call for Brown pled, "Our Sabbaths [are] wasted in melancholy Silence at home, or sadly broken and profaned, by the more thoughtless amongst us; Our Hearts and Hands discouraged & our Spirits broken with our Mournful Condition." [16] David Rice, born in Virginia and educated at Princeton, became in 1767 minister to a territory near the foot of the Peaks of Otter, two mountains in Bedford County, Virginia. After the American Revolutionary War he moved to Kentucky, and his activities there earned for him the title "Father of Western Presbyterianism." [17]

About the same time that Presbyterians were pushing into western Virginia, they were also planting communities in the frontier sections of North Carolina. As early as 1740, scattered families were found on the Hico, Eno, Haw, and Catawba rivers. Into the region between the Catawba and the Yadkin rivers many people were coming from north Ireland by the way of Pennsylvania and Virginia, and Presbyterian Highlanders were settling along the Cape Fear River.[18] Throughout the western half of Virginia, North Carolina, and South Carolina Hugh McAden preached. Graduating from Princeton in 1753, he was two years later in North Carolina, where there were some Presbyterian meetinghouses. He went on a missionary tour to the Catawba Indians and then into northwestern South Carolina, where lived an old man who had once complained to the governor of the colony that he "had never seen a shirt, been in a fair, heard a sermon or seen a minister." McAden was not the first preacher in these parts, however, for the governor had earlier sent a minister there.[19]

Members and ministers of the Presbyterian Church were active and prominent in supporting the revolutionary cause of the American colonies, in securing colonial liberties, and in forming a constitution for the new government.[20] In January 1775 the Scotch-Irish in Virginia met in a council near Abingdon and adopted an address to the delegates of Virginia. In bold and emphatic statements they declared: "We are deliberately and resolutely determined never to surrender any of our inestimable privileges to any power upon earth but at the expense of our lives. These are our real though unpolished sentiments of liberty and loyalty, and in them we are resolved to live and die." [21] The synod which met at Philadelphia, May 17, 1775, has been said to be the first body "to declare itself in favor of open resistance and to encourage and counsel their people, who were then ready to take up arms." Of the fifty-six signers of the Declaration of Independence, one writer claims to recognize at least fifteen as having been of Scotch-Irish or Huguenot ancestry.[22] John Witherspoon, the renowned Presbyterian clergyman and president of Princeton College, was the only minister to sign the immortal document.[23]

In addition he signed the Articles of Confederation and worked actively on the finance committee for the newly established government.[24]

When the battle area in the Revolution was shifted in the main to the South, the Scotch-Irish became intensely active in the conflict. Gideon Blackburn,[25] pioneer Presbyterian minister of the Watauga settlements in east Tennessee, met an assemblage of about one thousand mounted riflemen from the Watauga and Holston communities on September 26, 1780, preparatory to the decisive battle which followed at King's Mountain on October 7. Tradition claims that he offered a prayer closing with the Biblical quotation, "The sword of the Lord and of Gideon," to which the soldiers, leaning on their rifles, responded, "The sword of the Lord and of our Gideons!"[26] From Presbyterian communities in the Carolinas, Virginia, Tennessee, and Georgia came many of the soldiers who destroyed Ferguson's army and brought collapse to the plans of Cornwallis.[27] Washington so completely believed in the strength and fortitude of the Scotch-Irish element in the West that he once declared that "if all his plans became overturned and but a single standard was left, he would plant it upon the Blue Ridge, and making that his Thermopylae would rally around him the patriots of the Valley and there lay the foundations of a new republic."[28]

Although hundreds of members were killed in the war and some fifty meetinghouses were burned,[29] the Presbyterian Church as a whole emerged from the conflict in good condition. Its organization was intact, its people were exultant over victory, and its determination to grow and expand was strong. Perhaps no other church gained a greater benefit from the successful prosecution of the war.[30] Of all the churches in the South during the Revolution, only the Presbyterian denomination maintained "a vigorous life."[31] When the Constitutional Convention secured a quorum in Philadelphia on May 25, 1787, the members of the Presbyterian synod, meeting in the same city only four blocks away, were debating the form of government for a church which sought to function on a national basis. Nine of the fifty-five men at the Constitutional Convention were Princeton graduates,[32] and it is no wonder that the fathers of the Constitution were impressed with the "compact, comprehensive and liberal system" of Presbyterian government.[33] This coincidence ex-

14

plains "a certain vague resemblance" between the Constitution of the United States and the Constitution of the Presbyterian Church.[34]

It is indeed singular that few revisions in the church constitution have been made since its conception. In order that the reader might better understand the history of the organization of the Presbyterian Church, its *modus operandi* should be examined at this point.

The Presbyterian Church received its name from the fact that it was governed by presbyters or elders. As the church developed, there soon were created two classes of elders—preaching elders and non-preaching or ruling elders. The church session, composed of the pastor and the ruling elders,[35] was the governing body of the church. The ruling elders (normally called elders), elected for life by the congregation, were primarily assistants "to aid the minister in the management of congregational affairs." The elders were required to profess faith in the Scriptures, accept the Westminster Confession, and approve of the government and discipline of the church.[36] Often the elder was not inferior [37] to the minister "in doctrinal and Scriptural knowledge." Sometimes as widely read, he was "as competent as his minister" to pass judgment on problems which came before synod and presbytery.[38] Although the individual church could issue a call to a particular minister chosen by the congregation, the presbytery decided whether or not there were valid reasons for withholding the call and ordering the session of the church to hold a new election. To his congregation the elected minister preached, administered the sacraments, directed the religious instruction, and exercised general supervision over the church.

Actually the session was a court with legislative, executive, and judicial powers and had authority to make necessary and appropriate rules and regulations, appoint commissioners or delegates, and receive new members. The session kept a close watch on the conduct of church members, reprimanded or excluded those who erred, and kept a register of marriages, baptisms, deaths, and removals.[39] The records reveal a variety of additional activities. One session bought four tin drinking cups; [40] another authorized the treasurer to lend money at eight percent; [41] a third session divided the church into three groups and over each placed an elder to visit the members.[42] Frequently the minutes of the session contained a commentary upon the state of the community. When two members died within a month from consumption, one clerk philosophically noted that the congregation had been preserved from cholera.[43] The clerk of another session wrote in his record: "The Church [is] shut and [its] members scattered by the prevailing disease."[44] The session records clearly divulge the church in operation. Often the records were badly kept; spelling was poor or exceedingly bad.[45] Twice each year the minutes were laid before the presbytery, which examined them and often ordered that some changes be made.[46] Mutilation to protect the accused from the prying eye of a reader was not rare.[47] On one occasion the clerk of the session left the church, took the records, and refused to return them or to permit them to be copied.[48]

In addition to the elders, the church elected deacons, whose work was essentially different from that of the elders. Answering a question from the Synod of West Tennessee concerning the function of the deacons, the General Assembly of 1833 replied that "Their duties are plainly made to consist in distributing the charities of the Church to which they belong, to the poor of that Church. Over charities collected for any other purpose than those specified, their office gives them no control. In addition to this, the temporalities of the Church generally may be committed to their care." [49] Perhaps the Tuscaloosa (Alabama) Presbytery made a fine distinction regarding the power of the deacons over the control of the church building. The presbytery believed that the duty of the session was to protect the church from desecration, but any injury resulting from the use of the building was a problem for the deacons to handle. The presbytery ruled that it was difficult to determine "the peculiar powers of their respective office," and, in case of doubt, the deacons should yield to the decision of the session.[50] The importance of the deacon varied greatly with the particular church.

In practice the presbytery, composed of one elder from each congregation and all the ministers in the district, was the most important governing body in the Presbyterian system.[51] Usually a presbytery met twice a year. The Tuscaloosa Presbytery was a typical one. Its meetings were held regularly in April and October; they began on the first Thursday and usually continued through Sunday.[52] A presbytery examined, licensed, and ordained candidates for the ministry, installed ministers over congregations, and provided for the supervision of all churches under its care. It served as a court of appeal from the session.[53] Sometimes a minister found it necessary to ask the presbytery to force a church to pay its pledge to him, as in the case of the Concord (Alabama) Church which was ordered "to take immediate and efficient measures to obtain and pay over the amount due." [54] Advice was often given on various subjects, such as that offered by the South Alabama Presbytery, which urged its members "to avoid all unnecessary traveling on the Lord's day." [55] The members of a presbytery varied from three to fifty or sixty, but at least three ministers were necessary to form any presbytery. In extent the presbyteries varied greatly; sometimes they were as much as two hundred miles in width. [56] On occasions boundaries were as undefined as those of the Elk Presbytery, which began at the mouth of Duck River, thence north to the top of the Tennessee Ridge, "thence eastwardly, westwardly and southwardly to undefined bounds." [57] As necessary and effective as presbyteries were, it was difficult for many of them to continue to meet from year to year. Often they met without a quorum and found it necessary to adjourn to a later date. [58] One presbytery, lacking a minister to constitute a quorum, pressed into service an out-of-state elder who happened to be present. [59]

Above the presbytery stood the synod, usually defined as "a convention of several Presbyteries, within a larger district." In 1804, however, the synod was made to "consist not of Presbyteries, but, as it ought, of Bishops and Elders." [60] Before the organization of the first General Assembly, the form of synodical government was highly significant since "It was the only instance in which the collective wisdom and discretion of the whole body was brought to bear continuously upon the affairs of an American church." [61] Containing all the ministers within its bounds and one elder from each session, the synod had the authority to hear and determine appeals from the presbyteries, to review records of the presbyteries, to erect new presbyteries, to unite or to divide those already erected, to force members, sessions, and presbyteries to conform to church rules, and to propose to the General Assembly such changes as seemed advisable. Unless called into special session, the synod met once a year and continued for about a week. Some synods had printed rules and a standing docket of business [62] which was followed throughout the meeting.

The highest judicatory in the Presbyterian Church was the General Assembly, whose first meeting in the United States was held in the year 1789. Required to meet at least once a year, the General Assembly was composed of delegates, called commissioners, from presbyteries originally in a ratio of one minister and one elder for every six ministers in the presbyteries. In 1819 the ratio was reduced to one for nine, and in 1826 one for twelve. The General Assembly had the power to review the records of the synods, to create new synods, to unite or to divide old ones, to reprove, warn or discipline, and to exercise general control over the entire church.[63]

Two decades before the first General Assembly was formed, settlers had moved beyond the Piedmont fall line—pioneers heading toward the Bluegrass region of Kentucky and the Nashville Basin in Tennessee.[64] In 1769 William Bean built his cabin on the Little Watauga River. Six years later Daniel Boone in the employ of Richard Henderson, the land speculator, led a company of settlers through the Cumberland Gap into Kentucky, where they established a settlement called Boonesborough. In the winter of 1779 and 1780 James Robertson made a settlement on the Cumberland River at the site of the present city of Nashville. Several attempts were made to establish self-governing states within Tennessee and Kentucky—such as Watauga (1772), Transylvania (1775), and Franklin (1784)—before frontier grievances were quieted. There was much similarity in the motives which prompted emigration from England to America and the motives which encouraged a tide of settlers to move rapidly from the Atlantic seaboard to the trans-Appalachian section. In both cases the dominating force was economic betterment. Those who plunged into the wilderness suffered much, but "whatever trials the men endured, the burden bore most heavily upon the women and children. The chance of being shot or scalped by Indians was hardly worth considering when compared with the certainty of malarial fever, or the strange disease called milk-sickness, or the still more depressing home-sickness, or the misery of nervous prostration, which wore out generation after generation of women and children on the frontiers, and left a tragedy in every log-cabin."[65]

Following these people over the mountains and supplying them with ministers was one of the most difficult tasks yet faced by the American churches. In 1773 two churches, Ebbing Spring and Sinking Spring, on the Holston River in southwestern Virginia[66] issued to Charles Cummings a call, signed by 136 people,[67] whereupon the forty-year-old preacher, a native of Ireland, accepted the offer of ninety pounds a year for his services and moved to a point not far from the boundary of Tennessee. Three years later Cummings accompanied an expedition led by William Christian against the Cherokees. As Cummings passed through the Holston settlements, he preached some of the first sermons ever heard in the forts and settlements in that section. For more than thirty years this hardy, fearless, pioneer preacher labored in southwestern Virginia and Tennessee.[68] On a Sabbath morning it was his custom to "put on his shot-pouch, shoulder his rifle, mount his dun stallion, and ride off to church." There he preached to an attentive congregation, every man of which held his rifle close to his side.[69]

In 1778 Samuel Doak, a graduate of Princeton, became the first minister to settle in Tennessee.[70] At first he preached in the present Sullivan County; two years later he moved to Washington County, bought a farm, and established the first literary institution in the Mississippi Valley.[71] This "stern, hard, God-fearing man became a most powerful influence for good throughout the whole formative period of the southwest."[72] To the aid of Doak, Hezekiah Balch[73] came from Mecklenburg County, North Carolina, and Samuel Houston and Samuel Carrick came from Liberty Hall Academy in Virginia. In 1785 the Abingdon Presbytery was erected and included the churches in the southwestern portion of Virginia and those on the Holston in east Tennessee.[74] Twelve years later there were twenty-six congregations within the eastern part of the present State of Tennessee.[75] Farther west in middle Tennessee, Thomas Craighead, a graduate of Princeton, reached Nashville in 1785 and settled at nearby Haysboro, where he preached for thirty years. The first Presbyterian congregation in Nashville was formed near the close of the century from a group of Scottish Seceders, to whom William Hume was sent by the Presbytery of Kirkaldy in Scotland.[76]

Probably the first Presbyterian minister to visit Kentucky was Terah Templin, a licentiate of the Hanover Presbytery in Virginia, who in 1780 spent a few months in Kentucky. Some three or four years later he moved to Kentucky, and there he lived the remainder of a long and valuable life.[77] In 1783 David Rice visited the region solely for the purpose of purchasing land for his large family. During his stay he preached on several occasions and received an urgent invitation to settle as a minister. A subscription paper, signed by three hundred persons living in Danville and nearby, led to his removal to Kentucky in October 1783. Greatly disturbed by the low level of religion, he spent a year gathering congregations which he organized into churches at Danville, Cave Run, and the Forks of Dick's River. In the following year Adam Rankin from Augusta County, Virginia, received and accepted a call from the Mount Zion Church, which was in the process of organization at Lexington.[78]

The population shift to Kentucky differed in few respects from that to Tennessee. Both sections were highly attractive to the Scotch-Irish settler who went West with enough money to buy good land.[79] Nature had been generous and had lavished the land with beauty and life-giving substances. The virgin soil produced bounteously, and the land-hungry pioneer was determined to annex in the briefest time as many acres as energy and ingenuity would permit.[80] Despite dangers from Indian fighting and the excitement from land speculating, the state of religion made some progress in Kentucky. By 1785 there were twelve Presbyterian congregations scattered through the central portion of Kentucky. In the following year four ministers—David Rice, Adam Rankin, Andrew McClure, James Crawford—and five ruling elders formed the Transylvania Presbytery,[81] which embraced all of Kentucky, the settlements on the Cumberland River in Tennessee, and a short time later the settlements on the Big and the Little Miami rivers in Ohio.[82] The presbytery grew rapidly, so that in 1799 it was divided into three presbyteries, Transylvania in central Kentucky, West Lexington in the territory east of the Kentucky River, and Washington in the region northeast of the Licking River and across the Ohio River. The three presbyteries combined had twenty-six ministers, and three years later they were formed into the Synod of Kentucky.[83]

By the turn of the century the Presbyterian Church had expanded to the north of Kentucky and to the south of Tennessee. A year after Cincinnati was laid out in 1789, Rice organized a church there and two years later erected a building.[84] A Presbyterian minister, John Evans Finley, preached in Kaskaskia about 1795.[85] In 1799 Joseph Bullen was sent by the Presbyterian Missionary Board of New York to visit the Chickasaw Indians in Mississippi. A year later he moved his family and settled about twenty miles northeast of Natchez.[86]

According to the census of 1800, Kentucky contained 220,955 persons while Tennessee had 105,602. There was considerable evidence of change and signs of progress. Frame houses were replacing log cabins, many of which had no floors. Glass could be found in windows instead of the wooden shutters that made a cabin dark and

20

gloomy. Food became more varied and acceptable. In spite of the harsh and grinding life people found time for intellectual interest. A few books circulated and kept alive the feeble light of education until schools began to dot the countryside. As a general rule the West was settled by people who were both irreligious and uneducated, yet there is evidence that much literacy existed among the earliest settlers in Kentucky and Tennessee.[87] Among the Scotch-Irish and German immigrants with recent contacts with continental cultures, the highly literate Presbyterian minister[88] seemed to have the necessary requisites to win a "complete ascendancy in religious thought and life" [89] among the frontier people. Later as the population was composed more predominantly of those born and reared on the frontier, the high rate of literacy fell and with it fell the advantages possessed by the Presbyterian Church over the Methodist and Baptist churches, whose uneducated preachers "proclaimed a passionate gospel of hell-fire and salvation that moved the hardest drinkers, boldest fighters, and meanest sinners of the hinterland to repentance, periodically at any rate." [90]

When large quantities of land were opened to settlers, the frontier interest in wealth-getting tended to increase.[91] General worldliness and desecration of the Sabbath indicated the low ebb of religion. Naturally, if unfortunately, religion was not a matter of extreme moment. Quarreling, fighting, swearing, and drinking consumed much of the people's time.[92] Efforts to preach and convert were often thwarted by the "spirit of avarice." [93] In its pastoral letter of 1789 the General Assembly "with pain and fearful apprehension" perceived that "profligacy and corruption of the public morals have advanced with a progress proportioned to our declension in religion. Profaneness, pride, luxury, injustice, intemperance, lewdness, and every species of debauchery and loose indulgence abound." With "a deep concern" the Assembly further feared "that the eternal God has a controversy with our nation, and is about to visit us in his sore displeasure."[94]

Only some great, soul-shaking experience promised to turn men's attention away from land and its material wealth to the church and its spiritual wealth. In Logan County, Kentucky, James McGready sensed the extent of prevailing evil and bound his congregation to pray every Saturday night and Sunday morning and all day on the third Saturday of each month for Pentecost, repentance, and redemption.[95] The Great Revival period was in preparation.

II

THE PRESBYTERIANS
AND THE CAMP MEETINGS

IN THE PERIOD following the American Revolutionary War most of the colonists settled into a comfortable attitude toward religion. Relaxed after the strain of fighting, the new Americans enjoyed the security which a victor feels, and they turned their attention to material affairs. Some were affected by the disturbing aftermath of war—immorality and infidelity; others, sympathizing with the French Revolution, accepted some beliefs which were not in accord with a conventional religion. Among the seacoast communities spiritual coldness was so general and so definite that all denominations were greatly alarmed.[1] Virgin lands beyond the Appalachians beckoned to those people who desired adventures or a fresh life in a new section. Reports of cheap, fertile lands lured Presbyterian families from their homesteads in the East. Many Presbyterian ministers were among the earliest immigrants to Kentucky and Tennessee,[2] but the number was too few to meet the demands of a rapidly growing population.[3] Before the turn of the nineteenth century it was quite evident to the Presbyterian Church that additional preachers were needed in the West, for other denominations were giving better religious care to the widely scattered people. Homes and churches were separated by great distances; months often passed without a family seeing a new face. Greed for acres was a sustaining force in a barren existence; both clergy and laymen grew so concerned with "amassing a fortune in land" that they left little time for "the spirit of the gospel."[4] James Smith, a wealthy preacher in the Republican Methodist Church making a trip from Virginia to Kentucky in 1795, was much disturbed over the region where "pride and profaneness" had led to "great decay of true and vital religion."[5] Two years later Bishop Asbury of the Methodist Church visited east Tennessee and, readily sensing the lack of interest in religion, wrote in his diary: "When I reflect that not one in a hundred came here to get religion; but rather to get plenty of good land, I think it will be well if some or many do not eventually lose their souls." [6]

This enthusiasm for greed could not long continue, and eventually the social nature of man would cry for nourishment. The frontiersman would become an easy mark for any new type of religious appeal that came his way.

The General Assembly of 1798, disturbed by the condition of the West, appointed a committee to inquire into the religious state of the frontier and to make plans for missions to be sent there.[7] Despite the apparent strength of the Presbyterian Church, there were several vulnerable points in its program. In sharp contrast to the procedure in the Methodist and Baptist churches, the Presbyterian ministers did little itinerating but remained close to their own churches.[8] In fact, they were seeking to hold and attract only Presbyterians and had little interest in proselyting other sects.[9] Furthermore, the Calvinistic doctrine was too cold and unpalatable for frontiersmen with many deep-seated ideas of liberty in all phases of life. To them there was a grave inconsistency in the personal responsibility for the soul and the doctrine of foreordination and unconditional election. Calvinism necessarily needed to be adjusted to fit the demands of the Westerners, or the denominations with more emphasis on evangelical creeds would gather in most of the converts. It is to be admitted that, as a type, the Presbyterian minister had become static [10] and needed the inspiration that could be supplied by a genuine firebrand of the revivalistic type.

Into the region came the force that changed and revitalized Western life; this force was supplied by James McGready, a Presbyterian minister in Logan County, Kentucky. McGready was born in Pennsylvania, had lived most of his youth in North Carolina, and had returned to Pennsylvania for an education. When he was licensed to preach by Redstone Presbytery in 1788, he was assigned to work in North Carolina.[11] On his way there he spent some time at Hampden-Sydney College,[12] where a religious revival had taken hold of the student body. Finding religion at low ebb in North Carolina, McGready resorted to the revivalistic methods he had so recently observed, and achieved such amazing results that he was accused of "running people distracted." In 1796 he received an invitation from Presbyterian families in Logan County, Kentucky, and accepted the charge of three churches there—Gasper River, Muddy River, and Red

23

River. In less than a year thereafter in this community a religious awakening was in evidence, which within three years completely modified and transformed the spiritual life of Kentucky and Tennessee.[13]

A spark had fallen among the tinder: at a revival meeting in May 1797 a woman "was struck with deep conviction, and in a few days was filled with joy and peace in believing." [14] The awakening had begun in Kentucky and through the years 1798 and 1799 spread rapidly. Pinched spirits and starved souls found relief through the wondrous ways of the revivals. To a four-day meeting held at McGready's church at Gasper River in July 1800, crowds came from such distances that it was necessary to provide some local accommodation for them. The suggestion of camping at the meeting ground was accepted; thus the "camp meeting" came into existence.[15]

Probably McGready would have accomplished little as a leader of the camp meetings had he and his fellow workers not preached a modified form of Calvinism. He talked endlessly of the new birth and demanded the absolute necessity of knowing when and where one's conversion occurred.[16] Prior to McGready's coming to Kentucky, the stiff, formal Presbyterian theology had converted few Westerners,[17] chiefly because "there was no vitality—no flashing of the electric sparks of human sympathy—no trumpet call to repentance." [18] Frightened by his "coarse, tremulous voice," [19] even the stoutest quailed from so many references to torment and turned to "a Wesleyan way of escape leading through conversion to rebirth." [20] Hell-fire and brimstone were ever present in his impassioned sermons, usually devoted to the three topics of regeneration, faith, and repentance.[21] To "the fierceness of his invectives" was added terror by "the hideousness of his visage and thunder of his tones."[22] The salvation of souls became the one consuming interest of this "son of thunder," until he was cut down by an untimely death.

Under the direction of McGready and with the co-operation of the Methodists and Baptists, the camp meeting rapidly spread throughout Kentucky and Tennessee.[23] During the revival season homes were temporarily deserted, stores were closed, crops were left untilled in the fields. "Age snatched his crutch; Youth forgot his pastime . . . bold hunters and sober matrons, young men, maidens, and little children flocked to the common centre of attraction; every difficulty was surmounted; every risk ventured, to be present at the camp-meeting." [24] Whatever reserve the Westerner had once soon faded, and he abandoned himself to the religious enthusiasms and emotional excesses.[25] Often instructed by people totally unacquainted with theology, "the excited persons were suffered to float without rudder or compass." [26] Presently the phenomenon of "jerks" appeared and affected every muscle of the body. One revolting exercise after another developed until many of the revivals reached a degree of grossness unheard of in the religious history of this country.[27] The Cane Ridge camp meeting in Kentucky in August 1801 marked the peak of the movement. Some writers estimated the attendance at 25,000,[28] and firsthand observers reported seeing men struck down "like corn before a storm of wind"[29] before the preaching of six or seven ministers.[30] Since the details of the camp meetings have been carefully treated elsewhere,[31] it is more important here to examine the participation of the Presbyterian Church in the camp meeting and in the revival movement.

Although eighteen Presbyterian ministers were reported present at the Cane Ridge meeting, it is difficult to find in Kentucky more than a half-dozen leading members of that ministry who held to the revivalistic program through its important years.[32] At first the mature clergy took part,[33] but, when the excesses became evident and the theological drift was toward the Arminian viewpoint, most of them withdrew and denounced the movement. On the other hand, the actual leaders of the movement were largely young ministers educated in the border colleges whose theology was in sharp contrast to the heavily impregnated Calvinistic theology taught at Princeton.[34] The groups to which the young ministers preached were in the main composed of young people, who came not from the intellectual or wealthy classes but from the lower rungs of Western society.[35] There is little to support, and much to contradict, the contention that camp meetings had any religious effect on the upper brackets of frontier society.[36] At this period travelers reported that the rich in Kentucky were infidels and the illiterates were "downright fanatics." [37] Four Kentucky newspapers publishing five hundred issues between 1788 and 1804 did not mention the revivals, and the *Knoxville Gazette* for 1791-1796 contains only two statements concerning religious matters.[38]

The official attitude of the General Assembly toward revivals blew hot and cold. The fluctuations paralleled those of several individuals, David Rice and John Lyle in particular, who were in the very midst of the revival scene. In 1803 the Assembly felt it should not express an opinion as to the origin of the revivals, yet declared there was much evidence that it was "the work of God." A year later the Assembly had "unspeakable satisfaction" with the influence and the spread of the revivals farther south and west, but lamented the extravagances, which were "various and unaccountable." In 1805 the commissioners of the highest judiciary plainly stated that "bodily affections have been of such a nature, and proceeded to such lengths, as greatly tended to impede the progress and to tarnish the glory of what, in its first stages, was so highly promising." And in characteristic Presbyterian manner the warning continued: "God is a God of order and not of confusion; and whatever tends to destroy the comely order of his worship is not from him, for he is consistent with himself." By 1806 the Assembly was still mildly supporting revivals, yet expressing its sentiment against "extravagant and indecent outrages against Christian decorum." The accumulations of restraints evidently brought too sobering an effect, for twenty-five years later the General Assembly passed a resolution urging congregations to arise "from their spiritual lethargy" and to partake of "those gracious visitations with which others are so remarkably blessed and distinguished." But fearful lest the extremes would recur, the Assembly summarized them in a word of caution: the churches must avoid "all bodily agitations and noisy outcries," guard "against every species of indecorum," forbid women "to preach and exhort, or lead in prayer," and permit no "apparent converts [to] be hurried into the Church." In final admonition the congregations were warned to "let no measures for the promotion of religious revivals be adopted, which are not sanctioned by some example, or precept, or fair and sober inference, drawn from the word of God."[39]

Sober and judicious men on the scene feared the extremes of the revival era. One of the best-known and most generally respected Presbyterian ministers in the West during the revival movement was David Rice. He and other members of the Presbyterian clergy warmly sympathized with the success the revivals had had in converting men and women to Christianity, but they openly objected to the excesses. As early as 1805 Rice published his opposition to the bodily exercises and attempted to discourage their continuance. In his "Second Epistle to the Citizens of Kentucky," published in 1808,[40] he continued his opposition to the exercises. He stated his conviction that

26

there had been "a revival of the spirit and power of Christianity amongst us . . . but we have sadly mismanaged it; we have dashed it down, and broken it in pieces." [41] John Lyle, who has been called "the most formidable witness against the revival," kept a diary for the years 1801, 1802, and 1803 in which he noted his observations and reactions to the revivals. In early entries there is evidence that Lyle, if not sympathetic, was not hostile to the new mode of conversion.[42] He soon, however, became convinced that the revivals "were not the effects of a Divine impulse" but rather "the evidence of human infirmity." At Paris, Kentucky, he preached on the text "Let all things be done decently and in order," and at Danville, Kentucky, he delivered a sermon on "Bodily exercise profiteth little." [43] Later in the turn of events Lyle was to be the actual leader of the anti-revivalist faction that desperately tried to prevent the formation of the Cumberland Presbyterian Church.[44] As early as 1803 Adam Rankin, minister of the Associate Reformed Church at Lexington, had issued a violent attack in his *Review of the Noted Revival in Kentucky*.[45] Therein he charged that a band of preachers and exhorters, with doubtful ability but much zeal, "dehorted from vice, and exhorted to virtue"; and that a band of comforters aided and cheered "the feeble of the flock who looked for some great and marvellous approbation from on high . . . saw strange things every day" and received "fresh news from the world of spirits every hour." Rankin concluded that the entire revival movement was a delusion and must be prevented from spreading.[46]

Lapping back eastward over the mountains, a second revival movement reached eastern North Carolina, and from there William C. Davis wrote in 1803 to a Presbyterian friend in Kentucky that he was afraid "too great indulgence will promote extravagance which will eventually encumber & dishonor the work . . . [and it will] eventually be stopped by the too great zeal and wild sallies of its own votaries." [47] From other places Presbyterians harshly condemned the revival. Samuel Miller, an instructor in church history at Princeton, was convinced that the revivals had scattered "the seed of deep and extended ecclesiastical desolation." Ashbel Green, minister of the Second Presbyterian Church of Philadelphia, believed that excesses would be disastrous "to the interests of vital piety." [48]

While there is a good deal of Presbyterian testimony favorable to the revivals, it ought to be pointed out clearly that most of this came in the early years of the revivals before they had fallen prey to the excesses of the Methodists and similar groups. Probably the most oft-quoted supporter of the revivals was George A. Baxter, president of Washington College in Virginia, who visited Kentucky at the height of the revival period of 1801. In a letter under date of January 1, 1802, he wrote: "I found Kentucky the most moral place I had ever been in . . . [and] from whatever cause the revival might originate, it certainly made the people better." Commending the movement, he continued, "Upon the whole . . . I think the revival in Kentucky among the most extraordinary that have ever visited the church of Christ, and, all things considered, peculiarly adapted to the circumstances of that country." [49] Later Baxter changed his opinion regarding the revival program and considered much of the work "false, erratic and unholy." When he learned that the *New York Evangelist* had printed his letter of 1802, he planned to print a reversal of his earlier, favorable views, but his intention was defeated by death.[50]

When relieved of its bias, there is much truth in Richard McNemar's assessment of the unwillingness of the Presbyterians to accept the revival which had originated with them. "The love of a Savior constrained them to testify, that one had died for all. This truth so essential to the first ray of hope in the human breast, was like a dead fly . . . to the Calvinist. . . . Yet these exercises would no doubt have passed for a good work of God, had they appeared as seals to their doctrine of election, imperfection, and final perseverance."[51]

In the earliest days of the revivals the Presbyterians in Kentucky and Tennessee, spurred by the lethargy of the church and the pressing immoralities of the West, were willing and eager to participate in the movement. Under the leadership of McGready the results were highly pleasing, but as the camp meeting progressed there were injected, largely by the Methodists, a religious fervor and a fanaticism that led to excesses, which the orthodox Presbyterian theologian could not accept. As a rule, the Presbyterian minister seldom deviated from the standards in the Confession of Faith—stern and unbending as it was.[52] Naturally, any side step from Calvinism was called heresy, and revision in procedure resulted in theological controversy and denominational divisions. Especially in Kentucky, where the control of the synod was firmly in the hands of the conservative element, the forces of revivalism [53] were smothered, and the chief protagonists were either driven out of the church or lured back into the fold of the regular Presbyterian way. The revival movement swept through most of the settled West. It brought both good and evil. "Infidelity was laid prostrate; but churches were rent in sunder. The deadness and the lethargy of religion were broken up; but Stoneites, Shakers, and the Cumberland schism sprang up out of the chaos."[54] The Presbyterian Church, which had come to the frontier best prepared of all churches to cope with the need, would, henceforth, never compete in numbers with the more intelligible doctrines of the Methodist Church and the more attractive type of Calvinistic faith of the Baptist Church.[55] Although the camp meeting was declared to be "peculiarly adapted" to the need of the West, it was not adapted to the creed and polity of a church that had no intention of changing radically its fundamental tenets or of altering its ecclesiastical structure in order to meet a temporary condition on the frontier. Other churches would make the adjustment, but the Presbyterian Church refused.

III

A SEQUEL TO THE REVIVALS

PRIOR TO THE DISSENSION over the revivals, the unity of the Presbyterian Church in Kentucky and Tennessee had been rent by Adam Rankin and Hezekiah Balch. The effectiveness of these two able ministers had been lost to the church in the doctrinal disturbances which centered around them during the decade 1785-1795.

Rankin had come to Lexington in 1784 and soon had a large, faithful congregation. At a conference held in 1785, a year before the formation of the first presbytery in Kentucky, Rankin began a fight in behalf of his views on the question of psalmody. He objected to the use of Watts' psalms instead of the literal version by Rousse. Unable to get a hearing from his colleagues, he went without commission to the General Assembly of 1789 determined to force the Assembly to repeal the resolution of 1787 which permitted the use of Watts' psalms. Again unsuccessful, Rankin returned home and proceeded to his self-appointed task.[1] Contending that he was "the subject of extraordinary Divine Revelation," he barred from the Communion table those people who had favored Watts' psalms. Because of his independent action he was suspended by the Transylvania Presbytery in 1792.[2] Rankin was supported by a loyal congregation, the majority of which he took with him into the Associate Reformed Church, and, surprisingly enough, he retained possession of his church building. Rankin was endowed with many talents and an enthusiasm that bordered on fanaticism. Sympathetic with his views or drawn by his personal magnetism, scarcely a congregation in Kentucky was not disturbed by him.[3]

In Tennessee the church had lost ground through the leadership of Hezekiah Balch in the Hopkinsian controversy. Balch was the third Presbyterian minister to move to east Tennessee, arriving there in 1785.[4] Ten years later while in New England seeking funds for his school, Balch accepted a doctrine known as Hopkinsianism,[5] which

30

was a departure from strict Calvinism. At first his church (Bethel) received impassively the new teaching, but soon a disquietude stirred the community. When the Abingdon Presbytery decided that his views were not heretical, a dissatisfied group withdrew and formed an independent presbytery which existed for a while.[6] The Balch case was heard by the Synod of the Carolinas,[7] and then, on appeal, reached the General Assembly of 1798. Although the Assembly exonerated him from the accusation of heresy, Balch was charged with "imprudent and unwarrantable conduct" and warned "against doing any thing in time to come that may tend to produce such serious and lamentable evils."[8] Despite his acceptance of the censure from the Assembly, Balch remained at heart a Hopkinsian.[9] His teachings, strange and persuasive, aroused such concern that an observer in 1797 was convinced that the disaster caused "by Balch and his party is almost beyond description."[10]

The modified Calvinism preached by the younger and more democratic element of the Presbyterian ministry in the West contributed equally to the success of the camp meetings and to the schism within the church. Although the spiritual tone of the country was enriched and the church rolls were increased by the revivals, the Presbyterian Church itself emerged from the sweep of events "bleeding at every pore."[11] From the very beginning of the revival movement the church membership was divided into revival and anti-revival factions. In September 1803 the Synod of Kentucky found Richard McNemar, who had been previously condemned by the Washington Presbytery, guilty of preaching anti-Calvinistic doctrines. While the trial was in process, four other revival preachers—Robert Marshall, John Dunlavy, Barton W. Stone, and John Thompson—aligned themselves with McNemar in protesting against the action of the synod and withdrew from its jurisdiction. When this group constituted itself into a separate presbytery (Springfield) and refused to comply with the synod, it was summarily suspended. The members of the seceding group drew loyal followers who in no time were designated New Lights, Stoneites, and Marshallites. Their churches were nominally under the new Transylvania Presbytery until June 1804, when its dissolution was made public by a unique pamphlet entitled *The Last Will and Testament of the Presbytery of Springfield*. For a while the new organization generally called itself the Christian Church, but its idea of absolute freedom in worship destroyed any thought of union.[12] Separate and independent, the leaders lost their purpose within a few years.[13] In the end, of the five who seceded, McNemar and Dunlavy joined the Shakers, Marshall and Thompson returned to the Presbyterian Church, and Stone, as late as 1832, joined with Alexander Campbell in the Christian Church.[14]

These rifts and splits worked havoc and took great toll among the Presbyterians. Even James McGready, who had departed noticeably from the Calvinistic doctrine of predestination, was by 1807 much disturbed over the outlook.[15] In a letter to Archibald Cameron he wrote: "I have no good news. . . . McNemar, Houston, and Bates have been in Gasper river, Logan County, with their testimony, and have been successful. Mr. Rankin and about 20 persons of his Congregation are now Shakers, and Shakerism is now beginning to show its head. . . ." [16] The hardest blow was yet to fall—the defection which is generally known as the Cumberland Schism.

Four important factors contributed to bringing into existence the Cumberland Presbyterian Church. First, from the standpoint of time, were the forces set in motion by the revival movement. In the Presbyterian Church the anti-revival groups were composed largely of the ruling elders and their families who remained firm in their acceptance of the Westminster Confession. The revival party recruited its following from those people of Arminian trend, who were mainly not from the well-to-do and educated Kentuckians and Tennesseeans.[17] Between these two groups the divergence was wide, and, unless bridged by a great deal of compromise, the deviation would lead inevitably to cleavage.

The educational requirement for the ministry was the second disrupting feature that led to the schism.[18] When the revivals were at their height, the supply of ministers was far less than the demands of the congregations.[19] In order to meet the tremendous need, the Transylvania Presbytery in 1801 lowered the normal educational requirements for the ministry[20] and accepted four men as exhorters and catechists.[21] At its next meeting this presbytery, influenced by petitions from vacant congregations, licensed to preach three of the four exhorters—Samuel King, Alexander Anderson, and Finis Ewing. To this action, however, there was a strenuous objection, expressed in resolution and signed by five members of the presbytery. The objectors claimed that the trials of the candidates "consisted only in one short sermon & an examination on experimental religion &

divinity, being destitute of classical learning," and that the men were without such "extraordinary talents as to justify such measures." [22] In 1802 at the first meeting of the Synod of Kentucky, the Transylvania Presbytery was divided into the Transylvania and Cumberland presbyteries. The latter was to lie on the south of the Bigbarren River to its mouth and from there to the mouth of the Salt River.[23] The Cumberland Presbytery began with ten ministers equally divided between the revivalists and anti-revivalists. Almost immediately the bars on educational requirements were let down so far within the presbytery that "Illiterate exhorters, with Arminian sentiments were multiplied, till they soon numbered seventeen." [24] When questioned by the Transylvania Presbytery on the propriety of licensing and ordaining men for the ministry who did not have a liberal education, the General Assembly made a reply so carefully worded that each side readily found justification for its views on the subject. The Assembly was of the opinion that a liberal education was not "absolutely essential to a man's usefulness in the ministry . . . but reason and experience both demonstrate its high importance and utility." Parrying further, the judicatory concluded, "we cannot lawfully and conscientiously depart from our present standards till they be changed. . . ."[25]

The third difficulty leading to disruption arose from the whole issue of doctrine, the phase on which several Cumberland Presbyterian adherents placed most of the blame for the trouble.[26] When many of the preachers in the revival era adopted the Confession of Faith, they made an exception of the idea of fatality.[27] It was inevitable that the new independence and freedom possessed by the frontiersman would turn him away from Calvinism[28] "with its God of inexorable decrees" to Arminianism with the idea of "free will,"[29] or cause him to turn, as did the frontier revolters against Calvinism, to a position midway between the two extremes.[30] Actually the revivalists, "free will preachers,"[31] differed so little from the Methodists that some of their leaders desired to unite with the Methodist Church, but, according to Peter Cartwright, they were not accepted.[32]

The final step leading to the Cumberland Schism, and that which made reconciliation virtually hopeless, was the controversy over the rights and powers of the synods and presbyteries. On this issue the Cumberland party definitely held the better position. The beginning of this controversy stemmed directly from the appointment of a committee of five by the Synod of Kentucky in 1804 to attend the next meeting of the Cumberland Presbytery and report on the proceedings, particularly in regard to the educational requirements for the ministry.[33] The presbytery denounced appointment of this committee as an unwarranted assumption of authority and branded as a spy the one committeeman in attendance.[34]

A committee appointed at the 1805 meeting of the Synod of Kentucky made a report on the "extremely defective" records of the Cumberland Presbytery. It mentioned numerous irregularities and made the criticism that "the mode of transacting business frequently violates our rules of discipline." After much debate on the report and disapproval of many actions of the presbytery, a committee of sixteen ministers and elders was appointed to compose "a Commission vested with full Synodical powers to confer and adjudicate" with the presbytery on its proceedings. The meeting was ordered to be held at the Gasper meetinghouse in Logan County on the first Tuesday in December.[35]

By moving into the stronghold of revivalists, the anti-revivalist commission had chosen a hornet's nest. Its coming was thoroughly advertised throughout the community, and its purpose was represented as threefold: to stop the licensing of non-college trained ministers, to abandon the circuit system, and finally to halt the progress of the revivals.[36] Lyle recorded in his journal that bitter opposition to the commission incited one congregation in the presbytery to collect and burn copies of the Circular Letter published by the synod. Hostility and resentment filled the air, and, when time came for the meeting, only one person in the neighborhood of the church offered hospitality to the commissioners. Undoubtedly the synod compounded its mistakes in choosing John Lyle to deliver the opening sermon. Being extremely hostile to the revival group, he had boldly described Finis Ewing as "one of the illiterate ministers of this presbytery."[37] Following Lyle's three-hour explanation of the qualifications expected in a Presbyterian minister, the commission proceeded to the task before it.[38]

The chief trouble, as was expected, centered on the twenty-seven men who had been licensed and ordained by the Cumberland Presbytery. The candidates had been permitted to adopt the Confession with the reservation "so far as they deemed it agreeable to the word of God," and no reference had been made to this in the minutes of the presbytery. The majority of the presbytery, with James McGready as spokesman, admitted the fault as stated by the committee, but pleaded the exception of the fourteenth chapter of the Form of Government and numerous precedents.[39] Meeting this rebuff, a committee of the synod resolved to examine and to judge the qualifications of each candidate; whereupon the majority of the Cumberland Presbytery refused to submit on the very proper ground that the presbytery had the exclusive right to examine and to license its own candidates. The commissioners from the synod then prohibited the recusants from preaching or administering the ordinances until they submitted to examination. Five members of the presbytery were ordered to appear before the next meeting of the synod and to answer charges of error or contumacy in refusing to force to examination the young men "who had been irregularly licensed and ordained."[40] Immediately after the commission had delivered its verdict and declared itself dissolved, the majority of the Cumberland Presbytery formed itself into a council which pledged its members to preach, to refrain from presbyterial actions, to keep the churches and the revivals alive, and to seek a reconciliation with the parent church.[41] Of five ministers ordered to appear before the Synod of Kentucky in October 1806 only two were present, and they went not in answer to the command but in an attempt to effect a reconciliation. The synod, in no mind for compromise, suspended from the ministry the two recalcitrants, dissolved the Cumberland Presbytery, and attached its church members to the Transylvania Presbytery.[42]

The dissension came to the attention of the General Assembly[43] through a "Letter of the Council of revival ministers to the General Assembly of 1807."[44] The high judicatory held diverse views and expressed some sympathy for the revival party. In a letter directed to the Synod of Kentucky the General Assembly of 1807 commended the synod on its zeal but suggested that much of the procedure of the commission was of "questionable regularity." Furthermore, the letter urged a review of the proceedings and the adoption of milder views. The Assembly, by a letter to four remonstrants from the Cumberland Presbytery, admonished that the licensing and ordaining of persons not possessed of qualifications required by the discipline was "highly irregular and unconstitutional." The presbytery was advised to return to the constitution of the church and to strive for peace. The General Assembly of 1808 received a second petition from the presbytery, but declined to consider the overture on the grounds that the Synod of Kentucky was the only constitutional body empowered to handle the dispute at the stage then reached.[45]

In 1809 John Lyle, a commissioner from the Synod of Kentucky, took with him to the General Assembly a letter defending the synod's action.[46] Undoubtedly Lyle's dramatic presentation of the case influenced the unanimous support for the rulings made by the Synod of Kentucky against the Cumberland Presbytery. Awestruck by the Assembly, Lyle was at first speechless, then bursting into tears, he gave so impassioned an appeal that his hearers reversed their previous judgments.[47] The case against the revivalists was closed by a decision which is now "almost universally admitted" to be contrary to Presbyterian rule and custom.[48]

The council of recusants met again in August 1809 and made one final appeal to the Synod of Kentucky. Although willing to be examined on doctrinal points, its members would adopt the Confession only if permitted to except that portion which appeared to teach the doctrine of fatality.[49] The synod refused to accept the terms and ordered a meeting for the purpose of restoring those members of the old Cumberland Presbytery who would submit to the requirements of the synod. This offer brought the return of William Hodge, Samuel Hodge, James McGready, and Thomas Nelson.[50] Finis Ewing, Samuel McAdow, and Samuel King were the only ordained members who remained faithful to the stand taken by the revivalist element in the Presbyterian Church.

On February 4, 1810, this saving remnant, meeting in the home of Samuel McAdow, in Dickson County, Tennessee, constituted the independent Cumberland Presbytery, which formed the nucleus for the Cumberland Presbyterian Church.[51] The newly organized Cumberland Presbytery adopted a constitution which accepted the confession and discipline of the Presbyterian Church, but made a provision for relief from the doctrine of fatality. In March the members of the presbytery, still hoping for a reunion with the parent church, agreed that unless a reconciliation could be reached by October no further effort would be made.[52]

Much effort was expended by the Presbyterians in warning people by circulars and pamphlets that the new church had no right to administer ordinances. Two samples will give the flavor. McGready, writing to Archibald Cameron, expressed grave concern over the extreme position of the new sect: "They have a flame of animation with them which they call the revival and this is what supports them and gives them importance, but this malignant Spirit against the old Presbyterian— the contempt with which they treat some of the doctrines of the Confession of faith . . . and the vain glorious boast . . . [of] their own Superior Successes seem . . . to differ from the Spirit of Christ. . . ."[53] Co-author of an accusing letter to the West Tennessee Presbytery of 1811, Gideon Blackburn sharply took to task on many points the followers of the Cumberland Presbytery. As a compromise he suggested that the church "will open the doors as wide as will be useful for the interests of Zion," but in conclusion he reiterated his opinion that the new conception of fatality was "totally denied by every well informed Calvinist."[54]

These attacks had little effect on the rapidly growing Cumberland movement. In 1810 the new church distributed a circular letter which explained "the origin, progress, and termination of the difference between the Synod of Kentucky and the former Presbytery of Cumberland."[55] Three years later the new church held a synod composed of three presbyteries and sixty congregations. At this time a committee was appointed to prepare a confession of faith and a discipline— the whole of which was presented to and adopted by the synod in 1816.[56] By 1820 the church had a thousand members in the State of Kentucky,[57] and the movement had spread to Alabama,[58] Arkansas, Illinois, Mississippi, and Missouri.[59] The first General Assembly was held in Princeton, Kentucky, in 1829. Six years later there were nine synods, thirty-five presbyteries, three hundred ordained and one hundred licensed ministers, and 75,000 communicants.[60] The phenomenal growth of the church resulted largely from the adopting of the revivalistic program, the borrowing of the Methodist system of circuit riding, and the modifying of the Calvinistic creed. Finally, the leadership of Finis Ewing was a great force in the earlier years. By no means as illiterate as pictured by Lyle, Ewing was "a majestic pioneer preacher,"[61] admirably equipped to meet the same problems faced by such noted Methodist circuit riders as Peter Cartwright and James B. Finley.[62]

Viewing now in appraisal the events of 1810, the student finds much evidence that the founders of the Cumberland Presbytery had no intention of creating a new church or even a schism[63] in the old.[64] Anticipating a spirit of compromise from the parent church, the dissenting group scarcely expected or desired the sudden exclusion and independence that faced it. They entered the ecclesiastical skirmishes perplexed and uncertain, and, if they had found some tolerance and kindness in the synod, there is little likelihood that the new church would have arisen. "Had Presbyterianism been as sagacious as Methodism in such matters, it might have harnessed the fiery enthusiasm of those frontiers-men into its chariot. Grant that those John Baptists in linsey-woolsey and leathern girdles were lacking in diplomas, and rather low in their Calvinism, and wild in some of their methods; yet Presbyterianism needed just such a corps of skirmishers and sharp-shooters for its frontier campaign."[65]

The separation was complete and finished before the respective sides began to temper their judgments. Shortly before James McGready died he is quoted as saying to his congregation: "Brethren, when I am dead and gone, the Cumberland Presbyterians will come among you and occupy this field; go with them [,] they are the people of God."[66] Most of the membership of his church followed his advice and joined the Cumberland Presbyterians.[67] An evidence of the cooling of passions is seen in the minutes of presbyteries such as that of the Alabama in 1824; it is recorded that the presbytery could not "hold fellowship" with the Cumberland Presbyterians, but it did not "wish to oppose or disparage their labors in the cause of Christ."[68] In 1828 the *Western Luminary*[69] issued a statement that it was willing to print news concerning the Cumberland Presbyterian denomination. A year later Finis Ewing, who had more cause to nourish ill will against the old church than any other member of the Cumberland Church, wrote for publication in the *Luminary* a gracious letter urging members of his church to subscribe to the paper, because it probably had the widest circulation of any religious paper in those states where Cumberland Presbyterians lived.[70] The widely traveled and fair-minded James Gallaher, a Presbyterian minister, had no hesitation in believing that "no body of Christian ministers in America, or even in the world, have *preached so much good, effective preaching,* and *received so little worldly compensation,* as the ministers of the Cumberland Presbyterian church."[71] This new church met a pressing need[72] by coping with a frontier religious situation in which the older church on numerous occasions had failed.[73]

IV

THE PRESBYTERIAN MINISTER

I F THE PRESBYTERIAN MINISTER did not accompany the
first immigrants to the West, as has been widely claimed for the
itinerant Methodist preacher,[1] he was not far behind thousands
who sought good lands and new homes in the great Mississippi
Valley. There is much evidence that he was prophet enough to foresee
the rapid and successful expansion of the American frontier, and there
is absolute proof that he was no mean judge of land. In 1783 David
Rice, prominent in the settlement of Kentucky, went to that country
in search of good land at a low price.[2] Some Presbyterian ministers
bought land through agents, as in the case of Edward Crawford who in
1786, before he moved to Kentucky, bought 2,670 acres on the Little
Guyandot River.[3] Other ministers without plans for migrating bought
land as purely speculative measures.[4]

Probably the majority of Presbyterian ministers went to the West
strictly upon invitations from congregations, as was true of the Little
Mountain and Springfield, Kentucky, churches, which in 1794 petitioned for the services of Joseph P. Howe, promising him one hundred
pounds sterling per year, one-third cash and two-thirds in "Marchant-
able Produce" provided he would settle with his family in the bounds
of the two congregations. Permission having been granted by the
presbytery, the two congregations sent to Howe an invitation which
contained the names of ninety-seven persons who pledged a total of
nearly one hundred pounds sterling.[5] It was not rare for ministers to
be called from great distances as was Daniel C. Banks, whom the
Louisville First Presbyterian Church, at the time of its formation in
1816, invited to its pulpit from his home in Fairfield, Connecticut. In
a letter of call, the clerk of the session wrote the usual invitation that
the congregation was "well satisfyed of the ministerial qualifications of
you Daniel C. Banks & having good hopes . . . that your administrations
in the gospel will be profitable to our spiritual interests do earnestly
call you and desire you . . . promising you . . . all proper support, en-

39

couragement and obedience. . . ." The arrangement must have seemed generous to Banks; he arrived with his family a few months later.[6]

The early Presbyterian ministers in the West experienced their full measure of the hardships and trials of a new country. The best dwellings were often mere cabins or huts: batten doors closed the large apertures, but cracks were wide, so wide in one preacher's cabin that hogs passed to and fro "with uninterrupted freedom."[7] Food was simple and the variety was very limited; pumpkins, potatoes, "hog and hominy" were staples.[8] Cabins, forts, and forests served as meetinghouses, and stumps quite often provided a stand for the pulpit. To travel on horseback across wild territory, to go hungry and half-frozen, to cross swollen streams so often it became a pastime, required an immense amount of courage, resoluteness, and devotion. Only ministers endowed with these qualities could hope to succeed in this environment. Danger from Indians was imminent for years, and fear added to physical discomforts. An experience of Samuel Doak was not singular, nor was his courage unique. While he was preaching one Sunday in east Tenneessee, a man rode to the church at full speed shouting, "Indians! Indians! Ragdale's family are murdered." Immediateley Doak closed the sermon, offered a short prayer, snatched his gun, and led the pursuit. On another occasion an alarm led Doak to dismiss his school at Salem and to take his pupils to the camp of Colonel John Sevier.[9] Because the Cumberland Presbyterian Church adopted the Methodist circuit system, its preachers suffered greater privations and indignities than those in the parent church. Some of the sections into which the Cumberland Presbyterian ministers ventured had not been touched even by the Methodists. In Alabama, for example, ruffians often threatened William Moore. While he was praying, they stood outside and made various disturbances. Once firing a volley into a room, they wounded two members of his family kneeling in prayer.[10]

Physical discomforts and dangers were so certain and so real that men could reckon with them by experience, but weakness of character and instability of purpose offered greater dangers to ministers in regions of loose and undisciplined social relations.[11] Not all were guilty of indiscretions and dissipations, but, from those who were, shadows fell on the clergy as a whole. According to an historian of the church in Kentucky, not all the ministers possessed traits of character required by the standards of the church. Of the first fifty Presbyterians preaching in Kentucky, nearly half were "subjected to church censures more or less severe; several being cut off for heresy or schism, two deposed for intemperance, one suspended for licentiousness, several rebuked for wrangling, and others for other improprieties unbecoming the gravity or dignity of the clerical character."[12]

The problems arising from the presence and general use of hard liquors involved ministers on numerous occasions. In a statement signed by fifteen people, John Gillespie was charged in 1821 before the Shiloh (Tennessee) Presbytery with being drunk on three occasions: in 1817 at a corn-shucking, aiming "to carve a ham or shoulder of pork," he had "missed the object & put his fork on the table instead of the pork"; the next year he was charged with being drunk at a school entertainment; and two years later he was supposedly in the same state at a "social" in his own house. Despite detailed evidence to support the charges, the presbytery not only ruled unanimously that they had not been sustained, but also warned the complainants to be more careful about charges in the future.[13] In 1827 Samuel Hunter, however, was suspended by the Pine Ridge (Mississippi) Church "from the exercise of his official duties, until time shall have tested the reality of his penitence" for the use of intoxicating liquors.[14] Theodore Porter, a candidate for the ministry in Alabama, acknowledged the guilt of intemperance and was suspended for six months.[15]

In 1825 before the West Tennessee Presbytery, John Keel of Bowling Green, Kentucky, charged Edmond Lanier with having refused to pay for three blankets which he had purchased for approximately four dollars. Felix Grundy[16] and Governor William Carroll[17] of Tennessee testified before the presbytery that they did not believe that Lanier would swear falsely. Keel charged that the minister was "a scoundrel and that his ears ought to be cut off and that he was an impostor and not fit for a missionary." The presbytery ruled that it was hardly probable that "a Christian minister would swear falsely for the paltry sum of four dollars."[18] In 1834 a committee appointed by the South Alabama Presbytery examined reports injurious to the character of Thomas P. Davis, who was accused of disregarding the truth, having a quarrelsome disposition, and being dishonest in secular affairs. Concerning the last instance, a statement in writing gave the details of a transaction in which Davis refused to give "good cattle" in payment of a debt but gave "wild cows" instead.[19]

Frequent cases involving accusations of indiscretion and immorality of ministers are found in the minutes of the presbyteries. In 1824

Jeremiah Abell was suspended by the Transylvania (Kentucky) Presbytery for taking "indecent liberties" with three women of his congregation. While hugging and kissing Mrs. Jane Rayburn, he had told her "he loved her as a child" but had thought it wise not "to let the world know how intimate he was with his sisters. . . ." Abell was restored to the ministry within five months after his suspension, but withdrew from the church a year later.[20] Serious charges were brought against Aaron Williams in the early days of Presbyterianism in Arkansas. A committee was appointed "to collect the Voice of Public Rumor." Williams was suspended after he had been found guilty of "improper conduct" arising from the "imprudence in boarding at a house where the mistress of it was suspected by many of impunity of character and continuing to remain there after he was informed that reports were in circulation prejudicial to his character . . . and to the chastity both of himself and the woman. . . ."[21]

From garrulous women unfair and dishonest reports circulated hurtfully to the reputation of the preacher, as in the case of Eli N. Sawtell of the First Presbyterian Church of Louisville. He was accused by a Mrs. Byars, in whose home he lived, of coming to the table in a cotton nightshirt opened at the collar, of coming to meals without waiting for Mr. Byars, of borrowing her horse without remunerating her, and of various other indiscretions. Although completely exonerated by the session of his church, Sawtell resigned his pastorate and formed the Second Presbyterian Church in Louisville.[22]

Beyond question the financial support of the Presbyterian ministers by the members of the churches was more generous than that of the Baptist and Methodist churches.[23] Yet the Presbyterians were often reluctant and even hesitant to enter into contracts that could not be dissolved readily. This accounts for an additional hesitancy to install formally a minister, for fear that in event of the death of signers to the subscription list those who remained would be fully responsible for the minister's stipulated salary.[24] The amount of salaries varied a great deal. The church in Washington, Mississippi, gave a preacher a collection of $29.75 because it felt a "duty to afford him some pecuniary aid," since he had no regular charge.[25] A Cumberland Presbyterian preacher received seventy-five dollars a year for preaching once a month seventy-five miles from home.[26] In contrast, however, the First Presbyterian Church in Nashville offered sixteen hundred dollars a year to John T. Edgar in 1833.[27] Some pastors even received more than the contracted stipend, as in the case of Robert H. Snoddy, who was promised twenty dollars for one-half time in 1835 and was paid $31.20.[28] Robert Marshall kept a careful account of payments for eight years of service at Bethel Meeting House (Kentucky) and found his yearly average was $62.34¾, while from a second charge at Woodford, Kentucky, he received an average of $77.73 for ten years.[29]

For the most part, the church supported the ministers so meagerly that the preaching became in many instances an avocation, while a secular job provided the necessities of life. One preacher worked as a day laborer on a farm,[30] several practiced medicine,[31] others owned and labored on their farms,[32] but by far the largest number supplemented their income by teaching.[33] Often the congregation felt that whenever a preacher owned a farm the church should be relieved of supporting him. David Rice, a fair-minded and capable judge, unhesitatingly believed that "The people are starving the ministers, and the ministers are starving the people for it."[34]

On the Nashville Circuit of the Cumberland Presbyterian Church the signers of a contract between Cabbin Creek Church and Stephen Lindsley agreed to pay the sums affixed to their names, one-third in "good and lawful currency" and the balance in produce such as pork, wheat, corn, wool, salt, flax, sugar, and other products, the value of which was to be agreed upon by trustees, one-half of whom Lindsley appointed.[35] Whisky, being a readily marketable product, was often subscribed to the support of a preacher. In 1807 the subscription list for Joshua L. Wilson, of the First Presbyterian Church of Cincinnati, pledged more than one hundred gallons.[36] Articles of wearing apparel were acceptable; certainly the suit of clothes given to Robert Baker by the "ladies aid" in Nashville was well received since he had no regular charge.[37]

If poor in material things, the Presbyterian preacher was rich in mental powers, educational training, and respect for learning. As immigrants to America the Presbyterians brought an educated clergy and a profound respect for the value of education. This was a heritage to which the Presbyterians in a new country adhered with pride and stubborn devotion. The requirements—the highest of any successful Protestant church of the frontier—demanded that a candidate for the ministry possess a Bachelor of Arts degree or a testimony of having successfully completed a regular course of study arranged by the presbytery and supervised by an approved minister.[38] A typical examination was that given to a candidate named Warren by the Alabama Presbytery in 1823. The candidate was examined on church history, natural and moral philosophy, astronomy, Latin, Greek, and geography.[39] If the examination was sustained, the candidate was assigned a thesis or discourse to prepare and to defend. At its 1828 meeting the South Alabama Presbytery ordered T. S. Witherspoon to prepare an exegesis from "Anne homo sit omnino corruptus"; another candidate, I. N. Caruthers, was required to prepare from "Anne Baptismus Johannis sit Christianus."[40] Not infrequently the candidate received an unfavorable report, as in the case of a Mr. Wallace, upon whose discourse the committee reported that there was not "sufficient closeness of attention, either in arrangement, or in the arguments, [and] they also think it faulty in precision and perspicuity, and that there are too many redundant words."[41] Upon the satisfactory execution of this exercise, the applicant received a certificate of licensure.[42] Then he usually supplied vacant congregations for a probationary period before he was ordained and called to a regular pastorate.[43]

With few deviations the Presbyterians adhered faithfully and rigorously to their educational standards,[44] as is exemplified in the case of Richard H. King, who, although the holder of an academic degree from Princeton and a practicing attorney, was refused a license to preach until he had studied theology for two years. He turned to the Methodist Church, from which he immediately received a license. After preaching in this church for several years, King again applied as a ministerial candidate to the Presbyterian Church. Successful in his request, he received a license and in the service of this church spent the remainder of his life preaching in east Tennessee.[45] Despite the danger of losing members through the formation of the Cumberland Presbyterian Church, the parent organization held rather steadfastly to its educational standards. An excellent case in point is found in the stand taken by the West Tennessee Presbytery in 1811. In discussing the preparation of ministers by "heart religion" rather than by study, the presbytery declared that "those who would deny the utility of Academical study to qualify men for business either in Church or state, must take leave of their senses; shut their eyes on the common occurrences of life, and add a momentum to the demoralizing principles of Illuminism."[46]

The procedure and the requirement in the Cumberland Presbyterian Church were far below that normally required in the older church. For example, on July 27, 1810, Thomas Cahoon was recommended and passed on English grammar and divinity. He, after accepting the Confession of Faith "except the Idea of Fatality,"[47] was licensed to preach. The wording of the minutes of the Cumberland Presbytery is an interesting commentary on the educational level. Under date of March 21, 1811, Mr. Reece was recommended to "Study english gramer." At times, however, even the older church found cause to relax the literary requirements. Two licentiates, Martin and Dunham, had served as missionaries for twelve months, during 1828 to 1829, under the care of the South Alabama Presbytery. Pressed by need, it passed a resolution that "in consideration of the desolate condition of our Country, it is expedient to ordain at this time the Brethren. . . ."[48]

Several of the early Presbyterian ministers in Kentucky and Tennessee were graduates of Princeton; others held either earned degrees or the honorary degree of Doctor of Divinity. A list of both groups would appear rather imposing.[49] The mixed attitudes toward an honorary degree are interesting: some men desired the degree, some hesitated to accept it, and others declined the offer. In 1822 Thomas Cleland wrote a letter declining an offer of a D.D. from Transylvania College. Later he decided to accept the degree, which he called "one of the most unwelcome honors, or burdens, that was ever put upon me in all my public career." He was convinced that the degree came to him through the interest of James Blythe and N. H. Hall, who had recommended him to the Board of Trustees of Transylvania College. Blythe, said Cleland, was "the only D.D. in Kentucky, and I suppose wanted company, and the latter [Hall] probably looked forward when he might obtain it himself."[50] When David Rice heard that the College of New Jersey proposed to offer the D.D. to him, he flatly refused to accept it on the ground that it presupposed a professional standing which he had not attained.[51] In 1820 a writer to the *Christian Spectator* suggested that those desiring degrees might purchase them from Western colleges, badly in need of funds.[52]

It is natural to be curious about the kind of sermon that came from the average preacher equipped with moderate capacities and a veneer of formal education. The sermons followed a general pattern: often written in full essay form they opened with a text, then compared the text with other Scripture, and concluded with numerous parables and prophecies to support the text. The vast files of sermons from many preachers attest the infinite care, pains, study, and mental discipline that produced the most systematic compositions. John Lyle, more evangelistic than most Presbyterian preachers in Kentucky, felt that a minister should "become mighty in the Scriptures," and that it was wise to read the Scriptures again and again in the original language, for it was "better to take from the fountain head than from the streams." Lecturing, he believed, was the most useful mode of preaching. When the chapter or page lectured on was memorized "it may be explained & applied very pathetically."[53] He realized there was great value in expounding the word of God since many parts of a sermon were "much less *profitable* than the *unadulterated* word."[54]

Although he had prepared the sermon with meticulous care, the preacher delivered it in a tedious way. Ordinarily read in a monotone,[55] without extemporaneous remarks, the sermon presented "a cold and lifeless discussion of doctrine" which was utterly unsuited to the need of an early Western audience.[56] At times, in some sections, the preaching was considered quite poor. "Unhappily," according to one church historian, "with two or three shining exceptions, the majority were men of barely respectable talents, and a few hardly above mediocrity; and so far from being patterns of flaming zeal and apostolic devotion, a dull formality seems to have been their general characteristic."[57] John C. Young, a college president, expressed his views in 1835 about the quality of preaching done in the Muhlenberg Presbytery in Kentucky. He thought the sermons were coming from ministers "utterly destitute of those attainments, which our church has always considered . . . as indispensable to those who undertake the responsible duty of interpreting the oracles of God to their fellow men."[58]

Among Baptist and Methodist congregations in the West there was universal opposition to a minister who read his sermon; even the Presbyterians often reacted against this custom. The untrained mind wanted a sermon spoken clearly and forcefully, with conviction and enthusiasm.[59] A visiting minister, William Burroughs of Philadelphia, was preaching "in City Style," that is, reading a manuscript sermon, to a congregation gathered in an old barn in west Tennessee when an eclipse of the sun prevented him from seeing the pages. To the great gratification of the congregation it became necessary for the minister to complete his sermon extemporaneously.[60] Charles Coffin, president of Greeneville College in east Tennessee and a highly effective preacher, correctly stated the need when, in 1822, he wrote: "Ministers, in all the Southwestern country, to be acceptable, must be prepared to preach without notes."[61]

Recognition should be made of either the magnetic power of the preacher or the courtesy of his listening congregation. Long sermons were the rule, rather than the exception. Having spent all the week writing down every word of a sermon, the preacher had no aim to be hurried in the delivery of his discourse. It was not uncommon for a Presbyterian minister to preach for two hours or more. John Lyle once preached for two hours and twenty minutes with "almost no time for reflection or meditation." It may be suggested that liberty and freedom were not denied the minister.[62] Gideon Blackburn held some fifteen hundred people for a two-hour sermon in a graveyard while "a constant but not hard rain" fell.[63] About 1820 Governor Carroll and Felix Grundy heard Blackburn preach in Nashville a sermon which lasted the amazing length of three and a half hours. Carroll, inquiring of Grundy how he stood a sermon of such length, received the reply that he could have listened until midnight.[64] Samuel Carrick, who preached in east Tennessee as early as 1789 or 1790, was "calmness and dignity personified, his articulation was clear and distinct, he was never vehement or violent, never gesticulated, even in the most earnest part of his discourse, he was impressive and motionless."[65]

Early Presbyterian ministers preached a stern and unbending doctrine largely devoted to the trinity, the covenant, regeneration, the nature of faith and repentance, election, and predestination.[66] In 1729, when the Philadelphia Synod passed the Adopting Act, American Presbyterianism thereby secured its first constitution, which was a compromise directed toward preventing in the colonies what had happened in England—a three-way split caused by the Act of 1705 requiring all ministers to subscribe to the Westminster Confession of Faith. Under the Adopting Act much latitude was permitted and many exceptions could be allowed either to a minister or to a candidate for the ministry who had scruples about an article or articles of the Confession or the catechism. Subscription was required only to the "necessary and essential articles."[67] Yet this compromise was so grudgingly and hesitatingly accepted by the clergy in the West that schisms and disruptions resulted in a large shift of members to the Cumberland Presbyterians and a smaller gain to the New Lights. The church seemed to many to be wholly inconsistent in its emphasis on the one hand on the personal responsibility for the soul, and on the other hand on the doctrine of foreordination and unconditional surrender. The general effect of this stern doctrine caused much dissension among both members and clergy.

In 1810 Thomas B. Craighead, a perennial storm-center in middle Tennessee Presbyterianism, published a blasting attack on Calvinism that caused James Blythe to write to a friend: "I have never felt so uncomfortable under any publication. . . '. It has proved to [be] a kindling flame, an overwhelming deluge."[68] In 1813 John Todd was suspended by a Kentucky presbytery because he was adamant in his adherence to permissive decrees in face of the presbytery's ruling that the decrees of God were absolute.[69] Two years later, after much study, Todd thought all differences of opinion between him and the presbytery could be related to one point, "the doctrines concerning the Freedom of the Will."[70] In 1815 James McChord, one of the most brilliant Presbyterian preachers in Kentucky, was suspended by the Associate Reformed (Presbyterian) Church not "on a flagrant heretical position but on a hair-splitting distinction in a speculative sub-head of an undisputed doctrine."[71] The eminent Timothy Flint, a Congregational minister in the Presbyterian Church on the frontier,[72] was so opposed to Calvinism that he wrote a friend: "I would infinitely prefer, could I command my own convictions, to believe in the utter annihilation of the soul, than in the gloomy & horrible dogmas, which John Calvin thought he found in the bible."[73] Later writers found incongruity between Calvinism and frontier religious ideas. Theodore Roosevelt was convinced that Calvinism was too cold for the frontiersman.[74] In seeking an explanation of the failure of Presbyterians to appeal to "crackers," "red necks," and the great unchurched element in the new cotton states, William E. Dodd stated that "the Calvinist meat was too strong" and "the Princeton faith too drastic."[75]

The role of the Presbyterian minister in a frontier community was varied with his many activities. In spite of individual aberrations, the minister was always respected; as spiritual guardian of the mature and intellectual guide of the young, he was held in high esteem. Finding escape in books, he could remove himself from the crude settlers and rough surroundings. He gave tone to community life, raised the level of any society he touched, and contributed many of the forces that promoted and yet stabilized the expanding West.

V

PRESBYTERIAN INTEREST IN EDUCATION

T HE PRESBYTERIANS who came early to America brought a deep and profound respect for the values of education.[1] In an effort to establish religion firmly on the rational basis of knowledge and thought, the church logically evinced great zeal for education; where education was at a low ebb, the church suffered. A learned ministry with a classical education was deemed absolutely essential to Presbyterian standards.[2] The church early required that all candidates for the ministry have as a minimum the Bachelor of Arts degree or its equivalent in the nature of a regularly pursued course in theology under an approved teacher.[3] The initial item of the printed minutes of the first presbytery of the Presbyterian Church in the United States contains an account of the examination of a candidate for the ministry. It was recorded that in 1706 John Boyd "preached a popular sermon on John 1.12; defended his thesis (*de regimine ecclesiae*); gave satisfaction as to his skill in the languages, and answered to extemporary questions; all which were approved of, and sustained." In 1712 in the same presbytery David Evans was refused ordination because of his lack of "proficiency in learning." He was ordered to continue his studies "under the inspection" of Jedediah Andrews.[4]

In 1726 William Tennent, a Presbyterian minister at Neshaminy, Pennsylvania, twenty miles north of Philadelphia, established a school which became known as "Log College."[5] Several of the graduates of this school established other "log colleges," two of which later became Hampden-Sydney College and Liberty Hall Academy.[6] Schools of this type were established in the main to train locally young candidates for the ministry. The expense of traveling to an Eastern seminary was prohibitive for most students[7] and overbalanced any cultural advantages that came from older institutions. In support of these new schools the rational mind argued that even if Eastern colleges were superior in culture, they "might prove inferior in point of efficiency

49

when compared with the less elaborate courses of young western institutions."[8]

When John Knox, in his native Scotland in the sixteenth century, placed a school under the shadow of his parish church,[9] he thereby established for elementary education a pattern that was widely copied by the Presbyterians in the Old South and Southwest. Sometimes the church building was used as a schoolhouse; at other times a separate building was constructed nearby.[10] Out of a score or more of pupils, some of the children boarded with the teacher's family. In case of a larger boarding school, the pupils occupied little cabins clustered around the school, or they boarded in the households of nearby farmers. In this type of school the curriculum and method of teaching followed a generally accepted pattern. Reading, spelling, arithmetic, and English grammar were taught in the lower grades.[11] Higher mathematics, Latin, and Greek were added to the studies of the more advanced pupils, who did not always share the enthusiasm of the teacher for the classical languages. With surprising success, however, the Presbyterian preacher-teacher convinced the youth that "the salvation of their souls depended upon the memorizing of thousands of heroic lines or upon explaining to their masters the intricacies of languages that had not been spoken by any considerable number of people since the fall of Constantinople."[12]

In making contracts with patrons the teachers often agreed in such manner as did Robert Marshall of Kentucky. His contract plainly stated that "no undue influence shall be used to alter the religious opinions of any student. But morality shall be strictly inculcated by precept, example & penalty."[13] Teaching not only provided a very much needed source of additional income but also became the normal contribution of a learned clergy to an unlettered West.[14]

Since many of the early Presbyterian ministers in the West were graduates of the seminary at Princeton,[15] the exertions of these men were responsible for a great part of the educational achievement on the raw frontier. In Tennessee,[16] where the Presbyterians took an early lead in fostering education, the five important builders of educational institutions were Samuel Doak, Hezekiah Balch, Samuel Carrick, Isaac Anderson, and Thomas B. Craighead. All were Presbyterian ministers of Scotch-Irish descent; Doak and Balch had been educated at Princeton.[17]

In 1776 Doak taught at Hampden-Sydney and in the next year

50

"He walked through Maryland and Virginia, driving before him an old 'flea-bitten grey' horse, loaded with a sackful of books; crossed the Alleghanies, and came down along blazed trails to the Holston settlements."[18] At Salem, in Washington County, he established a log college named Martin Academy, the first school in Tennessee and the first literary institution in the Mississippi Valley.[19] In 1783 the Assembly of North Carolina chartered Martin Academy, and two years later it received from the State of Franklin a charter which is believed to be "the earliest legislative action taken anywhere west of the Alleghenies, for the encouragement of learning."[20] In 1795, by a charter from the Territory South of the Ohio River, Martin Academy became Washington College.[21] James G. M. Ramsey, the historian of early Tennessee, was a student of Doak and spared no praise in writing about his old teacher. "The acquisition of knowledge,—mere literary attainment, was not the sole or even primary object of Dr. Doak's instruction—it was mental discipline—it was to train the intellect,—to teach the young man how to think,—to think accurately and profoundly,—to think for himself, and to beget a spirit of manly reliance upon his own powers of independent investigation and vigorous thought."[22] This philosophy of teaching falls in quite well with "progressive education"; the pupils were not divided into classes by years, but were permitted to complete any course as quickly as possible and then proceed to another.[23]

While on a trip to the General Assembly in 1798, Doak collected a library which greatly strengthened the quality of his college.[24] In 1806 his son John, a graduate of the first class in 1796, was appointed financial agent of the school, for which he managed to raise two thousand dollars in two years. In 1818 he became president when Samuel Doak resigned after thirty-five years devoted to the academy and the college.[25] In the same year Samuel Doak, with the aid of his second son, Samuel W., opened in Greene County, Tennessee, a private school to which he gave the name of Tusculum Academy. Here he taught until his death in 1830, when the school was suspended until 1835 and then reopened by Samuel W. Doak.[26]

Hezekiah Balch, a graduate of Princeton in 1762, moved to Greene County, Tennessee, about 1783.[27] He early saw the great need for education in the region and determined to establish a school. After purchasing a plantation three miles from Greeneville, he received in September 1794 a charter from the Territory South of the Ohio River

51

for Greeneville College, of which he was president. At this time the nearest college was over the mountains, 175 miles away.[28] In the same year Balch made a tour through the East, where he collected $1,350 in cash, $350 in subscriptions, and a large number of books.[29] Although the college was not opened until 1802, the enrollment was one hundred students in the second year. Within a decade students from nine states were enrolled—a testimony to the fame of the school. When Balch died in 1810, Charles Coffin became his successor.[30] Coffin raised twenty thousand dollars for the college, but resigned in 1827, partly because of a fierce factional fight from which the college never recovered, and partly because of a tempting offer of the presidency of East Tennessee College at Knoxville.[31]

Samuel Carrick, a graduate of Liberty Hall in Virginia, was the pastor of the first Presbyterian church established in Knoxville[32] in 1793. During the same year he began in his home a seminary in which he offered instruction in a wide variety of courses—Greek, Latin, English, rhetoric, logic, natural and moral philosophy, geography, and astronomy.[33] A year later his school was chartered by the territorial government of Tennessee as Blount College.[34] The preamble of the legislative act defined the interest of the territory in promoting "the happiness of the people at large . . . by instituting seminaries of education, where youth may be habituated to an amiable, moral, and virtuous conduct and accurately instructed in the various branches of useful science, and in the principles of ancient and modern languages." The trustees were directed to make proper provisions "that students of all denominations may and shall be admitted to the equal advantages of a liberal education, and to the emoluments and honors of the college, and that they shall receive a like, fair, generous, and equal treatment during their residence therein."[35] This, despite the Presbyterian background and Presbyterian president of the college, was a clear declaration of non-sectarian intention. Without very necessary funds the college struggled on until 1807, when it transferred its money and property to East Tennessee College, which had just been chartered by the State of Tennessee. Because of the inability to realize adequate funds from the sale of lands and because of the death of President Carrick in 1809, the new college suspended operations and did not reopen until 1820. Twenty years later the institution became East Tennessee University and in 1879 the present University of Tennessee.[36]

Isaac Anderson studied at Liberty Hall for several years before moving to east Tennessee with his father in 1801 in search of cheap land.[37] The next year he established, near Knoxville, Union Academy, which served the same people as his Grassy Valley Presbyterian Church.[38] In 1811 he succeeded Gideon Blackburn as pastor of the Presbyterian Church at Maryville, where he remained until his death forty-six years later.[39] Anderson, concerned over the need for young ministers in the West, visited Princeton Theological Seminary in 1819 in order to invite and to urge graduates to go to east Tennessee. When he asked for volunteers, he was faced with the question, "What salary do they pay their ministers?" In reply he answered, "Go there and ask such a question, and as ministers of the gospel you are ruined." Discouraged by the results of his trip to the East, Anderson pondered the notion of a seminary in the new country. Soon after he returned home, his ideas took concrete form with the opening of a private school of theology in a small house in Maryville. Beginning with a little class in 1819, the seminary enrolled ninety students a decade later.[40] After the Synod of Tennessee decided to adopt Anderson's school, it was located permanently at Maryville, and named the Southern and Western Theological Seminary.[41] In 1826 the institution bought a farm of two hundred acres, thus reducing the cost of boarding each student to twenty dollars a year. In 1833 a new building was erected, and three years later the name was changed to Maryville College. By this time more than sixty men had been sent from the school to carry the gospel to regions destitute of preachers. This was a rich compensation to Anderson, who had taught for many years without monetary compensation.[42]

The first Presbyterian minister who located in the Nashville region was Thomas B. Craighead. In 1786, about a year after his arrival, he opened Davidson Academy in a stone church at Spring Hill, five miles north of Nashville.[43] The legislature of Tennessee appointed in 1803 a committee composed of Thomas B. Craighead, Andrew Jackson, James Robertson, and others to establish Davidson College at Nashville. Craighead was elected president. In 1806 an act of Congress gave Tennessee 100,000 acres of land for the support of two colleges, one in east and one in west Tennessee. In the latter section, Davidson College was consolidated with the new Cumberland College, which opened in 1809, closed in 1816, and reopened in 1825 as the University of Nashville,[44] with Philip Lindsley,[45] the learned Presbyterian preacher-educator, as its president.[46] Eventually this institution became the present George Peabody College for Teachers.

In 1810 Gideon Blackburn moved to Franklin, Tennessee, some sixteen miles south of Nashville. Here he took charge of Harpeth Academy and afterwards presided over Independent Academy in the same county.[47] Blackburn's teaching was typical of a host of other Presbyterian preachers who moved to various sections of the state and devoted a large part of their efforts to educating the young in communities almost barren of opportunities for schooling.

Recognizing the great need for education, the Synod of West Tennessee in 1828 took steps for the erection of a synodical academy. After hearing an extensive report, the synod resolved to locate the academy on three hundred acres of land on Rutherford's Creek in Maury County. The constitution of the school, called the Manual Labor Institute, stated that the institute was intended for "pious young men of all denominations who hold the essential principles of our holy religion. . . ." Students admitted were required to perform a full share of labor, and in return they were not expected to pay more than sixty dollars yearly for expenses.[48] So rapid was the progress of the institute that by 1835 it had been converted into Jackson College, at which time its lands, buildings, and apparatus were valued at seventeen thousand dollars.[49]

The establishment of schools in Kentucky was almost simultaneous with that in Tennessee. In 1780, four years after Kentucky was formed into a county, the legislature of Virginia set aside some public lands for educational purposes through "An Act to vest certain Escheated Lands in the County of Kentucke in Trustees for a Public School."[50] Under the leadership of Caleb Wallace, a graduate of Princeton and a Presbyterian minister from Virginia, a board of trustees for the proposed Transylvania Seminary was incorporated in 1783. Two grants of land gave the new institution twelve thousand acres as an endowment.[51] On February 1, 1785, David Rice[52] was elected chairman of the board, and two years later the seminary was opened in his home near Danville.[53] The endowment was so unproductive it furnished only a small salary for a single teacher, and this lack of money largely prevented the school from becoming more than a grammar school. In an effort to raise very necessary funds, the school was moved in 1788 to Lexington, where it was quite well received.[54] In 1794 James

54

Moore, once a candidate for the Presbyterian ministry but now an Episcopal rector, was removed from the principalship of the seminary by the board. To the newly created office of president of the seminary, the board elected Harry Toulmin, a Baptist minister who possessed Unitarian sentiments, liberal political views, and, according to some, French infidelity. Against this action the Presbyterians within the region protested loudly. So instrumental had they been in the Transylvania movement, they considered it largely their institution and were indignant when Moore was replaced by Toulmin.[55] Because of this radical change in leadership the Transylvania Presbytery immediately began preparation for an institution under its immediate direction.[56]

Within a few weeks, largely through the efforts of David Rice, a charter was secured for an institution known as Kentucky Academy. In addition to a grant of six thousand acres from the legislature, subscriptions and donations from individuals and churches amounted to more than a thousand pounds sterling. Rice and James Blythe, acting as solicitors in the Atlantic states, collected nearly ten thousand dollars. The subscription list indicates that the solicitors called on practically every prominent person in the East. George Washington, John Adams, and Robert Morris gave an attentive ear and each donated one hundred dollars.[57] Barton W. Stone was sent to solicit in the South, but, since he gave no report of his work, it is quite likely that he had little or no success.[58]

The purpose of the academy was "the promotion of Science, Morals, and Religion, in a young country, whose population is rapidly increasing, and where all the evils, both political and Moral, which flow from Ignorance, must in a great measure be experienced, unless the means of instruction are possessed within its bosom."[59] The academy was opened in the fall of 1797 at Pisgah, Kentucky, largely because Pisgah had offered fourteen hundred pounds sterling and land, an amount in excess of the offers from Harrodsburgh and Danville. Plans called for one tutor and one assistant tutor. Fees were five dollars at entrance and ten dollars every half-year, three-fifths of the revenue went to the tutor and two-fifths to the assistant tutor. In 1798 plans were discussed for a proposed building to accommodate fifty students and a lodge for twenty.[60]

In an effort to secure "many singular advantages," Kentucky Academy and Transylvania Seminary were united in December 1798 under the imposing title of Transylvania University. The board of trustees consisted of twenty-three members, a majority of which was to be Presbyterians.[61] Its first president was James Moore, a former teacher of Transylvania Seminary. Under the most promising auspices the university opened with a staff of three professors, each of whom was to receive five hundred dollars yearly. In 1799 law and medical departments were added. The library contained more than thirteen hundred volumes, and the university owned twenty thousand acres of land. Moderate success was enjoyed until clashes over religious and political philosophies threatened the life of the university. James Moore was removed from the presidency in 1804, and James Blythe was the head for the next fourteen years. During this period the curriculum was almost identical with those of Eastern colleges.[62] The Presbyterians, according to Davidson, "relaxed their vigilance" over Transylvania. When vacancies occurred on the board, they were filled with politicians. Soon it was realized that only seven of the twenty-one members of the board were Presbyterians. Quarrels and bickerings grew louder until some changes became inevitable.[63]

Liberals in Kentucky could see little cause for joy over the record of the university prior to 1812. Blythe had severely criticized the War of 1812, denounced the leading politicians of the state, and made himself generally obnoxious to the liberal element. A determined group demanding a very different type of president pushed through to acceptance the name of Horace Holley, a graduate of Yale and a distinguished Unitarian divine,[64] who led Transylvania to the border of greatness. Holley had smooth sailing for a number of years during which he assembled a remarkable faculty.[65] His popularity was general throughout Kentucky except among the Presbyterians, who were convinced that Holley was determined to crush them.[66] Even before Holley had been installed as president of Transylvania, the Presbyterians threatened withdrawal of all their support for the university on the ground that they would not support an institution in which the training of young ministers would be imperiled by infidelity.[67] The conflict between liberalism and Calvinism in Kentucky became inevitable. After ten years of constant and wearying struggles[68] Holley resigned in 1827, and the glory of Transylvania faded forever. "As Holley had been the chief proponent of liberalism in the state, his defeat was that of liberalism in general."[69]

In order to recoup its loss of Transylvania University, the Synod of Kentucky had sought in 1818 to recover control of education within the state by petitioning the legislature of Kentucky for a charter for a new college to be located in Danville. After the state chartered Centre College and offered it to the Presbyterian Church, the charter was so altered by the legislature that control was not given to the synod but to the legislature. The church particularly objected to the clause in the charter that "no religious doctrine peculiar to any one sect of Christians shall be inculcated by any professor in said college." The offer was rejected by the Presbyterian Church, and Centre was established and remained under state control until January 27, 1824. At this time the charter was amended and complete control was given to the Synod of Kentucky.[70] The college struggled along for several years until John C. Young became president in 1830, after which the institution became one of the best colleges in the West.[71] In the ten years between 1831 and 1841, Centre increased its endowment from three thousand dollars to fifty thousand and its student body from thirty-three to 150.[72] After half a century of visions, dreams, and disillusions, the Presbyterians were now in control of a college which they were absolutely free to manage as they felt disposed.

Although the question of education was a contributing factor in the Presbyterian schism of 1810, the first official act of the newly organized Cumberland Presbyterian Church was the establishment of educational standards for its ministry.[73] Leaders in the new church, conscious of the need for educating its ministers, brought before the Cumberland Synod in 1825 plans for establishing a college. Largely because the people of Princeton, Kentucky, pledged $28,000 in subscriptions, Cumberland College was located there. A large farm of some five hundred acres was bought on credit for six thousand dollars. Less than one-fourth of the subscriptions made by the people in Princeton was paid, and the school was in financial trouble during its entire existence. The manual labor feature of the school was chiefly the idea of Franceway R. Cossitt, its first president. The institution opened about March 1, 1826, with six students and had sixty by the end of the year. A large hewn-log house was the main building of the college—really a "log college." Other structures were likewise simple and unpretentious; President Cossitt lived in what was little more than a cabin. When a professor of philosophy was employed, he was guaranteed a house that would cost the college no more than fifty dollars. In 1833 a dormitory having all the appearances of a Pennsylvania barn was built of brick, sixty-five feet by thirty-nine and two stories high. The faculty dressed in long black gowns, a practice which gave a touch of formality and ceremony to the simple and austere surroundings.[74] When parents and guardians complained of extravagance in the dress of students, a resolution was adopted at the General Assembly of 1832 requiring uniform dress "as soon as the present stock of clothes be worn out."[75] The synod prescribed the course of study, selected the textbooks, and made laws to govern students—even to prohibiting the use of featherbeds.[76]

Originally the Cumberland Presbyterian Church had hoped to finance its educational efforts through a subscription of fifty cents from each member. When this request was only partially heeded, James Smith was appointed "to ride and solicit donations throughout the United States, for the benefit of Cumberland College,"[77] which was sorely in need. The returns were not gratifying, for Smith and a second agent had, after paying expenses, $78.47 left to aid the college.[78] When various schemes of financing failed,[79] the college sold in 1842 all its land but a ten-acre plot on which were the buildings and the spring. In this year the General Assembly of the Cumberland Presbyterian Church severed connections with Cumberland College, but the school managed to continue until 1860, when it gave up after thirty-five years of desperate struggling.[80]

As the frontier became more stabilized, the control of the "regular" Presbyterians over education in Kentucky grew stronger, and "the passage of years saw Kentucky becoming increasingly an orthodox Christian state," through the conservative leadership of men like James Blythe.[81]

To a degree the early westward drive of the Presbyterian Church seems to have spent its force largely in Tennessee and Kentucky. The North Alabama Presbytery did not appoint until 1827 a committee to study the possibility of establishing a literary and theological seminary in Mobile. The efforts of the committee, however, bore no results.[82] Six years later the South Alabama Presbytery accepted a report from its committee on education which recommended the establishment of a Manual Labor Institute in Dallas or Perry County in Alabama. The report asked for several items: a subscription of fifteen thousand dollars for the purchase of a plantation and erection of necessary buildings; a co-operative labor plan by which students would work a maximum of five hours a day; and a board of sixteen trustees, only one-third of which would be clergymen. The McKinney plantation, located three miles west of Marion in Perry County, was selected as an advantageous site for the new school. Under an extremely generous arrangement with the owners the purchase price of the plantation was set at eighteen hundred dollars and the last payment was to be made in 1837.[83] The institute was progressing so well at this date that the presbytery was able to rejoice in its "present flattering prospects."[84]

At a meeting of Presbyterian ministers in Baton Rouge, Louisiana, in April 1829 the question of education was discussed thoroughly. Most disturbing was the fact that there was not a single Presbyterian college within Louisiana, Mississippi, and the Arkansas Territory—an area containing more than 300,000 people and 145,000 square miles. After considerable correspondence and study within a committee, a meeting of the friends of education was called at Bethel Church near Rodney, Mississippi. Subscriptions were opened for funds, and twelve thousand dollars were contributed for buildings and grounds. The Mississippi Presbytery, containing all the Presbyterian ministers in the above region, appointed a board of trustees, elected Rev. Jeremiah Chamberlain president, and fixed a location for Oakland College in Claiborne County, five miles east of the Mississippi River. On May 14, 1830, the school opened with three students, and by the following March sixty-five had enrolled. In the winter of 1831 Oakland College received a charter from the State of Mississippi, and two years later held its first commencement. The singular position which this college enjoyed in the lower Southwest is shown by its spectacular growth in twenty years. By the end of this time the physical plant contained thirty cottages for the occupancy of the students, residences for the president and the professors, two halls for the literary societies, a library of four thousand books, and a large main building, one hundred feet by sixty.[85]

To James Blythe, reflecting over the state of education in the West, the picture may have been personally disturbing in 1836, when he wrote: "Among the many gloomy prospects that must overwhelm the mind of every reflecting man among us, as to the real and threatened desolations of the land, none strike me with so much horror and dread as the ignorance and darkness which I see fast settling around the almost innumerable cabins and log houses scattered over the valley of the Mississippi."[86] Although the situation was not satisfactory to Blythe, hundreds of private schools and academies organized and taught by Presbyterian ministers in this great valley bear complete evidence of their consuming interest in the cause of education. The newspapers and church periodicals were actually crowded with notices regarding private schools. With amazing regularity the session records tell the story of contributions on the part of individual members to worthy enterprises.

The influence on higher education of Presbyterian efforts is more readily evident in cold statistics. Of forty permanent colleges and universities founded between 1780 and 1829 in the United States, thirteen were Presbyterian in origin. Of the forty, fourteen were located in the West, and of the fourteen, seven were established by the Presbyterians.[87] By 1840 the Presbyterians had organized eleven colleges in the South. Perhaps a "college ideal was not indigenous to the frontier" and not a "product of local demand";[88] nevertheless, by this time the Presbyterians had contributed much to intellectual progress.[89]

Probably the Presbyterian insistence on a highly trained ministry stemmed from "the scholastic shape in which the doctrines of the church were presented in its confessions and catechisms, and the influence of these upon preaching and teaching." Although right in setting a high standard, the church was apparently unwise in failing to recognize occasions when circumstances demanded a relaxation of the adopted course. On the frontier the adherence to a strict rule resulted in Baptist and Methodist churches swelling their ranks at the expense of the Presbyterians.[90] The refusal, however, to lower standards ultimately resulted in the founding of many schools and colleges throughout the West, and gave to the Presbyterian Church, in the matter of education, a decided advantage over other denominations.

Beyond question the contribution made by the Presbyterians to education in the Old Southwest far exceeds that of any other religious organization. Quite naturally the highly educated Presbyterian minister took his place as a leader in this line of endeavor. He possessed learning, interest in its furtherance, and a definite insight into the value education would bring to all people.

VI

THE PRESBYTERIAN CHURCH
AMONG THE INDIANS

I N MAY 1742 the Synod of Philadelphia announced that Azariah
Horton had been ordained as a missionary since the last meeting
of the New York Presbytery.[1] About the same time David
Brainerd began his notable work among the Indians, and two
years later he was ordained by the Presbyterian Church.[2] In 1751 the
Synod of New York urged the collection of money yearly in its several congregations for "the great affair of propagating the gospel
among the heathen."[3] These efforts are probably the first made by
this church for civilizing and Christianizing the Indians in the United
States.[4] This missionary zeal early characterized the Presbyterian
Church, and it may be assumed that in this respect on the frontier
this organization was "surpassed by no group among Protestants in
the eighteenth century."[5]

Three years after its formation the New York Missionary Society of
the Presbyterian Church resolved in 1799 to establish a mission among
the Chickasaws of "West Georgia." To that end it selected Joseph
Bullen to perform this arduous task. Bullen was accompanied by his
seventeen-year-old son on the long and hazardous journey, which
finally terminated in Mississippi. Companionship was fine, for the
distance was overwhelming and travel conditions, which high waters,
poor food, and widely separated lodgings made more complicated,
were most difficult. The strength of Bullen was exhausted upon arrival in Mississippi, and he was very ill for some while. He found that
the Chickasaws were people "without any kind of religious observance,
and without temple and priest" except for images which carried little
meaning for them. Gaining confidence of the Indians at times and
receiving great disappointment on other occasions, Bullen completed
the year with reasonable success. By the fall of 1800 he was worn out
and returned north by the way of Maryville, Tennessee, where he
conferred with Gideon Blackburn, who was earnestly determined to
begin a similar work among the Cherokees in east Tennessee.[6]

The General Assembly of the Presbyterian Church meeting in 1800 recognized the urgent need for "gospelizing of the Indians on the frontiers of our country," and stressed that its evangelical program should be "connected with a plan for their civilization." In order to accomplish this twofold instruction of the Indians, as well as that of the blacks and others unacquainted with religion, it was suggested that "an order of men under the character of *catechists*" who, not enriched with a liberal education nor "clothed with clerical functions," should go among the Indians, instruct, lead devotional exercises, and prepare the way for the later organizing of churches. Responding to this plan, the Synod of the Carolinas in 1802 sent out a missionary who spent part of his time among the Catawba Indians in South Carolina. Three years later the General Assembly reported that interest in this plan had spread and that additional workers were in the Catawba Nation, a school had been established, and "several young men of different tribes" had received or were receiving education through the efforts of the Synod of Pittsburgh.[7]

Gideon Blackburn,[8] as early as 1799, had sought in vain to get his presbytery (Union) to begin work among the Cherokees, who originally claimed some forty thousand square miles of territory, much of which was fertile and all beautiful, located in what later became parts of Alabama, Georgia, South Carolina, North Carolina, Tennessee, and Virginia.[9] Spurred by the success of Bullen, Blackburn presented the need to the General Assembly of 1803, which replied favorably by appropriating two hundred dollars and commissioning Blackburn as part-time missionary to the nation. Among his friends in east Tennessee he succeeded in raising $430.[10] After receiving letters of recommendation from the President of the United States and from the Secretary of War, Blackburn had several interviews with the principal chiefs of the nation. In October 1803, at the time of the distribution of the annuity, some two thousand Indians assembled, and before them he outlined his program. He received their approval in writing, together with a declaration that they would send their children to a school to be established at Hiwassee, in that part of the nation which was "most likely to be civilized."[11]

The school opened in September 1804 with twenty-one children enrolled. The Shorter Catechism was readily learned, and many hymns were committed to memory since singing was found to have a "remarkable tendency to soften" the Indian mind. Through a system of granting prizes for accomplishments, greater progress was attained than through the simple desire to learn. Visitors to the school found advancement that "exceeded all belief." The entire school of twenty pupils went on the Fourth of July 1805 in large canoes down the Hiwassee River to witness a treaty-signing between the United States and the Cherokees. Upon seeing the children, Governor John Sevier of Tennessee remarked with much emotion to Blackburn: "I have often stood unmoved amidst showers of bullets from the Indian rifles; but this effectively unarms me. I see civilization taking the ground of barbarism, and the praises of Jesus succeeding to the war whoop of the savage."[12]

This public exhibition of Blackburn's pupils prompted urgent requests from the Cherokees for a second school in the lower portion of the nation. The desired school opened with some thirty "scholars" on August 26, 1806, at Richard Field's house on South Sale Creek.[13] When Blackburn appealed for aid to the committee on missions of the General Assembly, he received the answer that support would be given for only one school. Although promised only two hundred dollars by the General Assembly of 1805, the school was given five hundred dollars for each year from 1806 to 1809.[14] In an effort to raise the needed funds for both schools Blackburn worked to the detriment of his health. While on a trip to the South to recover his strength, he sought donations for his schools and received some fifteen hundred dollars, which relieved a highly discouraging financial situation.[15]

Blackburn, cheered with the results of his Southern canvass and the extra aid from the General Assembly, was convinced that the fame of his work had spread sufficiently to secure funds from sympathetic people in the Northern states. In 1807 on a tour of seven months he secured $5,250 in addition to many books and much clothing. Dividends from the investment brought gratifying results. Within four years from the initial effort more than three hundred children had received instruction at the school. Blackburn not only had established schools and churches but also had encouraged the development of agriculture and the formation of civil government.[16] He jubilantly wrote to a friend in Tennessee: "The period has at last arrived, on which I have long fixed my eager eye. The Cherokee nation has at length determined to become men and citizens."[17]

Strangely enough, the blush of enthusiasm paled, and Blackburn by 1810 decided that the financial strain and general debilitation of health necessitated his leaving the mission work.[18] In the fall of that year he moved to middle Tennessee, and the mission scarcely lasted his leaving. Forces that contributed to the beginning of the War of 1812 brought complete ruin to this successful mission work among the Cherokees.[19]

Although the missionary emphasis was evident in the Presbyterian Church from its earliest days in the United States, not until 1802 was a standing committee on missions formed.[20] In 1801 the Congregationalists and the Presbyterians had entered into a Plan of Union by which they were to co-operate in establishing churches and furthering missionary endeavors. In 1810 the Congregational Church formed the American Board of Commissioners for Foreign Missions and invited the Presbyterians to have a part in its labors. Eight prominent Presbyterians were elected to the board in 1812, at which time the organization, known as the American Board of Commissioners for Foreign Missions,[21] was incorporated by the legislature of Massachusetts.[22] From its beginning this board had as its chief aim the advancement of missionary work among the Indians,[23] and until 1837 it was the common agency for the Congregational, Presbyterian, Dutch and German Reformed churches.[24] In the Old Southwest, where the missionary work of the board was especially active, it is not easy nor necessary to draw a hard and fast line showing the portion of the work contributed by the Presbyterian and Congregational churches.

The earliest school established in the South by the American Board was first known as Chickamauga Mission and later as Brainerd.[25] It was located within the city limits of present-day Chattanooga, Tennessee, in 1817 by Cyrus Kingsbury, a native of New Hampshire. The site included 160 acres, for which five hundred dollars were paid by the United States. President Monroe, accompanied by General and Mrs. Edmund P. Gaines, visited the mission in 1819 and was so pleased with the plan and the instruction that he ordered the Indian agent to pay the accumulated debt and also the cost of the erection of a good two-story house to be used for the teaching of young girls. A sketch of the mission made in 1821 shows a cabin and schoolhouse for the boys and the same for the girls, a mission house, barn, farmer's house, carpenter's house, sawmill, garden, and graveyard.[26]

From Brainerd, the parent institution, additional missions were established in Tennessee, Alabama, and Georgia. Among these were

64

Carmel in Georgia, sixty miles southeast of Brainerd, founded in 1819; Creek Path at Guntersville, Alabama, in 1820; Hightower, eighty miles southeast of Brainerd, in 1823; Willstown near Fort Payne, Alabama, in 1823; Haweis near Rome, Georgia, in 1823.[27] In 1824 the churches which had been established at Brainerd, Carmel, Hightower, and Willstown were admitted to Union Presbytery in east Tennessee. Four years later there were 219 members of the Presbyterian Church in the Cherokee Nation, to which one thousand copies of the Gospel of Matthew in Cherokee and eight hundred copies of Cherokee hymns had been distributed.[28]

The success of these missions may be measured by the Indians who identified themselves with the active work of the church. In 1828 John Huss, speaking only his native Cherokee language with a remarkable knowledge of the Bible, conducted a sacramental meeting at Haweis with some two hundred people in attendance.[29] For several years he had been highly successful in holding religious meetings for the American Board, and in 1831 the North Alabama Presbytery licensed him to preach the gospel "within [the] bounds of this presbytery and wherever else he may be regularly called." At the same session John Wayne, a Cherokee member of the church at Haweis, was licensed to perform the duties of a catechist in the Cherokee Nation.[30] The great demand and need for workers among the Indians had prompted the North Alabama Presbytery in 1828 to grant licensure to James Holmes "although he has never pursued a systematic course of study."[31]

Upon hearing about the mission among the Cherokes, the Choctaws in Mississippi petitioned the American Board for a mission in their country. In answer to this urgent plea Cyrus Kingsbury was sent from Brainerd in 1818 to the Choctaws, who numbered some twenty thousand and lived in central Mississippi in three groups called Upper Towns, Lower Towns, and Six Towns. The first mission was established in Upper Towns at a point called Eliot, eight miles west of the present town of Grenada, on the Yalobusha River. In less than a year log cottages, a mill, stable, carpenter shop, blacksmith shop, school, and storehouses had been built. By 1820 a second mission was established in Lower Towns at Mayhew in present-day Oktibbeha County. Additional stations were founded at Emmaus, 140 miles south of Mayhew near the Alabama border, and another at Goshen, equally as far south but fifty miles farther west.[32]

By 1828 the American Board had five missionaries working in all sections of the Choctaw Nation,[33] but results from this work were slow. The Indians were passively reluctant to be converted to Christianity; within the first ten years of this missionary endeavor only four Indians had joined the churches of the mission despite the additions of a sizable number of Negro slaves and "white vagrants." The Indians, however, came to the meetings for various reasons. About 1828 a wave of interest, generally denominated as religious, spread through the nation. It was not uncommon to see four or five hundred Indians at a meeting. As many as two hundred were classed as "inquirers" about Christianity at a single service.[34] The religious zeal of the Indian increased during 1829, and conversions to Christianity were numerous at meetings that often were attended by some five hundred Choctaws. It was estimated that there were three thousand inquiries about religion and that "more than 2000 had begun to pray."[35] There is, however, little evidence to indicate that any large number of Mississippi Choctaws were actually added to the churches. In 1831, for example, slightly over three hundred Choctaws in the entire nation belonged to churches sponsored by the American Board. At this time the Choctaw Mission had expanded until it contained eight stations, four missionaries, and nine male and eighteen female assistants.[36]

As a general rule the Indian women were seated at a service on one side of the building and the men on the other. Unless the preacher spoke the native tongue, he stood with his interpreter fronting the audience and spoke a few lines that were immediately translated. At the end of each sentence the men in the congregation responded in unison, "Yum-ma!" (very good). Often some man would quietly leave the building, fill his pipe with tobacco, and resume his seat. After smoking a few whiffs, he would pass the pipe to his neighbor—from one to another the pipe would pass until the tobacco was consumed. The one who took the last draw would leave, refill the pipe, and return to the preaching.[37]

In addition to the large schools at Eliot and Mayhew, a number of smaller schools were established at various missions and even at the homes of some of the Indians. As a whole the schools were considered definitely successful. So efficiently had the schools at Eliot and Mayhew been managed that Kingsbury in 1823 offered to relinquish an appropriation of one thousand dollars made by the American Board to the Choctaw Mission.[38]

Excited by the activity and success of the Indian missions of the American Board, the missionary urge was taking form in various synods of the Presbyterian Church. In May 1820 the Synod of South Carolina and Georgia sent T. C. Stuart and Daniel Humphreys on a trip to determine the prospects of establishing missions among the Creeks and Chickasaws in Alabama and Mississippi. Furnished with documents from the War Department and a letter from John C. Calhoun, Secretary of War, the two missionaries went westward by way of Milledgeville, Georgia, Fort Jackson and Tuscaloosa, Alabama, Columbus and Cotton-Gin Port, Mississippi. By the middle of June they had entered the Chickasaw Nation, whose principal villages were located along the Pontotoc Ridge and Natchez Trace in the present-day counties of Pontotoc, Lee, and Chickasaw. Spending a short while at the hospitable home of Levi Colbert, the most important man in the nation, they later attended a meeting of the chiefs at the home of James Colbert. Here the missionaries outlined their plans for schools, to which the Indians readily consented. Articles of agreement were formulated, signed, and deposited with the Indian agent of the United States. After looking for a suitable location for a school, Stuart selected a site which he named Monroe, two miles southwest of James Colbert's home and not far from the present town of Pontotoc. With the survey finished, Stuart and Humphreys returned to their homes in August.[39]

Stuart was chosen by the Synod of South Carolina and Georgia to develop the tentative plan and to take charge of the Monroe Mission. With his family and two other families as assistants, Stuart reached Monroe in January 1821. Two years were devoted to clearing a farm of a hundred acres and erecting the necessary school buildings. Although a school was opened in 1822 for seventeen children in the neighborhood, boarders were not admitted until a year later, at which time the school formally opened with an enrollment of fifty, most of whom lived at the school. It continued until the Chickasaws ceded their lands in 1834.[40]

The Chickasaws, pleased with the enterprise, requested the organization of additional schools under the care of the synod. In 1823 another school called Tokshish was opened two miles north of Monroe. During the following years the chiefs appropriated five thousand dollars for two more schools and half as much yearly for their support.[41] One school was erected on Pigeon Roost Creek, near the present town of Holly Springs, and the other school on the Tennessee River in Alabama. In the four schools there were over one hundred pupils, of whom many seriously learned to read and write and others watched only for the opportunity to run away.[42] In 1827 these schools along with the missions were transferred to the American Board, a union to which there was no objection by the missionaries and teachers.[43]

In the same year that the Chickasaw mission was begun, a church was founded at Monroe, originally composed of the members of the mission families and a black woman named Dinah. For years Dinah, who spoke the Chickasaw language, was used as an interpreter by Stuart when he preached to the Indians.[44] By 1831, ten years after its establishment, the mission had three stations, two missionaries, one licensed preacher, and two male and five female assistants. The churches contained more than a hundred converts, of whom at least half were Negroes.[45] Often some fifty persons assembled for meetings conducted entirely by Christian slaves who spoke the Indian language and sang hymns which they had memorized.[46] In October 1827 the missionaries to the Choctaw and Chickasaw nations met at Mayhew and formed an association, which became in 1828 the Tombigbee Presbytery in the Synod of South Carolina and Georgia. At the meeting of the presbytery in the next year, Loring S. Williams "requested ordination as an Evangelist." In response the presbytery directed him to write in both Choctaw and English languages a lecture on the Parable of the Sower, and to deliver it at the next meeting of the presbytery. In March 1830 Cyrus Byington was assigned to Bokpalaia, Wika Shobaba, Apokta Chito, Nerha, and Okayanali.[47] Knowledge of or even acquaintance with the languages of the Indians counted heavily in missionary work.

Although the Cumberland Presbyterian Church was organized as late as 1810, its Elk Presbytery sent Samuel King and William Moore in October 1818 to survey the possibility of work among the Indians on the Tombigbee River. In response to their recommendation the missionary board of the presbytery sent King and Robert Bell in 1819 as evangelists to the Chickasaws and Choctaws. In May 1820 Bell opened a school on the eastern side of the Tombigbee. After teaching there for a month, he was ordered by the missionary board to move his school into the Chickasaw Nation and to receive the assistance of two commissioners in making the arrangements. The three went to the house of Levi Colbert where an assemblage of chiefs signed an agreement for the establishing of a school at Cotton-Gin Port. The federal government gave the school some three hundred dollars a year, and the church contributed twice this amount. The chief reliance for support, however, came from the farm of thirty cleared acres which students helped to cultivate. The school was opened in a hut belonging to Levi Colbert, but a building, deserving the name Charity Hall, was soon completed at a cost of fifteen hundred dollars. As a rule the school had thirty-five pupils, some ten or twelve of whom paid their expenses and the remainder had to be provided for. Levi Colbert was so pleased with the work of Bell's school that he promised to enlist the aid of the wealthy of his nation in giving assistance to the poor in getting an education.[48]

A committee representing the church visited the school in 1825 and found a small class of beginners spelling in two syllables and a more advanced class learning in the back of the same spelling book. Some classes were reading the New Testament and two "scholars" were studying English grammar and parsing. Irregular attendance among the pupils constituted the chief problem of the school.[49] The free life of the forest was difficult to mold into one regulated by more sedentary habits.

For two or three years before the 1832 Treaty of Pontotoc, by which the Chickasaws ceded all their possessions east of the Mississippi River, large numbers of whites were pushing into the Indian territory and causing much trouble, especially with huge quantities of liquor. Aid to the mission from the government and from the church ceased in 1830. For two years Bell tried to carry on but found the job impossible and had to close the school.[50]

Immediately after the War of 1812 the lands in Mississippi were opened rapidly, yet the whites demanded greater and greater slices of Indian lands. The federal government was highly sympathetic, as a rule, with the demands of the frontiersman; Indian treaties ceding the lands followed each other in rapid succession. In 1830, despite much resistance from a group of humanitarians, Congress passed the Indian Removal Bill, which followed a policy earlier advocated by President Monroe. A half-million dollars was appropriated to make possible the exchange of Indian lands in the East for the public domain in the West. Although no interpretation of the law seemed to give the President the power to force the Indians to move, the determined Andrew Jackson left few stones unturned. Within a decade the entire region containing the three nations under consideration had been cleared of all Indians except a relatively small number who had eluded the agents of the state and federal governments.[51] At the first meeting of the Synod of Mississippi and South Alabama, held at Mayhew, Choctaw Nation, November 11-13, 1829, a resolution was adopted regretting any attempt to remove the Indians. Concern was felt because the teachings of the Gospel had "begun to dispel the darkness of heathen ignorance, degradation and sin." A year later the narrative of the synod reflected the conditions that preceded the removal. "Intemperance begins again to appear. Murder, in some of its most flagrant forms, has been committed, without being inquired into. Great attempts have recently been made secretly [,] by unprincipled white men, to produce apostacy among the native converts." In its narrative for 1831 the synod seems to have lost hope, for instead of some vigorous action it merely recorded its desire "to bring the cause of these Indian converts before the churches; and in their behalf, ask an interest in their prayers; that the pillar of cloud by day, and of fire by night may conduct these our red brethren in their wanderings through the wilderness of this world . . . to their eternal home."[52]

By the treaty of Dancing Rabbit Creek, September 27, 1830, the Choctaws surrendered their title to all their lands in Mississippi. Members of the American Board had so strenuously opposed the treaty that they were refused permission to attend the signing.[53] Several thousand Choctaws left the state in 1831; two years later most of them were in their new lands in the West. Spurred by the Removal Bill, Mississippi quickly extended her laws over the Chickasaw Nation, and the country was soon overrun by the whites. In this intolerable condition the Chickasaws signed in 1832 a treaty by which they surrendered their lands for a doubtful home across the Mississippi.[54]

Resolutely determined to drive the Cherokees from Georgia, the legislature of that state in 1830 passed a law requiring that all white men living in Indian territory must take an oath of allegiance to the state and obtain a permit to live there. In a test case, Samuel A. Worcester and Dr. Elizur Butler, two missionaries to the Indians, ignored the requirements made by Georgia. They were arrested, imprisoned, and sentenced to four years in the penitentiary. Despite a reversal of the action of the Georgia court, Worcester and Butler remained in prison for fifteen months.[55] By playing one faction against another the United States commissioners secured at New Echota, Georgia, in 1835 a treaty by which the Cherokees ceded all their holdings in the East. When a majority of the Indians opposed the treaty, an army of seven thousand troops was sent to overawe them. In the winter of 1838-1839 they were literally driven to the West in a most shameful and degrading manner. Some four thousand out of a total of sixteen thousand were estimated to have died from exposure and bad food.[56]

The Presbyterian Church and the American Board followed the Indians to their new homes and increased the work already established there. As early as 1819 the United Foreign Missionary Society[57] had sent two men on an exploratory trip among the Indians of the Mississippi Territory. A mission site had been selected twenty miles from Port Gibson, to which in the following year nine men and eight women had been sent by the society to work among the Osage Indians. The next year a second mission had been formed, and by 1823 missionaries at several places in Arkansas had formed a presbytery called New Harmony, which became identified with the Synod of Missouri.[58]

In 1818 the American Board promised a mission to the Cherokees in Arkansas. Because of a delay Alfred Finney and Cephas Washburn did not reach Arkansas to begin work until July 1820. After a meeting with the important chiefs, a place was selected on the west bank of the Arkansas Creek, some five miles from the Arkansas River, and was given the name Dwight. By 1823 a school of some sixty children was in operation and continued to flourish for about fifteen years.[59] In 1831 a religious revival of consequence occurred among the Cherokees in Arkansas. A three-day union meeting of Methodists, Presbyterians, and Cumberland Presbyterians resulted in many conversions. Even a temperance society among the Indians made considerable progress.[60] Viewing richer yield in new fields, the church abandoned by 1836 its program in Arkansas for mission work that promised greater results still farther west.[61]

Contemporary appraisers of the missionary work vary in their estimations. Timothy Flint, extremely familiar with the Mississippi Valley, was very skeptical about Christianizing the Indians. He was convinced that "Protestant exertions . . . have not been in these regions marked with apparent success." Furthermore, he believed that radical changes could come only "among the children, whose inclinations and habits are yet to form."[62] An opposite point of view came from a representative of the United States government visiting the Cherokees in Georgia in 1829. He reported that "the advancement the Cherokees had made in morality, religion, general information and agriculture had astonished him beyond measure. They had regular preachers in their churches, the use of spirituous liquors was in a great degree prohibited, their farms were worked much after the manner of the white people and were generally in good order."[63] Evidence of values accruing from the work of the American Board can be found in the testimony of the trustworthy Cyrus Byington, who contrasted the Indian in Mississippi when first visited by missionaries of the American Board with the Indian a third of a century later. Much improvement had been made[64] even though the cost to the Indian was generally regarded as unnecessarily high.

The difficulty of estimating the contribution of the Presbyterian Church toward civilizing and Christianizing the Indians of the Old Southwest is clearly evident. Beyond question the sympathy and support of the church as an institution stand out in stark contrast to the greed and injustice of men who saw only material gain from driving the Indian westward. Thousands of Indians who were once semi-wild and found in the war whoop their chief joy became peaceful, industrious, and interested in the religion of the white man. In many places the war drum summoning Indians to battle was replaced by the church bell calling them to prayer. Unfortunately the work among the Indians in the Old Southwest was supported largely from a distance and carried out by New England missionaries[65] and workers sent into the region. There is evidence that the Presbyterian churches established in the Indian nations objected rather strenuously to the removal program, but theirs were weak voices against the land-hungry population that was pouring into Mississippi. Religion had been temporarily brushed aside for land—the dominant reason for moving to the West.[66]

VII

THE SLAVERY QUESTION

HARRIET MARTINEAU, in one of the most scathing invectives against slavery, lashed the Presbyterian Church for its attitude toward the Southern institution. She said that "from the lips and pens of Presbyterians in the south, come some of the defenses of slavery which evince the deepest depravity of principle and feeling. . . . Of the Presbyterian, as well as other clergy of the south, some are even planters, superintending the toils of their slaves, and making purchases, or effecting sales in the slave-markets, during the week, and preaching on Sundays whatever they can devise that is least contradictory to their daily practice."[1] Stephen S. Foster, in early life a student of divinity and later an active participant in the antislavery movement, charged that the Presbyterian clergy was "among the most active and energetic in arousing the people to determined and obstinate resistance. No sect in the land has done more to perpetuate slavery."[2] Having recognized some truth in these and various other charges, leading ministers of the church sought to find justification for slavery and for the position of the church. At the General Assembly of 1836 a reprint of an article, written by Archibald A. Hodge of Princeton Theological Seminary and printed in the *Princeton Repertory,* was circulated among the members of the Assembly. It declared: "The assumption that slaveholding is, in itself, a crime, is not only an error, but it is an error fraught with evil consequences."[3] James H. Thornwell, professor of didactic and polemic theology at the Presbyterian Theological Seminary in Columbia, South Carolina, declared in 1850, "Slavery is a part of the curse which sin has introduced into the world and stands in the same general relations to Christianity as poverty, sickness, disease, or death." A decade later he defended the slaveholder against the charge that slavery was immoral by contending that Christianity taught sympathy for slaves. Benjamin M. Palmer, popular Presbyterian preacher in New Orleans, delivered on the eve of the Civil War a sermon, "The South:

73

Her Peril and Her Duty," with the theme "in this [slavery] struggle, we defend the cause of God and religion."[4]

In 1787 the first official resolution on slavery, adopted by the Synod of New York and Philadelphia,[5] recommended that its members "give those persons who are at present held in servitude such good education as to prepare them for the better enjoyment of freedom" and "use the most prudent measures, consistent with the interest and the state of civil society, . . . to procure eventually the final abolition of slavery in America."[6]

David Rice, generally accepted as the father of Presbyterianism in the West, assumed leadership of the opponents of slavery in early Kentucky. Rapidly acquiring a position of trust among the people, he was elected to the constitutional convention in May 1792.[7] Before this body met, he published his convictions on the slavery issue in a pamphlet in which he urged the convention as its first duty to put an end to involuntary servitude in Kentucky.[8] Although Rice's proposal was not adopted, Kentucky sentiment against Negro bondage was still strong. In 1794 the Transylvania Presbytery, embracing all of Kentucky, ordered Presbyterian slaveholders to teach all "not above the age of fifteen years to read the word of God & give them such good education as may prepare them for the enjoyment of freedom."[9]

The Transylvania Presbytery's action so disturbed the General Assembly of 1795 that a committee was appointed to draft a letter warning the presbytery "that differences of opinion with respect to holding Christian communion with those possessed of slaves, agitate the minds of some among you, and threaten divisions which may have the most ruinous tendency." Furthermore, the Assembly stated that it had taken all steps "expedient or wise, to encourage emancipation, and to render the state of those who are in slavery as mild and tolerable as possible."[10] Apparently this rebuke failed to convince the Transylvania Presbytery that it had spoken too vehemently. In the next year it adopted another resolution "earnestly recommending" that Presbyterians "emancipate such of their slaves as they may think fit subjects of liberty" and prepare others for eventual freedom.[11] In 1797 extenuating circumstances had taken effect: this presbytery again discussed slavery, declaring it "a moral evil," but refused to consider all slaveowners guilty.[12]

To some people concerned over the problem of Negro servitude the church provided a solution that would be superior to any state law. In 1799 Rice wrote to James Blythe that he preferred to see Christians adopt "a rational plan for the gradual abolition of slavery: and do it under the influence of religion & conscience, without any regard to law . . . because then it would appear to be the genuine effect of the power of truth and the justice & benignity of the religion of Jesus."[13] But Rice later relinquished much of his buoyant and optimistic faith in the unique position of the church. As he lay dying, he took a parting shot at a slaveholding society which withheld from its slaves "instruction and grace" and deprived them of liberty: the whole institution was "the crying sin of our country . . . now bleeding at a thousand veins."[14] Fearing for the personal safety of emancipated Negroes, Rice kept his slaves but hoped in time they would have greater security. He willed his daughter a Negro woman whose children were to be freed at age twenty-five for the males and twenty-three for the females. "Freedom is a natural and unalienable right," he wrote, "belonging to them, as well as others, of which the proprietor of man has not authorized me to deprive them."[15]

Other leaders in the church believed as Rice did about slavery. As early as 1793 Blythe wrote in his journal: "I spoke to a number of poor black people. Their ignorance and inattention is so truly to be lamented. O God display thy arm and work powerfully in their behalf."[16] Barton W. Stone, while on a visit from his home in Kentucky to Charleston in 1797, received impressions of slavery that firmly fixed his distaste for the institution. He was sickened at the horrible sights, the worst that he had even seen, and commented, "Poor negroes! some chained to their work—some wearing iron collars . . . distress appeared scowling in every face." No longer a Presbyterian in 1828, he was preaching and writing that slavery was morally and politically wrong. In desperation, to free himself from its immediate presence he moved to Illinois in 1834.[17]

In 1818, two years after the death of Rice, the Presbyterian General Assembly approved the most outspoken legislation against slavery which it had passed for many years. It declared Negro bondage "a gross violation of the most precious and sacred rights of human nature," and "totally irreconcilable with the spirit and principles of the gospel of Christ." After sympathizing with that portion of the church affected by the evil, the resolution exhorted Presbyterians "to increase their exertions to effect a total abolition of slavery." The significance of this action was made ambiguous when the Assembly reminded the churches that regard should be taken for "the safety and happiness of the master and the slave."[18] The church had stated its position, but there was little evidence that the resolution would ever be enforced. Here was a compromise between the church's principles and the slavery forces that so thoroughly controlled sentiment in the Old Southwest.[19] "The effect of this temporizing and procrastinating policy," said William Goodell, "was precisely as might have been anticipated. The 'mournful evil' only struck its roots deeper under such pruning."[20]

There is evidence that the impending extension of slavery from Kentucky to Missouri prompted the declaration of 1818.[21] At this stage religious and secular arguments against the Missouri Compromise bill were based on "justice and duty and the law of Christ" in contrast to the "defense of slavery on principle."[22] The latter theme was soon to be advanced with the expansion of cotton culture and the rise of abolitionism.

During the first third of the nineteenth century cotton and slavery brought rapid changes to Southern life and thought. Penniless immigrants became small freeholders, and native farmers often became planters. The mania to own slaves spread to the extent that James Smylie, a Presbyterian clergyman in Mississippi, claimed that three-fourths of all Presbyterian Church members in the South were slaveholders.[23] The force of expansion pushed the cotton frontier to the very edge of profitably productive lands. By 1833 the four states of Tennessee, Mississippi, Alabama, and Louisiana produced far more cotton than the remainder of the country.[24] As cotton and slavery strengthened their grip on Southern life, there came a halt to the growth of democracy and liberalism. This condition was true in older states at earlier times;[25] in 1817 Robert Finley, Presbyterian minister and president of Franklin College, had blamed money, cotton, and slavery for lack of religious zeal in Georgia. "Slavery chills every ardor," he had asserted.[26]

Despite the humanitarian emphasis of the Presbyterian Church, records of the different judicatories are peculiarly lacking in cases of discipline or reprimand for violations of the Negro's accepted rights. A few cases, however, were recorded. In 1809 the Concord (Kentucky) Church suspended a member for selling a Negro boy at public auction. This decision was upheld by the Synod of Kentucky, which overruled a reversal by the Presbytery of West Lexington.[27] In 1823

John Curry was found guilty by the church of Paris, Kentucky, of selling a Negro man and thereby separating him from his family. Although the session felt "bound to lift their Testimony against the inhumane and unfeeling practice," it found extenuating circumstances and ruled that the case did not call for its "judicial interference."[28] William Thompson admitted in 1827 before the Pisgah (Mississippi) Church that he had cruelly whipped a slave but denied any intention of being "unmerciful." After an admonition, the session acquitted him.[29] These cases indicate the difficulty of securing convictions against a white member of the church; the breadth of permissible interpretation usually operated against the slave.

The American Colonization Society, established in Washington in 1817, had as its chief object the removal to Africa of Negroes who were already free and of others who might later be emancipated. State colonization societies were also formed.[30] Much interest in the movement was evinced by slaveholders who honestly sympathized with the Negro's plight and by others who hoped to rid the states of the undesirable free Negroes. Still others hoped colonization would eventually lead to emancipation of all slaves. Seven years after the founding of the Colonization Society, the Synod of Kentucky appointed committees to promote its work within the churches. Recommendations urging participation in and contribution to the enterprise were made from year to year.[31]

Records of the different judicatories of the Presbyterian Church in the Old Southwest reveal considerable interest in colonization. In 1826 the Louisville (Kentucky) First Presbyterian Church gave $25.25 for the program.[32] The New Providence (Kentucky) Church made contributions of $11.25 in 1826, $8.37½ in 1827, and $14.50 in 1828.[33] A meeting of the North Alabama Presbytery in 1830 recommended that a collection for the Colonization Society be taken in the next July.[34] The Synod of West Tennessee in 1833 recognized the failure of the sessions to comply generally with its recommendation for a collection but urged that it be taken during July 1834.[35] Two years later the New Orleans *Observer* sought to interest Presbyterians in the activity of the Mississippi Colonization Society, which had been authorized to purchase territory on the African coast.[36]

Only in Kentucky and Tennessee did the idea of the emancipation of slaves flourish in the Old Southwest. Antislavery workers appeared in east Tennessee with the coming of the first settlers and sought converts to their ideals. As late as 1827 that region contained nearly one-fifth of all the antislavery societies in the United States and almost one-sixth of the total membership. In the antislavery endeavor in Tennessee the early lead was taken by the Quakers, ably assisted by the Presbyterians.[37] The first religious newspaper in the Southwest was the *Western Luminary,* a Presbyterian journal capably edited by Thomas T. Skillman, in Lexington, Kentucky. From the establishment of this paper in 1823 until his death in 1833, Skillman fought slavery so courageously that William Lloyd Garrison praised him in the *Liberator.* The antislavery efforts of the *Western Luminary* and of two other Kentucky papers inspired Benjamin Lundy with "the hope that the day of political and moral redemption is drawing near."[38]

In 1832 and again in 1833 the antislavery members of the Synod of Kentucky introduced a resolution that "slavery, as it exists within our bounds, is a great moral evil, and inconsistent with the word of God, and we do, therefore, recommend to all our ministers and members who hold slaves . . . to favor all proper measures for gradual voluntary emancipation." Upon its tabling for the second year, Robert J. Breckinridge, one of the antislavery leaders in the synod, walked out of the house with the words, "God has left you, and I also will now leave you, and have no more correspondence with you."[39] About the same time he wrote for a church periodical that slavery was "utterly abhorrent from every law of God. . . . The man who cannot see that involuntary domestic slavery, as it exists among us, is founded on the principle of taking by force that which is another's has simply no moral sense."[40] Inertia likewise characterized church action in Tennessee. At the Synod of West Tennessee in 1833 the question was asked, "Is there any inconsistency under existing circumstances in professors of religion owning slaves?" After some discussion the topic was indefinitely postponed.[41]

Although there is little evidence that the Cumberland Presbyterian Church differed from the parent body to any extent on the slavery question,[42] its official organ, *Theological Medium,* maintained a strong opposition. In the issue of March 19, 1834, there was a ringing editorial on "Gradual Emancipation," declaring, "The hope that slavery will be perpetuated is a delusion—a desire that it should be is a disgrace upon humanity. The negro will be freed; and we *must* liberate him, or God will do it at our expense."[43] Finis Ewing, the only one of the three founders of the Cumberland Presbyterian Church who owned slaves, preached a sermon in Tennessee that was widely printed. In this he said, "Lest some of my readers say, 'physician heal thyself,' I think it proper to state in this place, that after a *long, painful,* and prayerful investigation of this subject, I have determined *not to hold,* nor to *give,* nor to *sell,* nor to *buy any slaves for life.*"[44]

For many Presbyterian ministers slavery cast such a shadow over the South that they felt a strong urge to move away from the region. Among such preacher emigrés were Hugh Bass, stated clerk of the Synod of West Tennessee, who moved to Illinois, and James C. Barnes, stated clerk of the Transylvania Presbytery in Kentucky, who moved to Ohio. A Kentucky minister commented that the best men were "flying from the South."[45] Will Breckinridge, worried over the disposition of his own slaves and disgusted with slavery in Kentucky, wrote to a good friend in Ohio: "I care little where I go—so that I may only get where every man I see is as free as myself."[46]

It is interesting to note that while some preachers left the South, others, shying from the fanatical efforts of abolition societies, became apologists for slavery. Joshua L. Wilson of Cincinnati in such a manner forsook his advocacy of emancipation.[47] There is much evidence to support Leonard Bacon's belief that the "southern apostacy" from the generally accepted sentiment on slavery may be dated from about 1833. At that time James Smylie, searching the Scripture to determine its teachings in regard to slavery, found to his surprise a marked variance from the popular notion.[48] Desiring to spread his discovery, Smylie delivered at Port Gibson, Mississippi, a sermon which "gave great offense" not only to the local church but also to the ministry, which cautioned him not to preach further along this line. In the meanwhile, the Chillicothe (Ohio) Presbytery addressed to the Mississippi Presbytery, of which Smylie was the stated clerk, a series of resolutions urging that the sin of slavery be forsaken. Irritated by the letter, Smylie was now determined to put his ideas and findings into printed form.[49] In an answer to the Ohio presbytery he contended that Negro slavery was justified under divine dispensation and that the duties of masters and servants were clearly stated in the New Testament. He further pointed out that "servant" meant "slave" and that, if it were a sin to hold a slave, he demanded proof from Holy Writ.[50] Although for a while Smylie "was covered with odium," his interpretation was so rapidly accepted that it became "not only prevalent, but violently and exclusively dominant" in most of the lower South.[51] In 1853 the Synod of Mississippi prepared a notice of Smylie's death; the committee acclaimed him for "giving the true exposition of the doctrines of the Bible in relation to slavery in the commencement of the abolition excitement."[52]

The growing strength of abolition was terrifying to Southern churches in the 1830's, and their fear contributed greatly to the surrender of important principles that formerly had been accepted by the higher judicatories.[53] From Tennessee to the Gulf, presbyteries and synods once silent on the slavery issue now united vigorously in a war against the abolitionists. In 1835 the South Alabama Presbytery resolved that "the Schemes and efforts of the Abolitionist [s] of the North are ruinous to the peace & happiness of our beloved country . . ., destructive to the comfort of the Slave population, the interest of the church and the Stability of established Institutions."[54] In the same year the committee on abolition of the Synod of West Tennessee reported that the emancipation movement was "disturbing its civil associations" and "alienating the affections of brethren."[55] Also in 1835 the Tuscaloosa (Alabama) Presbytery considered the abolitionist interference as "wicked and fanatical," "cruel and uncalled for," and, if continued, certain to "rend the union" and to lay "our country in ruins." Furthermore, it declared, slavery was so interwoven into the life of the South that it could not be suddenly abolished without great disaster.[56]

Although rigid opposition to slavery began to weaken in Kentucky about 1830, the Presbyterian Church there resisted slavery at least a decade longer than in any other Southern state. Cotton was a far more important crop in Tennessee than in Kentucky; hence the churches in Tennessee had remained discreetly silent on the "peculiar institution." The antislavery element in Kentucky, however, had regained control of the Synod of Kentucky by 1835.[57] In a lengthy and able document a committee of ten presented a report which lucidly and fearlessly described the horrors of the slave system and recommended a plan for emancipation.[58] This was far in advance of the prevailing sentiment in the remainder of the South. Even in Kentucky it contributed to the disturbance of religious meetings of Negroes and to the closing of some of their Sabbath schools.[59] This statement generally expressed the view of the synod, but it was not acted upon because of the fanaticism that prevailed in the North at this time.[60] The plan, however, later was discussed by some of the presbyteries.[61]

A contrasting action was that of the Synod of Mississippi in 1835. In a resolution it denied that a church judicatory had the right to interfere in any of the political or civil relations of society, and confined church authority to the realm of conscience.[62] Two years later the South Alabama Presbytery took similar action. Its commissioners to the General Assembly were instructed that this body had no right to interfere with slavery matters and that they should seek to prevent any action on the subject.[63]

In 1836 twelve memorials on the subject of slavery were brought before the General Assembly.[64] A special committee on slavery reported that Negro bondage "is inseparably connected with and regulated by the laws of many of the states in this Union, with which it is by no means proper for an ecclesiastical judicatory to interfere." A vigorous minority report, however, held that "buying, selling, or holding a human being as property, is, in the sight of God, a heinous sin."[65] Immediately forty-eight slaveholding delegates met and agreed that they would not submit to the acceptance of this or a similar report.[66] By vote of 154 to 87 the matter was closed by the adoption of a resolution indefinitely postponing action.[67]

In 1836 the majority in the General Assembly had been composed of New School representatives, but in 1837 the situation was reversed and the Old School delegation was safely in control.[68] Slavery did not enter into the discussion of issues in the Assembly of 1837,[69] but it was a latent force drawing the line of cleavage sharper and clearer.[70] Many who so strenuously and plainly had condemned the acts of exscinding were leaders in the repudiation and condemnation of antislavery legislation.[71] Amidst some rejoicing, especially in the South,[72] the action of the Assembly led to a schism—each part of the church retaining the same name, the same standards, and almost the same field of activity.[73]

Despite the fact that the national antislavery movement began among the Presbyterians,[74] they, like the Methodists and Baptists, receded from an earlier position of attacking slavery and compromised with it. As cotton and slavery took a firmer hold on Southern society and economy, Presbyterian orthodoxy became an important factor in establishing a "social oligarchy" whose convictions on the justice of the adopted position seldom wavered. Presbyterian clergymen, recognizing in Calvinistic theology the rational premise of master and slave, were among the ablest defenders of the moral and Scriptural basis for slavery.[75] In accord with expediency,[76] the Presbyterian Church, "the most influential religious body in the United States,"[77] took its stand with an expanding slavocracy. Expediency produced compromise; compromise gave energy and stimulation to an institution which, without the direct and indirect support of the churches in the early South and Southwest, might have been short-lived.[78]

As with similar topics in Southern history, the general outline is familiar, a retelling of the old theme—cotton and slavery, expediency and compromise.

VIII

THE NEGRO SLAVE
IN THE PRESBYTERIAN CHURCH

THE TOTAL of all the care and attention given to the Negroes by the Presbyterian Church in the Old Southwest is highly significant.[1] In the states of Kentucky and Tennessee, where there was no legal restriction against the education of Negroes, the work of the church was varied and diverse. In Mississippi, Alabama, and Louisiana, where there were legislative prohibitions, the church managed to find devious ways to teach the individual slave. In general, the chief interest of the church was directed toward an effort to give religious instruction so that the Negro might enjoy the benefits of Christianity.

As early as 1787 the Synod of New York and Philadelphia urged Presbyterians to give Negroes all the advantages of a good education.[2] Seven years later the Transylvania Presbytery in Kentucky ordered all persons under its care to teach their slaves under fifteen years of age to read the Bible and to instruct in the Christian religion all others "as far as they can find it practicable."[3] In 1803 the General Assembly "observed, with great pleasure, that the desire for spreading the Gospel . . . among the blacks . . . has been rapidly increasing during the last year. . . ."[4] Six years later the Synod of Kentucky ordered the presbyteries in Kentucky and Tennessee to take steps which "may seem prudent to secure the Religious instruction of Slaves" so that they may have "a human and Christian treatment."[5] In conformity with this order the Transylvania Presbytery in 1811 urged its members to pursue the proper course in order to guarantee the fulfillment of this very acceptable ruling.[6]

The commissioners to the General Assembly of 1816 discussed at length the subject of missions to the Negroes, but no plan was put into effect.[7] Four years later the Board of Missions of the General Assembly reported that a man of color, George M. Erskine, had preached for four months in east Tennessee to audiences composed of whites and blacks who were "attentive and sometimes solemn."[8] Interest in missions to Negroes began to fade by 1830;[9] however, references in church records to activities of local preachers became rather frequent about this date.

Encouragement was given by the Assembly of 1818 to provide religious instruction for slaves, together with liberty to attend preaching and to receive opportunities for learning through Sabbath schools.[10] Despite this gesture, little was accomplished in the West for several years. In 1825 the Synod of Kentucky ordered its ministers to provide greater religious instruction for the slaves.[11] In response to this edict, fifteen schools were established in the synod within a year.[12] In 1825 the General Assembly commended the prudence and zeal in religious instruction and evangelization of slaves, especially in the presbyteries of South Carolina, Georgia, Alabama, and Mississippi. By way of inspiration the Assembly stated that "No more honored name can be conferred . . . than that of Apostle to the American slaves. . . ."[13] Beyond question the most successful worker in any church among the Negroes of the South was Charles C. Jones, a Presbyterian minister in Georgia, who sought to convince slaveowners that religious education tended to reduce the possibility of insurrection. He cited the Southampton Insurrection as a product of ignorance and misunderstanding by Negroes who had been misled by the false prophecy of Nat Turner.[14]

The North Alabama Presbytery lamented in 1829 the neglect of its members to provide religious instruction for slaves and recommended that thereafter each church member "attend to it as he may have the opportunity."[15] Two years later the Synod of Mississippi and South Alabama, in its narrative for 1831, felt encouraged over the interest in Negroes but begged for a faithful compliance with the resolution of the synod to provide missionaries for oral instruction to slaves on the plantations, with permission of the owners.[16] The South Alabama Presbytery in 1832 recommended a plan by which each church should be required to divide the colored members into two or more classes, appoint a teacher for each, catechize the members, and explain the Scriptures.[17] Two years later the narrative of the Synod of Mississippi revealed the deep interest in the Negro and the efforts to teach him religion. Despite the laws in Mississippi, Alabama, and Louisiana against teaching the Negro to read, oral instruction was used.[18] The

South Alabama Presbytery in the same year proposed three methods by which the Negroes could be taught "their duty to God and man": first, attend at preaching; second, assemble in families to hear the Scriptures read; third, meet in classes convenient to several families on the plantations for lengthier oral instruction.[19]

The Synod of Kentucky became so concerned about the enslaved black men that it believed the Negroes were doomed *"to hopeless ignorance"* unless drastic steps were taken in their behalf.[20] Following this warning, the Transylvania Presbytery in 1836 recommended to its members the synod's plan which called for instruction "in the common elementary branches of education" and the teaching of the Scripture through Sabbath schools and domestic tutoring.[21] In the next year a committee on the education of slaves appointed by the West Tennessee Presbytery reported a plan quite similar to that of the Transylvania Presbytery. The only significant difference was a recommendation that a catechism prepared by Charles C. Jones be used.[22] In 1839 the Synod of Mississippi commissioned two of its ministers, James Smylie and John L. Montgomery, to write a catechism for the instruction of the slaves under its care.[23]

A striking generosity toward the education of the Negro is found in the individual case of Robert Marshall, a Presbyterian minister and schoolteacher in Kentucky. He sent a child of one of his servants to a subscription school. The schoolmaster insisted that this action was "contrary to the customs of the country," and he refused to teach her.[24] Marshall's curt letter in reply is a gem from the pages of early liberalism. "I'm sorry," he wrote, "that any difficulty should occur respecting one child merely because her skin is not of the same colour with others—I have not imposed her on you without your prior consent, & the consent of the trustees. . . . I feel conscientiously bound to teach all blacks, whom I raise to read the scriptures; & I know not how any person who professes christianity can . . . do otherwise. If I must teach her at home, I can also teach the rest of my family . . . when we mix in the family continually with slaves it can be no dishonor to mix with them at school."[25] Many Negroes received a smattering of reading and writing from schools conducted by such men as Marshall and James Blythe. The latter had a slave Jefferson who on Sundays taught fifteen to twenty black children to read in Blythe's kitchen.[26] Negro members of the churches were used to catechize

Negroes in the churches. This fact is evident in the permission granted by the South Alabama Presbytery to the Government Street Church at Mobile.[27]

As a general rule in the Presbyterian Church, Negro slaves were encouraged to attend preaching in the morning along with their masters. Galleries or back seats on the lower floor were used by the Negroes when convenient, otherwise they "must catch the Gospel as it escapes by the doors and windows."[28] In 1816 Daniel Smith, a Presbyterian minister at Natchez, was distressed because he found no place assigned to the blacks. "The poor creatures were hanging about the doors, afraid to enter."[29] Special sessions were usually arranged for the afternoon, at which time the minister preached solely to his black congregation.[30] Joint arrangements were sometimes made by the churches and by the plantations to employ a minister for the whole or part of his time to itinerate from one plantation to another.[31] On a few of the large plantations a minister devoted all of his time to preaching and giving religious instruction. Some planters who formerly had been ministers preached regularly to their own slaves.[32]

In 1832 the session of the Pine Ridge (Mississippi) Church resolved that its minister should devote alternate Sunday evenings to the religious instruction of the blacks "by preaching for their benefit in the church, in a style more simplified and more suited to their capacity." The session further agreed that Negroes who gave "evidence of piety" and sought admission should be organized into a branch of Pine Ridge and that sacraments should be administered in the presence of the Negro congregation. A week later the congregation was organized with seven members, six of whom were slaves belonging to William Bisland, an elder in the white church. However, "on account of their ignorance . . . it was thought expedient to defer the administration of the Lord's Supper to them until a future occasion."[33] About the same time George G. M'Afee began his ministry in Henderson, Kentucky. Finding the Christians in a "cold state," he decided to preach to the slaves in the afternoons. Soon he had a congregation of 150 attentive but ignorant blacks, about whom he was able to say that they constituted "the most hopeful part of my charge and through them I think the whites may be reached."[34]

The scene was not so promising everywhere. In 1833 a committee of the Synod of South Carolina and Georgia felt that the Negroes were *"destitute of the privileges of the Gospel."*[35] In the following year this synod recorded in its narrative that there was little opportunity to preach to the Negroes separately and at stated times.[36] In peculiar contrast, in the same year the Synod of Mississippi and South Alabama was pleased over its religious efforts on behalf of the Negro.[37] Although the laws in these states were strict in the matter of teaching slaves to read, there was no opposition to preaching to them.[38] In the synods of Kentucky, Tennessee, and West Tennessee—free from restrictive legislation—it was the prevailing practice to preach to the Negro once on Sunday and once during the week. Reports from all sections, however, insisted that the abolitionist excitement interfered with the program.[39] Now from a better perspective there are evidences that the abolition movement impelled the planters and the churches to give more attention to the religious life of the slave.

From the slave ranks came preachers and missionaries of considerable stature, many of whom went to Africa to work among the natives. One of the most interesting was George M. Erskine, whose freedom was purchased by a group headed by Isaac Anderson of east Tennessee. Receiving in 1818 a license to preach, Erskine served as a local missionary for ten years. Within this period he accumulated $2,400 to buy the freedom of his wife and seven children so that they could go with him to Africa.[40] Another and better known case is that of the slave Ellis of Alabama whose freedom was purchased by the Alabama and Mississippi synods. Skilled as a blacksmith, Ellis commanded attention with his quick mind, alert manner, and confident bearing. When a leader for his people was sought, the choice readily fell on Ellis. Learning came easily, and he quickly secured an elementary education. In preparation for the ministry he studied Latin, Greek, and theology, and, following an examination by the Tuscaloosa Presbytery, he received ordination for the ministry. In 1846 he, with his family, was sent to Liberia as a missionary.[41]

The First African (Presbyterian) Church in Philadelphia, founded in 1807, had for its pastor John Gloucester, a former slave of Gideon Blackburn, by whom he had been converted to the Presbyterian faith. After a short while Blackburn saw the great possibilities in the Negro and released him from slavery. Later Gloucester was able to secure money necessary to purchase the freedom of his family. He possessed a powerful frame, a strong and musical voice, and a tireless and unabating store of energy. Highly successful as a preacher, he remained at the First African Church until his death in 1822.[42]

87

In preaching to the Negroes, the Presbyterian minister talked much about sins—quarreling, drinking, stealing, and loose living.[43] Urged by the master, the minister often fashioned his sermon to fit the need of the particular occasion and the particular plantation.[44] Some planters even required their slaves to be present at the services arranged for them.[45] The wise Charles C. Jones felt that most of the owners hindered religious work among slaves since the owners were mainly interested in combatting the vices that were to a large degree incidental to slavery.[46] In a report of a committee on religious instruction of the Synod of South Carolina and Georgia in 1834, the claim was made that proper attention to the gospel for Negroes would advance *"the pecuniary interests of masters,"* because the Negro would become less addicted to crime and laziness, and would be more saving and more obedient.[47] Probably three-fourths of all cases of church discipline of the Negro by the Presbyterians concerned sex relations.[48] The pages of many session records are replete with charges of adultery, fornication, and illicit relations among the Negroes.[49] Some of the typical records run: Tobias was found guilty of "fornication in several instances" and was excommunicated. Five years later he was restored to church privileges.[50] A Negro named Washington was charged with "improper intercourse" with Ebe. The latter acknowledged her guilt and charged Washington with being the father of her child. At the same time Ebe said her husband had not forsaken her but had simply "taken up with another woman." Washington also confessed guilt; both he and Ebe were expelled and both readmitted somewhat later.[51] On one day the session of the New Providence (Kentucky) Church considered three cases of fornication involving one white woman and two colored women. All three were suspended.[52]

A variety of charges against Negroes is found in the church records. Whisky was the cause of the greatest number of disciplinary actions taken by the Presbyterian Church, as was true of other churches on the frontier. As a rule simple intemperance was considered little more than a censurable offense, though there were numerous exceptions. The procedure became then as in Polly's case. She was lectured for her intemperance. After she repented, she was admonished, and advised to refrain from future use of intoxicating beverages.[53] The Paris (Kentucky) Church excommunicated Billy for theft and Fanny for "Night-stroling, breach of promise and a false oath."[54] Stealing, habitual lying, and profane swearing were often regular offenses.

"Living in open rebellion against God"[55] was a general charge that often brought expulsion. Sometimes charges were for more violent forms of transgression against the social order. For example, Jacob, a member of the Bethany (Mississippi) Church, was found guilty "of beating his wife and giving threatening languages to his mistress," for which act he was suspended.[56]

The Presbyterian Church courts seldom resorted to disciplinary action against the whites in order to secure redress for wrongs against the slaves. Although a session of the Paris (Kentucky) Church felt "itself bound to lift their Testimony against the inhumane and unfeeling practice of separating slaves from their husbands or wives," the session did not feel that the case against John Curry for the sale of a Negro man called "for their Judicial interference."[57] Charges of the cruel whipping of a slave were usually dismissed after "suitable admonition" had been given.[58]

Since slaves were owned by both church members and preachers who bought and sold them throughout the South, condemnation of the institution and censure of treatment came timidly and slowly. The session records contain surprisingly few entries concerning inhumane, barbarous, or unfair treatment of slaves.[59] In 1834 the Synod of Kentucky adopted a report which contained a description of the horrors of the internal slave trade. "There is not a village or road [in the state] that does not behold the sad procession of manacled outcasts, whose chains and mournful countenances tell that they are exiled by force from all that their hearts hold dear." "Cases have occurred in our own denomination where professors of the religion of mercy Have Torn The Mother From The Children, And Sent Her Into A Merciless And Returnless Exile. Yet acts of discipline have rarely followed such conduct." Sick with disgust, a ruling elder from Illinois declared before the General Assembly of 1835: "Elders, ministers, and Doctors of Divinity, are, with both hands, engaged in the practice."[60] His disgust was fomented by such preachers as Joseph L. Howe, who once failed to perform a marriage ceremony because he was attending the sale of Negroes who had been willed to the children of some of his relatives.[61] Yet in defense of many ministers it should be pointed out that they inherited slaves and kept them because they honestly pursued what seemed to be the more humane course.[62]

A few Presbyterian churches as corporate bodies held slaves for an investment. By hiring out slaves, money was raised for salaries of pastors and current expenses of the church. In 1836 more than $94,000 of the funds of the Presbyterian Church were invested in banks in the Southwest in anticipation of a high rate of interest made possible by a lively trade in slaves.[63] In 1845 eight Negroes were sold at public auction, together with some cattle and furniture, for the benefit of the Theological Seminary of the Synod of South Carolina and Georgia.[64] There can be little denial that individual churches dodged the issue, closed their eyes to the deplorable situation, and by silence sanctioned slavery as an institution.[65] The influence of individual persons was weak; the indignation of some went into sermons and of others into entries in their diaries. Charles Coffin, a Presbyterian preacher in east Tennessee, noted in his journal that he had seen a company of male and female Negroes handcuffed together with iron. "In the rear travelled a mounted Negro driver, whose countenance bespoke as complete destitution of every noble and humane feeling, as did his employment."[66] Countless sermons, mild and ineffectual, were preached by Presbyterian ministers on the duties of masters and slaves.[67] Books on the subject were written by such forceful and dynamic figures as Charles C. Jones.[68] Catechisms in both the historical and doctrinal form were prepared for the special use of the Negro.[69] Essays on the moral and religious condition of the colored people were read before white audiences[70] and published in the church journals.

The evangelical appeal of the Presbyterian preacher, however, had only slight effect on the Negro. Preaching man's depravity, the minister had no fresh attraction to a slave who already had suffered ignominy and shame. A rational accounting for slavery made the yoke no lighter on the slave. The Negro with his limited training was better equipped to feel than to think; the earnest and intense, though poorly trained, Baptist and Methodist preachers asked far less intellectually of the Negro. Probably the Methodist advantage is best explained by Benjamin T. Tanner, bishop of the African Methodist Episcopal Church, who said the Presbyterian Church "strove to lift up without coming down and while the good Presbyterian parson was writing his discourses, rounding off the sentences, the Methodist itinerant had traveled forty miles with his horse and saddle bags; while the parson was adjusting his spectacles to read his manuscript, the itinerant had given hell and damnation to his unrepentant hearers; while the disciple of Calvin was waiting to have his church completed, the disciple of Wesley took to the woods, and made them re-echo with the voice of free grace. . . ."[71] On the other hand, the Baptist Church contained more Negro members than the Methodist, probably because of the attractive form of baptism by immersion and the privilege of preaching.[72]

The Negroes joined the Presbyterian Church under the same entrance regulations to which the whites conformed. They were both subject to the same discipline, although it was more leniently applied to the Negro.[73] A typical session entry recording the admittance of a Negro to membership is found in the records of the Shiloh (Tennessee) Church for 1834. "Delphiny, a slave of Samuel McMurray, appeared before the session and was examined on experimental religion, whereupon she was admitted to the privileges of the church, and it was resolved that she make a public profession of religion tomorrow morning (Sunday) and receive the ordinance of baptism."[74] On occasion Presbyterian ministers agreed to baptize by immersion. John Morgan, a Cumberland Presbyterian minister, once was requested to immerse a large Negro man. At the moment when Morgan attempted to immerse the Negro, he lost his foothold on the slippery bottom of the creek and let the Negro slip from his grasp. For several years afterwards Morgan refused to baptize by immersion.[75]

The General Assembly of 1816 discussed the question, "Ought baptism, on the profession and promise of the master, to be administered to the children of the slaves?" The Assembly ruled that masters owed to the children of slaves the duty of presenting them for baptism; furthermore, it was the duty of the ministers to baptize all children who were presented by their masters.[76] As a rule the masters were willing to have slaves baptized into the church. On May 21, 1826, John Hunley presented seven of his servants for baptism by the First Presbyterian Church of Louisville and "he sealed the covenant on their behalf."[77] Six younger children of Friday and Venus were admitted to baptism by the Salem (Mississippi) Church at a single meeting in 1833.[78] In some cases the slaves were received at the white services and baptized at the colored.[79] The Bethesda (Tennessee) Church wondered if masters of slaves who refused "to bring them forward and give them to God in baptism" were not censurable.[80]

The marriage ceremony was a sacrament of the church which little concerned the Negro members. The Southern states did not give legal sanction to marriages between slaves, and the planter seldom had any peculiar feeling on the subject. An isolated exception is found in a letter to the Synod of Kentucky in 1827 urging that marriages be encouraged and that Negro families be kept intact.[81]

Existing statistics on the Negro and his church affiliations are variable and inconsistent. One writer has estimated that in the 1840's there were formally connected with churches in the South 260,000 Negroes, of whom only seven thousand belonged to the Presbyterian Church.[82] Another authority thinks twenty thousand was the largest number of Negroes who were members of the Presbyterian Church at any time before the Civil War.[83] Accepting either source, it is clearly evident that the Presbyterian Church held only a small percentage of the Negroes. Failure to attract the Negro to membership did not lessen the church's interest in his physical and spiritual welfare. This great social interest of the church was significant. Despite the restrictions placed by some of the Southern states on instructing slaves, the Presbyterian Church sought various means of giving oral instruction in religious education. In states free from restrictions much was accomplished in the elementary education of the Negro. When due consideration is given to the problems that inevitably arose from the very nature of slavery, the position of the Presbyterian Church in its relation with the Negro is one of generosity and studied attempts to raise the general welfare of the enslaved people.

IX

THE CHURCH ELEVATES
WESTERN MORALS

WHEN THE FIRST PIONEER from the coastal region crossed the Alleghenies and looked at the vast region before him, a new sense of independence surely swept over him. Here lay in the great forests, rich grasslands, and fine rivers the opportunity for which every man dreams—a kingdom for the taking. But the taking called for a feat of physical strength which "seared his moral sensibilities and coarsened his aesthetic appreciations."[1]

The Presbyterian Church on the frontier was a vigilant protector of peace and order and an exacting judge when its erring members strayed from its Confession of Faith and rules of conduct.[2] The governing body of a local church was composed of the board of elders and the minister, and in this session were vested the powers to control officers and members.[3] At regular intervals the entire church membership was tested on the articles of faith and acquaintance with the Scripture. This public examination was made by the minister prior to Communion.[4] The members who satisfied the examiner received tokens, wooden or metal, which gave them admittance to the Communion table.[5] The session books are filled with records of reprimands, reproofs, warnings, and actual character trials of church members. When rumors of theft,[6] drunkenness,[7] fornication,[8] adultery,[9] and slander[10] came to the ears of the session, the body organized itself as a grand jury and later into an ecclesiastical court. Here justice was summarily meted to offenders of the moral law. The decision of the session was read by the minister to the entire congregation, and this public denouncement was frequently more humiliating than dismissal from church membership. The church was usually on safe ground, because it considered cases which involved neither civil nor criminal courts.

The church did not hesitate to raise its voice against the amuse-

ments of dancing, theatergoing, horseracing, and cardplaying. The
General Assembly of 1818 condemned dancing as "a fascinating and
infatuating practice" which "dissipates religious impressions, and
hardens the heart."[11] It further warned in ambiguous terms that
dancing in "highest extremes" leads to "ultimate consequences"
which are "fatal."[12] Local churches were not so vague in substituting
"immoral" for "fatal." Sentiment was much the same in Tennessee,
Alabama, Missouri, and Ohio; dancing was considered major among
the minor vices, and promiscuous dancers were expelled from the
church.[13] From Murfreesboro, Tennessee, came the resolution that
dancing was contrary to the spirit of the discipline, and parents who
permitted their children to attend dancing parties were threatened
with disciplinary measures.[14] The West Tennessee Presbytery stated in
1817 that the dancer was guilty of "decidedly criminal" conduct and
should be banned from the church.[15] A similar opinion was later
expressed in a pastoral letter from the church in Courtland, Alabama.[16]
Many of the church members meekly accepted the reprimands from
the sessions, but some were rebellious and altered their ways but little;[17] one defender of his actions presented Biblical support.[18]

The General Assembly denounced gambling and lotteries at numerous meetings. It denominated gambling as an "infatuating and
destructive vice . . . maintaining its accursed sway over thousands of
its hapless victims."[19] Since the pioneer was so dependent on luck and
chance, he did not meekly accept the condemnation of them. In its
opposition to lotteries the church received little support from congregations in the West. Too frequently funds for benevolent and religious organizations had been raised by lotteries: the erection of the
church buildings in New Orleans[20] and Natchez[21] had been financed
chiefly by monies acquired in this way. Despite this use of income, the
General Assembly disapproved of its source and in 1830 restated its
disapproval of "legalized gambling."[22] Local sessions, however, closed
their eyes to the business.[23] A quiet gentlemanly game for money went
almost unnoticed among church members; a Mr. Aldrich of Baton
Rouge was cautioned by his session "to reflect upon the course he was
pursuing," but the session took no further step.[24] Bets placed on horseracing fell into the category of mild gambling; the sport had too many
devotees in all sections of the South for a preacher to speak very
loudly against it. When Robert Henderson, preaching in Nashville,
condemned all kinds of fashionable amusements, he was waited on

by a group of "sportsmen" from the audience. General Jackson, a lover of the race track, was present and defended Henderson against his would-be attackers.[25]

Although the theater was seldom found in the West, the church regarded it as "a school of immorality" and viewed it as an iniquity which would "blunt the delicate sensibilities of the female mind."[26] Beyond such warnings there is no evidence from Western church records that the theater played any part as a disciplinary problem.

By the 1820's some spokesmen for the church were concerned over the growing love for fashionable dress. In the *Western Luminary* frequently appeared letters or articles commenting on the excessive use of bracelets, finger rings, ribbons, feathers, and "the trimmings worn by the daughters of Zion." Copying a column from a New England paper, the *Luminary* printed "The Misfortunes of Flora," which recounted the sad story of a young woman who "in order to be a lady, thought she must be pale as a sheet, slim as a pipe's tail, and straight as a candle." She achieved erect posture by wearing "an instrument, which may properly be termed a *consumption board.*" The text of this article was evidently as pertinent to the Western woman as to the New England miss.[27]

The church sessions worried themselves greatly over the relationships of contracting parties in marriage. Advice and Biblical interpretation were sought from higher judicatories on the questions: May a man marry his brother's widow? May a man marry his former wife's niece? These situations did not merit dismissal from church privileges, but the man who married the widow of his uncle was suspended.[28] Marriage between a man and his dead wife's sister always brought severe rebuke and loud disapproval.[29]

Extra-marital relations of church members were the frequent subjects of many session meetings and numerous pages of minutes. The cases were recorded with unexpected frankness, and the findings were made public with equal harshness.[30] No doubt, fear of the session rather than fear of the Lord kept many people in the straight and narrow path.

The initial entry in the session book of the church at Paris, Kentucky, indicates the formal and ominous procedure by which the session tried a case for immoral conduct. "WHEREAS fornication is a henious [*sic*] sin and scandal contrary to the word of God, and to the profession of the Church founded thereon; repugnant to the Christian

95

Character, and injurious to the religion of the Lord Jesus; yet true it is, that you Elizabeth Beckett a member of the Presbyterian Church are Charged of being . . . the parent of an illegitimate offspring . . . you ought therefore to be proceeded against. . . ." The offender, acknowledging her guilt, was barred from church membership, but later was restored. An extremely grave case against Dr. Joseph H. Holt is contained in fifty pages of the session book of the Paris (Kentucky) Church. Charged with living in adultery with Eliza S. Jones, "a female of lewd character," Holt further damaged the "Character of the church" by passing "clandestinely through fields and unusual ways of passage" to a farmhouse in the neighborhood.[31] The case against Polly Gibson of New Providence (Kentucky) Church was recorded with extreme candor. The statements of character witnesses contained unusually intimate details, startling even to the modern, uninhibited reader. Charged with the act of fornication with a man whom she later married, Polly was suspended from the church by the session, which looked "more to the operations of nature than to oral Testimony because in general they lead to more certainty."[32] A female member of the Mount Bethel (Tennessee) Church, confessing that "she had very much ignored the cause of Christ" by having an illegitimate child, was suspended until she gave evidence of an "honest repentance."[33] It was hard to let past sins lie forgotten. When the minister of the First Presbyterian Church in Nashville learned that one of its members had been guilty of fornication, he had the woman and her father appear before the session, where she "frankly and penitently confessed her previous fall."[34]

As a rule, suspension from church membership was meted to the woman, but the man was often let off with words of rebuke and reproof. Two members of the Shiloh (Tennessee) Church were convicted of adultery. The woman was excluded from membership in 1845, but not until 1847 was the name of the man struck from the church roll.[35] After several hearings the Kentucky Presbytery of the Associate Reformed Church in 1802 acquitted John Snodgrass of the accusation of two sisters who claimed he was the father of their children.[36] Unusual charity was shown to John Paul and his sister, who admitted guilt of incest upon applying for admission to the church at Honey Creek, Kentucky. Baffled, the church appealed to the presbytery, and the presbytery to the synod: the synod advised that the Pauls should be admitted on the provision that they live separately.[37]

Judging from the frequent charges that the Southern slaveholder lived in perpetual sin with his female Negro slaves, the reader of the records will be surprised that only two cases were found in the many minutes examined. In Kentucky a Mrs. Tull, evidently in a fit of anger, accused her husband of "holding an improper intimacy with his negro woman," but, when the accusations were brought before the Transylvania Presbytery in 1798, Mrs. Tull completely retracted her previous statements.[38] Upon "common fame" Harry Emerson was questioned by the Pisgah (Alabama) Church about illicit relations with one of his female servants, but he was acquitted of the charge.[39]

The preacher did not always hold a position above reproach in the community. He easily became the center of unfavorable criticism— some earned, but much unearned. "The voice of public rumor" allowed few indiscretions to go unnoticed in the neighborhood. When receiving criticism from the congregation and session, the preacher was responsible for his actions to the presbytery. The minutes of the various presbyteries in the region under consideration contain frequent charges of immorality of ministers. There were recorded against the preacher many petty and malicious accusations of imprudence, improper dress, impolite manners, and minor infractions of social customs. "Common fame," too often from the tongues of garrulous women, received exaggerated value in most cases and formed the basis for severe judgments.[40]

The church did not confine its disciplinary power to infractions of the moral code. Holding its members to a strict standard of conduct, it stepped in as a modifying force whenever emotions or actions became violent and uncontrolled. The church frowned upon fighting, an "endemic vice" of the frontier, and attempted to curb its members who used fists too frequently and freely. The instances of the church reproving its members for fighting or quarreling are numerous, but a few pointed examples will clearly reveal the temper of the early West. When R. H. Simmons refused to appear before the session in answer to a charge of having fought Dr. David Barber, he was excluded by the Lasting Hope (Tennessee) Cumberland Presbyterian Church.[41] Before the Apple Creek (Missouri) Church session John Cowan admitted that he had struck at James Rosebrough with a cooper's adz and would do it again under similar circumstances.[42] The Baton Rouge Church was embarrassed by a hot-headed elder, James Cooper, who was repeatedly involved in fights and brawls.

Within four years the session record contains portions of thirty-two pages devoted to the misconduct of this belligerent officer of the church.[43] Plum Creek (Kentucky) Church listed three charges at one time against J. N. Allen, who had settled his differences by fighting.[44]

Women indulged in petty and even mean quarrels; malicious gossip was as potent a weapon as fists. Margaret Anderson, refusing to attend the same church with her daughter, was suspended for a year.[45] Caroline Tucker admitted assault and battery on Jane Lightfoot, but confessed in "a most unchristian and unforgiving temper," so that the church suspended her.[46] A session excused Edward English for striking his wife, but suspended Mrs. English because she refused to appear before the session.[47]

Rumors or accusations of theft by or from a church member were generally investigated by the local church sessions. Often the church could settle a matter outside of civil court. Bryant Ferguson, upon being accused of taking stray hogs, asked his church to investigate the charges. When the accuser would not come before the session, the case was dropped.[48] The Apple Creek (Missouri) Church accused William B. McNeely of stealing corn, but took no action as McNeely left the neighborhood.[49] The Murfreesboro (Tennessee) Church acted as mediator between two elders, one of whom accused the other of stealing wood.[50] Andrew Kelly was acquitted by the church of charges of petty thieving,[51] but Jane Write was suspended by her church when it decided she was "taking things she had no business with."[52] A decision of unintentional fraud was given in favor of the seller of four kegs of butter which arrived in New Orleans in extremely rancid condition.[53] A "shady trade" always brought complaints, and the session or the presbytery was often hard put to render a fair decision. Church members too often drove hard bargains, and their honesty was sometimes questioned. In a reversal of its earlier decision, the West Tennessee Presbytery exonerated John Frierson in a dispute over a boundary line.[54] James McGready was so involved in a property dispute that the matter passed from presbytery to synod and back to presbytery. The second presbytery ruled that the first one had given "a false, iniquitous & malicious representation of the conduct of the Rev. James McGready."[55]

Perhaps the widespread use of whisky among all people on the frontier accounts for the generous attitude toward the excessive use of intoxicants. Whisky was present on all occasions—weddings, funerals, births, baptizings, corn-huskings, house-raisings, and elections.[56] The host who failed to provide whisky, brandy, or bounce was a poor one indeed, and it was a reckless homemaker who did not have corn whisky on the shelf as a medicine. The national consumption of liquor was estimated in 1812 to be five gallons per person. This large consumption of whisky has a basis other than gastronomics. Whisky was tied up with the economics of the frontier:[57] a horse could transport twenty-four bushels of corn in liquid form but only four in grain. Distilling and selling was a respectable home industry, conducted by laymen and sometimes by clergymen.[58] Gideon Blackburn was at one time a large-scale dealer in liquor. Two contemporaries made interesting comments on Blackburn's enterprise: John Sevier noted in his diary that some Creek Indians about 1807 had "seized upon & took away Parson Blackburn's whisky,"[59] and M. W. Trimble, upon hearing Blackburn preach a temperance sermon in Mississippi in 1834, said, "If any man ought to preach of temperance it ought to be Gideon Blackburn."[60]

The attitude of the church toward the making, vending, and using of whisky is not so positive as might be expected.[61] Early in the nineteenth century the General Assembly of the Presbyterian Church began a series of resolutions expressing disapproval of intemperate drinking.[62] But judicatories less remote from the Western scene—synods, presbyteries, and sessions—were not so bold in condemnation of a staple commodity. The synods of West Tennessee and of Mississippi and South Alabama expressed disapprobation of the making, selling, and frequent use of liquor.[63] In 1832 a presbytery in Alabama refused to ordain a candidate for the ministry who continued to distill, retail, or drink the "inebriating fluid."[64] About the same time a presbytery in Kentucky sought "to affectionately warn" its churches of the dangers of "liquid fire"[65]—a moderate and tolerant attitude that was typical in Kentucky, of which the limestone soil produced peculiarly good grain and sweet spring water. Subscriptions to preachers' salaries were often paid in gallons of whisky, a payment adaptable to personal and commercial use.[66] Ample indication of personal use is found in the censures and suspensions of preachers for drunkenness. Ephraim McLean was criticized for appearing somewhat "elevated and too light";[67] William Mahon, guilty of many offenses, was never reinstated as a preacher;[68] James Hamilton, an eloquent and gifted preacher, was deposed because of his love of grog.[69] Mem-

99

bers were likewise brought before the church sessions, but reproval and probation, not suspension, were generally given to the layman[70] unless his conduct had been too improper.[71] The Pisgah (Alabama) Church excluded from communion John Murphy, who accompanied his drinking with fighting;[72] John Smiley, an elder, injuring himself and the cause of religion, was suspended by the Bethany (Mississippi) Church;[73] John Miller in repentance promised "to walk in newness of life";[74] and concerning Israel McGready a character witness stated that intemperance had caused him to "depriciate in property & credit."[75]

Not only was drunkenness discountenanced, but some sessions severely reprimanded the seller of whisky. The Murfreesboro (Tennessee) Church sent a committee to confer with Jonathan McElroy, who was selling liquor in his store. He promised to stop as soon as he could make necessary arrangements.[76] A rather infamous character in middle Tennessee made a living largely by selling whisky at various camp meetings. In 1832 he went to a Cumberland Presbyterian meeting at Lebanon, Tennessee, where he found customers so scarce he took a seat on the outskirts of the congregation. His vocation suffered permanently when he "fell prostrate before the throne of grace."[77]

Organized efforts for temperance took several forms about the same time. In 1828 at Lexington, *The Temperance Herald of the Mississippi Valley,* the first paper in the West "devoted exclusively to temperance," was sponsored by the Presbyterian Church. In the same year the General Assembly appointed a day of prayer for temperance and a year later encouraged the organization of temperance societies in individual churches. Neither of these efforts was well received by the Westerner, who regarded the whole movement as an infringement on his civil liberties. In 1837 the General Assembly, being aware that members "still manufacture and still sell ardent spirits," lamented the fact with the terse statement, "these things ought not to be so."[78]

While the church leaders might close their eyes to frequent imbibing of "the cheering juice," they took no foolishness about the keeping of the Sabbath Day holy. They zealously prosecuted the letter of the fourth commandment and filled the minutes of the sessional and presbyterial records with transgressors of the day. Church people were cautioned "to guard against the pernicious ways of the world . . . either by riding out, walking abroad, or visiting friends. . . ."[79] For a long time Sunday travel and Sunday mail were anathemas to pious

Presbyterians. To the churches in the Mississippi Territory Gideon Blackburn and Robert Henderson sent in 1816 a circular letter concerning the desecration of the Sabbath. Church members were warned that "without the Sabbath, there will be no religion. Without religion, no morality and without correct and sound morality, the bonds of society must be dissolved and hatred and jealousy, with all the crimes and miseries to which fallen nature is incident must ensue."[80] The General Assembly ruled in 1819 that business or commerce on Sunday was a bar to Communion;[81] and various synods, presbyteries, and sessions subsequently cited violators for driving hogs,[82] trading,[83] patronizing steamboats,[84] and traveling.[85] The Synod of West Tennessee declared that Sunday travel disturbed the "Cherokee brethren."[86] The South Alabama Presbytery urged all people and particularly ministers to avoid leaving a protracted meeting on Sunday.[87] The North Alabama Presbytery said that free movement over the country was an "awful profanation of the Christian Sabbath."[88] The *Western Luminary* gave a strong warning to Sabbath breakers by featuring the fate of a Mr. Babcock who, while moving a cannon on Sunday to celebrate General Jackson's election, met an accidental death.[89] The General Assembly regularly petitioned Congress to prohibit the transportation of mail on Sunday and systematically published propaganda against it.[90]

The efforts of the Presbyterian Church to regulate the moral life of the Western folk were manifold. Until civil authority was fully established on the frontier, the Presbyterian Church, with Argus eyes, was constantly vigilant for all manner of infractions of the moral code and, with other churches, contributed a stabilizing force that assured decency, law, and order to an ever receding frontier.

X

THE LOCAL CHURCH: ITS PHYSICAL
STRUCTURE AND SOCIAL SERVICES

THE SELECTION OF A SITE for a church building was dependent on several factors: a central location for a community, the proximity of a spring or running water,[1] and a good location for a graveyard. Regardless of denomination the church with a burying ground served the surrounding neighborhood, and the close relation between a church and a graveyard gave solemnity to early religious life.[2] An account of the evolution of one church tells the story of any on the frontier. The Presbyterians built the first house of worship[3] in Marion County, Kentucky, in 1789. Constructed five logs high and sixteen feet square with an earthen floor, it contained no windows, but unchinked cracks between the logs let in sufficient air and insufficient light. Within six years when a larger building was needed, a new church was erected measuring twenty by twenty-eight feet, equipped with a floor, benches with framed backs, and a small window behind the pulpit. Nine years later a still larger church was necessary, and the new structure, measuring twenty-eight by thirty-eight feet, was a frame, not log, building with several windows.[4] The Pine Ridge (Mississippi) Church is typical of a later period and a more elaborate structure. In 1827 a committee raised the necessary money to meet the contract of $4,410 for a building thirty-six by fifty feet, with a gallery on each end and windows in both sides and the front end. It was completed in about a year, and the session voted money for attaching a cistern to the church—ample evidence that there was neither well nor spring nearby.[5]

The interior of the church building was plainer than the family cabin. In general the earlier churches had no windows and the only light came through the cracks or the single door. Slowly glass came into use in windows which had been covered by batten shutters. Flares, lanterns, and lamps were used as artificial light, but this was seldom needed, for most church meetings were held in the day. When the New Providence (Kentucky) Church bought a "Brass Chandilier,"[6] an era of extravagance began. Little provision was made for heating the building. When heat was provided, it usually came from a fire on the outside in front of the door,[7] sometimes from a charcoal fire built in the center of the house.[8] A few people brought hot bricks wrapped in flannel on which they warmed their feet[9] during the long sermons. Stone or brick chimneys capable of holding huge logs were later additions to the meetinghouses.[10] Stumps left by the clearing of new ground were not removed from the area inside of the church. Benches were made by laying slabs from one stump to another; these seats were called "log-sittings."[11] Some people, desiring more comfortable seats, brought split-bottom chairs, marked with their initials, and left them for their personal use.[12] A tree cut off about waist high was the pulpit, and on the stump the preacher laid his Bible and his manuscript sermon.[13] In one instance when the length of the church was doubled, the pulpit, not being moved, stood in the center of the building.[14] As better churches were built, the pulpits became more elaborate: some had a sounding board at the back, others were raised and boxed, accessible on two sides by four or five steps; and an octagonal pulpit with eight or nine steps was an extreme rarity. Directly in front of the pulpit in some churches stood the "precentor's box," from which the precentor led the singing. The seats immediately in front of the pulpit were designated as the "elders' benches,"[15] or in seasons of revivals were called the "anxious seats" and reserved for those people "who appeared [to be] seeking the salvation of their souls."[16] When the congregation gathered,[17] decorum demanded that men sit on one side of the building and women on the other. There were diverse opinions concerning the legitimate and proper uses of the church building. One session decided that the "church edifice" should be lent only for sacred purposes and that it would not "tolerate any of those varied measures which excite associations inimical to religious worship."[18] Another congregation strangely questioned the propriety of bringing bodies of the dead into the church for burial services.[19] The buildings were frequently inadequate to accommodate the crowds that gathered for sacramental occasions or "big meetings," and the services then had to be held outdoors.

The usual manner of raising money for a church building was a subscription paper circulated among the members. Additional funds were supplied from various sources. The sale of an old church sometimes aided in financing a new one. At rare intervals somebody left by will a sum of money to a church.[20] Mount Zion (Kentucky) Church asked the Board of Education of the General Assembly to donate fifty dollars toward finishing the church building.[21] In several instances, especially in the lower South, money for churches was raised by lottery. As early as 1815 the legislature of Mississippi Territory passed an act authorizing a lottery, not exceeding five thousand dollars, for the benefit of the First Presbyterian Church at Natchez. In this particular case, an opponent of the lottery commented that "men were so bent upon temporal concerns that racy stimulants were resorted to to awaken a gleam of piety in the multitude."[22] When Theodore Clapp was offered the pastorate of the New Orleans church in 1822, he refused to accept the offer until the $45,000 indebtedness on the building was cleared. More than half of this amount was raised by a lottery, permission for which was granted by the state legislature.[23] Enough money was realized in 1815 from the sale of pews in the Second Presbyterian Church, Lexington, Kentucky, to cover the entire expense of the building. With the price of a pew ranging between $203 and $212, the sale of half the pews brought at auction a total of six thousand dollars.[24] In 1821 the New Providence (Kentucky) Church held a public sale of pews that had been "ranged and classed," and collected seven hundred dollars beyond the debt of the church. The surplus was spent enclosing the graveyard and buying stoves for the church.[25] In 1831 the trustees of the Tuscaloosa (Alabama) Church fixed the price of pews, but later increased it by fifty percent. Much dissatisfaction resulted, so that the price was immediately restored to the original amount.[26] In 1832 a dual calamity hit Nashville, Tennessee—fire destroyed the First Presbyterian Church and Asiatic cholera killed nearly two hundred people. With money scarce and collections slow, the times were difficult for rebuilding the church. The session resorted to the "questionable expedient of selling pews" to the highest bidders.[27]

Some of the Presbyterian congregations provided the minister with a manse, but the majority did not. In 1825 the Cabbin Creek (Kentucky) Church agreed to add fifteen feet to the length of the manse, raise it three logs higher, put on a good roof, add "an upper & under floor & make the whole close & comfortable."[28]

104

The earlier church records contain few references to the amount of money received for specific purposes, but they frequently included a list of subscribers to the general support of the local church and preacher. The Washington (Mississippi) Church in 1807 had a subscription list of forty-five names with pledges ranging from five to thirty dollars. Apparently these names included all the male white members of the church.[29] As the years unfold and particularly by the 1830's, the session and presbytery records contain many references to contributions and supply much evidence that the giving was commensurate with most of the pressing needs. As a general observation, the Presbyterians represented a financial level considerably higher than that of the Baptists and Methodists. An examination of the minutes of a session, such as the New Providence (Kentucky) Church, reveals much in regard to various contributions and donations. In 1829 a donation of $260 was made to the theological seminary of Centre College and $117 to the education fund. Two years later the women of the church subscribed $42 to the American Education Society and the church gave $105 to Centre. It is hardly probable that a church no larger than New Providence would make today similar gifts to education.[30] Missions were rather generously supported. In 1829 the Pine Ridge (Mississippi) Church appropriated $125 for the missionary to the Choctaw Nation.[31] In the same year the Louisville Church gave $1,300 to the missionary fund,[32] and in 1839 Tuscaloosa Presbytery promised $1,500 yearly to send Daniel Baker as a missionary to Texas.[33] In the same year the Plum Creek (Kentucky) Church gave $255 for foreign and domestic missions.[34] The missionary board of the church assisted struggling churches as in the case of the Baton Rouge Church which received two hundred dollars to aid its minister.[35]

Most of the early Presbyterians brought with them to the New World three books—Bible, catechism, and hymnal.[36] Their church had no hymn writer who approached the greatness of Charles Wesley. Although singing constituted a vital and important aspect of worship, the Presbyterians were far less productive in hymn writing than the other democratic churches. "They contributed little to the rapid development of poetry and imaginative prose which characterized the national life at this time."[37] Perhaps this is best explained by their satisfaction with the ways of their fathers and a consequent reluctance to substitute new hymns for the psalms and older hymns. Usually the precentor, with the aid of no musical instrument except the tuning fork,[38] led the singing and parceled out the hymns two lines at the time. After the precentor had "set" the tune by singing a couple of lines, the congregation joined in.[39] Often when the minister was not present, hymns or psalms were sung until the formal service began.[40] As hymnbooks came into common use, opposition arose to lining out the hymns[41] and this method was gradually forsaken. Later churches employed music leaders,[42] who greatly improved the quality of the singing.

Some of the most violent disputes in the church arose over the extreme determination of some members to sing only the psalms of the Old Testament. The chief protagonist of this group was Adam Rankin, who introduced the subject in a Kentucky conference held in 1785. Before the termination of this fight practically every Presbyterian church in Kentucky had become involved in some degree.[43]

Fifty years later some of the Presbyterian churches were even objecting to the hymnbook that was recommended by the General Assembly. As late as 1842 the Tuscaloosa Presbytery appointed a committee to report on the hymnbook. The members believed that "Some of the Hymns . . . are not well suited to the public, social or private worship." "Others are deficient in poetic merit or lyric character. . . ." "Others though not liable to any specific objection are not of sufficient merit to have a place in a work designed to be permanent and of general use. . . ."[44]

The first collection of hymns made for the Cumberland Presbyterian Church was not printed until 1824. It contained the stirring songs which were vital to the procedure of the camp meeting. When a minister walked to the stand and led the singing of

> "O Lord, revive Thy work
> In Zion's gloomy hours,"[45]

results were not long to be awaited.

In early Missouri much of the singing in Presbyterian churches resembled that of the Methodist camp meeting. Tunes were often impromptu. Some of the ministers, like David Nelson and James Gallaher, had voices "like silver trumpets" and often brought tears to many eyes. The singing was sometimes accompanied by handshaking led by the minister, who passed through the entire crowd shaking hands as the singing continued.[46]

The church member was tested during the Communion period on

his mastery of the catechism and careful reading of the Bible. It was an occasion of receiving grace from above and approval from fellow men. As a general rule the Communion service in the Presbyterian Church was held less frequently than at the present time.[47] Invariably the sacrament followed the culmination of a series of meetings, called a protracted or a three-day meeting, which usually began on Thursday and continued through Sunday. The action sermon, which preceded the taking of the sacrament, was regularly preached by a minister, who, by announcing the rules, "fenced the table."[48] The rules applied to the distribution of tokens, which were small pieces of lead resembling coins with something stamped thereon. Handed to worthy members on Saturday or Sunday,[49] the token permitted the holder to participate in the sacrament of the Lord's Supper.[50] The tokens were collected after the communicants had gathered at the tables and before the distribution of the elements. The long Communion tables,[51] covered with white cloths and laden with vessels containing bread and wine, were set near the altar or pulpit. While the congregation stood, a short prayer was said and a psalm was sung. A much longer prayer, a second psalm, and a sermon constituted the order of the service, which culminated in the communicants seating themselves on the benches around the tables.[52] On occasions several ministers participated in the sacramental services, which for convenience were held in the open when the weather permitted. Each table had a different minister and each gave a fresh exhortation to his group. When a long succession of communicants came to the tables, "the services were protracted until sunset, and became extremely tedious and fatiguing."[53]

No definite date or occasion can be said to be the beginning of the Sunday school movement in the Presbyterian Church in the West. As early as 1805 fourteen men in Kentucky entered into an agreement to supply Negroes and others with "an opportunity of learning to read the Holy Scriptures."[54] Some writers have claimed that the first Sunday school in Kentucky was founded in the spring of 1810 by Mrs. John Brown at her home, Liberty Hall, in Frankfort.[55] Apparently she persuaded Michael Arthur, a Presbyterian minister and schoolteacher, to devote an hour each Sunday to teaching the catechism and Scripture to the children. When Arthur left Frankfort in 1819, Mrs. Brown and six teachers opened a Sunday school with eighteen girls. Largely supported by public donations, the school prospered and added a boys' department in 1828.[56]

In order to broaden the efforts of the local churches, the General Assemblies repeatedly discussed methods by which religious observance of Sunday could be improved.[57] Viewing the success of Sunday schools in Eastern cities where thousands of children were in attendance,[58] the General Assembly of 1824 urged the extension of the program to "new and destitute regions of the Church."[59] Plans were discussed for the establishment of schools and Bible and missionary societies throughout the Mississippi Valley, and suggestions were sent to the Western churches.[60]

Within the bounds of the Synod of Tennessee numerous Sunday schools had been established by 1819 for the "instruction of the ignorant," especially the Negroes.[61] A report from the Alabama Presbytery in 1827 praised the "increasing interest in the cause of Sabbath Schools."[62] Three years later the South Alabama Presbytery appointed a committee to find an agent to establish schools throughout its bounds.[63] About the same time a Sunday school in Greene County, Tennessee, reported more than 150 pupils.[64] In 1834 a church in Blount County, in the same state, had established within its territory fourteen schools that had 558 children in attendance.[65] In addition to the Bible and the catechisms, primers and spelling books were taught. The children were drilled in the A B C's as well as in such questions as "Who was the first man?" Many of the books used were "dull, prosy biographies of unnaturally good children, who all died young," yet they were read in spite of style and content. The committing to memory of Bible verses was the usual exercise. Bright scholars often recited whole chapters of the Bible or entire hymns.[66] One girl within a single year memorized 3,394 verses of the Bible.[67] Not many of the schools were held in the church buildings, because the country was so sparsely settled. As a result of the scattered population, the schools were taught at convenient locations in the different neighborhoods.[68] One church in Louisiana reported that the school was the only force that held it together during some very trying days.[69]

The individual churches and communities benefited from the numerous actions of the General Assemblies to distribute books, Bibles, catechisms, and religious material throughout the West. In 1800, with special reference to the frontier, the Assembly agreed that the "purchasing and disposing of Bibles, and also books and short essays on the great principles of religion and morality" deserved attention. The Synod of Kentucky in 1803 asked permission of the General Assembly to print one thousand copies of the Confession of Faith for distribution in Kentucky. These were later offered for sale at fifty cents a copy.[70] In 1806 the Transylvania Presbytery received from benefactors in Philadelphia two hundred copies of the Shorter Catechism for free distribution.[71] In 1804 the General Assembly had sought to alleviate this literary drought by publishing a magazine "sacred to religion and morals," but this undertaking was short-lived, and publication of the *Evangelical Intelligencer* was suspended in 1810. Making another attempt to supply religious literature, the General Assembly of 1811 decided to furnish books and tracts to missionaries for distribution and requested the presbyteries to select places for deposits.[72]

The local churches were relieved of some large responsibilities by the organization of the American Bible Society in 1816 and the American Tract Society a year later. These societies were organized to provide religious literature for Western people, and their success depended upon co-operation from all denominations. One writer claims that the Presbyterians gave to the American Bible Society "men and means beyond any other American church."[73]

Since there was no religious paper edited by the Presbyterian Church in the southwestern portion of the country and "no paper circulated with the express design of exhibiting the Calvinistic view," the Synod of Tennessee encouraged its churches to support the *Calvinistic Magazine,* the first issue of which was published at Rogersville, Tennessee, in January 1827. For four years this magazine was filled with essays and dialogues concerning doctrine and polity. Much of the material was "controversial and belligerent" in good Presbyterian style. Although contributing much to the church, the magazine was discontinued in 1831.[74] During the year 1830 the *Presbyterian Advocate* was published monthly by Thomas T. Skillman, in Lexington, Kentucky. Its purpose was "to exhibit correct views of the doctrines and government of the Presbyterian church, to support their truth and scriptural authority and defend them against objections and misrepresentations." Because the *Advocate* interfered with the circulation of the *Western Luminary,* an interdenominational journal which he also edited, Skillman decided to cease publishing the *Advocate.*[75] In February 1830 the Cumberland Presbyterian Church sponsored the *Religious and Literary Intelligencer* which was printed in Princeton, Kentucky. Devoted to religion, literature, science, agriculture, and general information, this weekly continued for about two years. Undoubtedly the claim was justified that it was "at least one among the very first efforts to excite and stimulate native talent. . . ."[76]

The local Presbyterian church as a community agency grew increasingly important in early settlements. Rising beyond the limits of walls and place, it had acquired a significant position. Its beginning had been laid out in heroic dimensions; from united endeavors had come strength, and co-operative efforts had widened the horizons through which had gleamed the first visions of Sunday schools, missionary and Bible societies, religious literature, and denominational periodicals.

XI

EXPANSION AND DIVISION

THE PRESBYTERIAN and Congregational churches sought to minister to the Western people, but both soon realized that neither church alone was equal to the task. The Plan of Union of 1801 permitted the pooling of their resources for the support of ministers in the new settlements. Under this scheme a large number of churches, presbyteries, and synods were formed partly of Presbyterians and partly of Congregationalists. A church of either body might call a minister from the other. In the event of a dispute the Presbyterians might be represented in the associations by elders and the Congregationalists in the presbyteries by messengers.[1]

Scarcely had the Plan of Union been adopted before the Louisiana Purchase of 1803 opened to all churches the vast region between the Mississippi River and the Rocky Mountains.[2] Thrilled with the great challenge, the Rev. J. Van Vecten at a meeting of the American Home Missionary Society said: "The strength of the nation lies beyond the Alleghany. The centre of dominion is fast moving in that direction. The ruler of this country is growing up in the great valley: leave him without the gospel, and he will be a ruffian giant, who will regard neither the decencies of civilization, nor the charities of religion. The tide of population will not wait till we have settled every metaphysical point of theology, and every canon of church government. While we are deliberating, the mighty swell is rising higher and higher on the sides of the mountain."[3]

During the years of the War of 1812 the Presbyterian Church, as was true of several other churches, lost ground in various ways, especially in membership. In 1812 the church had 37,699 members; four years later it had 37,208.[4]

Probably the latter figure would have been still lower had the church not received a boost from a series of earthquakes that rocked the central part of the Mississippi Valley during four weeks begin-

111

ning December 16, 1811. Intermittent vibrations continued for more than a year. The area of greatest destruction lay along the Mississippi River between the thirty-sixth and thirty-seventh parallels. Although the whole of Caruthersville and a part of New Madrid, Missouri, were destroyed, the loss of life was very small.[5]

Some people accepted the theory of the "direct agency of Jehovah in these convulsions and consider[ed] them as intimately connected with the moral guilt of the world."[6] A focus on New Madrid was not difficult, for its people "had been noted for their profligacy and impiety. In the midst of those scenes of horror, all, Catholics and Protestants, praying and profane, became of one religion and partook of one feeling."[7] John Allan, who was teaching school in Christian County in the southwestern part of Kentucky during the winter of the earthquakes, expressed a desire, when the first tremor came, to feel another shock. His wish was almost instantly fulfilled. Standing in the door of his house, he heard "the distant lumbering," felt the house "shake and everything that was in it," and saw the yard fence "distinctly waving back and forth." The whole community was frightened so that for weeks "religious meetings were frequent and numerously attended. They were accompanied with a great deal of noisy excitement. Multitudes appeared for a time to be serious, many made a profession of religion." Although many people lost interest in religion as soon as the quakes ceased, others sought and kept a religious faith long after the period of excitement.[8] A committee on the state of religion appointed by the Synod of Kentucky in 1812 expressed gratitude for "providential dealings such as Earthquakes and War that . . . increased attention to the Scriptures and all means of Grace— that many additions have been made to the Church the last year—that some have returned to our Communion who formerly went out from us—that Infidels in general have been more silent, and in some instances reclaimed. . . ."[9]

Reflecting the state of society, Susan L. Martin in Kentucky wrote to a friend in Ohio: "We have heard of earth quakes in many places and felt some of them; and now we have war in all its horrors, war with the Indians and war with the British."[10] The demoralizing influence of the war on a new people in a new section was great indeed. Political strife "drew lines so sharp that men would not tolerate in the pulpit a minister whose political opinions differed from theirs . . . and to crown it all the church was tormented by a virulent outbreak

112

of unbelief and skepticism."[11] In 1814 Daniel Smith and Samuel J. Mills visited Kentucky and the Southwest on a mission for the American Bible Society. While in Kentucky they spent two Sundays in a town of some three thousand inhabitants where it was impossible to collect a congregation to which they might preach. They noted that the only difference between Saturday and Sunday was that the noise, profanity, and general evidences of wickedness were considerably greater on the Sabbath.[12] The General Assembly of 1816 was deeply disturbed about the "secular pursuits" on the Sabbath and the failure to keep the day holy. A report, however, commended "the harmony, the union, and the peace of the church; the fidelity of its ministers, and the instances of exemplary piety, of fervent zeal, and of generous and devoted attachment" of its members to the work of the church.[13] Isaac Reed made a tour of seven hundred miles through Kentucky in 1817 and 1818. He found that jerks and exercises still persisted among the Presbyterians in the remote sections of the state. In Frankfort, a town of twelve hundred people, he found no member of the Presbyterian Church and only one house of worship—a Roman Catholic chapel. In more than thirty counties, with large populations, there was no Presbyterian minister.[14] By 1820, according to one writer, there were probably not over 2,700 Presbyterians and one thousand Cumberland Presbyterians in the entire state.[15] All in all the religious situation was rather gloomy.

In 1814 the Presbyterians had seventy-nine churches and twenty-six ministers in Tennessee.[16] In this year Gideon Blackburn organized the First Presbyterian Church in Nashville, which had a population variously estimated between nine hundred and thirteen hundred. Four years later the church had forty-five members, only two or three of whom were men.[17] In 1820 a missionary in east Tennessee reported that the section was practically destitute of ministers.[18] Nine years later another missionary, writing from the Sequatchie Valley in east Tennessee, "found but one Presbyterian and that a female." Still another reported five "densely inhabited" counties that contained not a single Presbyterian preacher.[19]

A few Presbyterians moved into west Tennessee when it was opened for settlement in 1818. An occasional sermon was preached, but no sacrament was performed by the Presbyterians in that region until Richard Beard, of the Cumberland Presbyterian Church, held a sacramental meeting on the Forked Deer River in 1822.[20] The first

Presbyterian church in west Tennessee was Shiloh, established near Humboldt in 1825. Three years later there was organized in Memphis a church which occupied a portion of a two-story building also used by the Methodists and Baptists. In 1832 the city deeded to the Presbyterians a lot on which they erected a church forty by sixty feet, complete with cupola and steeple.[21] Five years later the Associate Reformed Presbyterians had gone into west Tennessee and constituted the Tennessee Presbytery at Salem Church in Tipton County.[22] Here in a section newly opened and lacking many of the refinements of older regions, the Presbyterians did not refrain from using the camp meeting. In 1830 the Synod of West Tennessee strongly urged its ministers and churches to arrange protracted meetings wherever they were deemed "expedient."[23]

During this period the Cumberland Presbyterians in Tennessee employed the camp meeting as an effective instrument of conversion to membership. Glowing descriptions of successful revivals appeared in the *Theological Medium*. A typical meeting was held in Wilson County in 1832. Rain dampened the prospects on Friday and Saturday, but the sun came out on Sunday. Success was evident on Tuesday, and Wednesday in a "mighty overwhelming torrent rolling from the mountains, it triumphantly prevailed in its rapid course over every obstruction. The long settled rocks were moved out of their places, the tallest oaks of the forest prostrated, and a highway indeed appeared for our God."[24]

In 1813 Robert Henderson was appointed by the West Tennessee Presbytery[25] to serve one Sunday each month in Huntsville, Alabama.[26] Five years later Gideon Blackburn organized a church in Huntsville. The work was extremely difficult in a section whose "people are carried away with the world, so that they talk of little else but corn, cotton, [and] the price of land," which then sold for from ten to fifteen dollars per acre.[27] Missionary efforts in the state progressed sufficiently to warrant establishing in 1821 the Presbytery of Alabama. At its formation the presbytery had three churches, five ministers, and about fifty members.[28] The citizens of Mobile in 1822 built a church and opened it to all Protestants. A Presbyterian minister named Bell preached there a few times. Although offered a salary of twelve hundred dollars, he served only a year and then moved to New Orleans.[29] Some six years later the city had eight or ten thousand people, whose single Presbyterian church was the only one within a hundred miles.[30]

114

By 1836 the Board of Missions of the Presbyterian Church had sent four missionaries to Alabama, a part of the great Western field whose inhabitants were collecting "from all parts of the world, . . . increasing with a rapidity unparalleled," and presenting to the church greater missionary problems than it had ever faced.[31] Camp meetings may have declined in many places, but the Presbyterians successfully revived them in such places as Tuscaloosa, where, for example, in 1828 a four-day meeting resulted in seventeen baptisms, "many affecting cases," and numerous "awakened sinners."[32]

Although a Presbyterian minister had arrived in Mississippi as early as 1799, the work progressed slowly so that by 1814, when the territory had some sixty thousand inhabitants, there were only six Presbyterian churches and four ministers. The state of society, according to a missionary, was deplorable. "You scarcely see a man ride without his pistol, or walk without a dagger in his bosom." He "believed that more innocent blood is shed in this Territory and in Louisiana, in one year, than in all the Middle and Eastern States, in ten years."[33] Although the Synod of Kentucky established the Mississippi Presbytery in 1815, progress beyond the work among the Indians was very slow. In 1826 a report to the General Assembly called Mississippi "a scene of spiritual desolation." There was only one Presbyterian minister to every twenty thousand people in the state.[34]

In Louisiana the Presbyterians were several years behind the progress of the more aggressive Methodists. Gideon Blackburn was in Louisiana during the winter of 1815 and 1816 seeking, he said, "those literally in the shadow of death." While there he met many people who had not heard a sermon for ten years.[35] Established Presbyterian missionary work in New Orleans began with the arrival in 1816 of Elias Cornelius,[36] who was appointed by the Connecticut Missionary Society to tour the Southern states. On the way Cornelius stopped at Princeton College, where he engaged the brilliant Sylvester Larned[37] to aid him in the new work. In January 1818 Larned reached New Orleans and soon succeeded in erecting an unaffiliated church which cost the amazing sum of $42,000.[38] In the summer of 1821 Larned at the age of twenty-three fell a victim to yellow fever, which scourged New Orleans.[39] Larned's work was assumed by Theodore Clapp, who found the church embarrassed by a debt of $45,000. A lottery raised $25,000, and the church building was sold for the remaining $20,000 to Judah Touro, a wealthy Jewish merchant and personal friend of Clapp. Touro permitted the Presbyterians to retain use of the building without charge. The early work of Cornelius and Larned had been purely evangelistic, and no formal church was organized until 1823, when Clapp gathered nine men and fifteen women into a church which adopted Presbyterian doctrines and petitioned the Presbytery of Mississippi for admission. Clapp disrupted an effective ministry by his lack of faith in the doctrine of eternal punishment. He soon became opposed to the entire body of Calvinistic theology and refused to "believe in, avow, teach, or defend the peculiar doctrines of the Presbyterian Church." After ten strenuous years of service, Clapp was tried by a church court and was removed from the Presbyterian ministry in January 1833.[40]

Timothy Flint did not find in 1823 "a single Protestant house of worship" between St. Francisville, Louisiana, and New Orleans, "a rich and highly cultivated tract" of country where plantation touched plantation.[41] In 1825 the Presbytery of Mississippi, covering Louisiana and Mississippi, had within its bounds about a quarter of a million inhabitants, thirteen churches, and thirteen ministers, eight of whom were missionaries.[42] A Presbyterian minister in 1830 was so despondent over the condition of his church in parts of Louisiana that he wrote: "The Hindoo on the banks of the Ganges is not more completely enveloped in moral and intellectual darkness than the Acadian Creole."[43]

John Carnahan, an exhorter in the Cumberland Presbyterian Church, preached in 1812 what was probably the first Protestant sermon in the Arkansas territory. His church ordered him to form a circuit "among the people where he lived," and for nine years Carnahan was the only Cumberland Presbyterian minister in all Arkansas.[44] In 1825 Benjamin Chase, a Presbyterian minister, reported that he had been in Helena and found that his sole predecessor had been "an ignorant Methodist" and that the people were so starved for religion they "listened as though it was for their lives."[45] Three years later James W. Moore, a missionary sent by a board from the General Assembly, reached Arkansas and found only two Presbyterians in the territory and no organized church of any denomination. During the year he organized a Presbyterian church composed of seven members.[46] A Cumberland Presbyterian missionary in Arkansas as late as 1832 wrote that he had agreed to ride a circuit 150 miles by one hundred miles which would consume eight weeks. "The poverty and scattered situation of the settlements . . . leave no room to doubt that hundreds of souls will perish here unless something, in the providence of God, is effected through the Church."[47] A Presbyterian minister in 1835 pleaded that young and hardy preachers who "can sleep on *scaffolds* and sit on *stools*" be sent to Arkansas, lacking in roads, sparse of population, and plagued with general sickness.[48]

Sumner Bacon, a native of Massachusetts living in Arkansas, requested the Arkansas Presbytery of the Cumberland Presbyterian Church in 1826 to accept him as a candidate for the ministry so that he might go to Texas where he felt he had been called. The presbytery did not think his appearance or his call warranted its permission. At a second meeting Bacon again was rejected. Nothing seemed to daunt him. In 1828 at his own expense he purchased some Bibles and began evangelistic work in west Texas. Finally in 1835 he was ordained not by Arkansas Presbytery but by Louisiana Presbytery of the Cumberland Presbyterian Church.[49]

In 1834 the New York Young Men's Home Missionary Society sent D. S. Southmayd as a missionary to Texas. Arriving at Galveston, he obtained a small boat and rowed to Harrisburg some twenty miles away. Soon he had succeeded in establishing preaching places at Harrisburg, San Felipe, and other points.[50] Also in the year 1834 a second Presbyterian minister, Peter H. Fullenwider, was sent by the Presbytery of Mississippi to work in Texas.[51] During 1837 Mississippi Presbytery commissioned four missionaries for service in Texas. Provided with horse, saddle, shawl, Bible, blanket or buffalo robe, long-barrel rifle, and sometimes a pistol or bowie knife, they were equipped to preach the gospel, hunt for meat, and protect themselves against the Indians.[52] The first Presbyterian church in Texas was organized by Hugh Wilson in 1838 at a place four miles west of San Augustine.[53] Undoubtedly the most important minister in either branch of the church in Texas was Daniel Baker, who went as a missionary in 1840. Eventually Texas became his home and the field of his extraordinary accomplishments.[54]

As the South expanded, the ties that held the nation began to weaken. The Presbyterian Church "in the full tide of her evangelistic efforts"[55] experienced a similar course of events. Reaction against the very forces that caused growth in the church explains many of the causes for her decline. The blow suffered in the Cumberland Schism of 1810 was a hard one, but the division in 1837 and 1838 was an even greater loss. In spite of controversies and divisions after the Camp Meeting-Revival Era, the Presbyterian Church, in step with the westward movement, expanded rapidly during the first third of the nineteenth century. Between 1831 and 1834 the average yearly addition of members to the entire church was approximately twenty-two thousand. In the years 1836 and 1837 the average was less than twelve thousand. Between 1833 and 1837 the church had suffered an over-all loss of thirteen thousand.[56]

Although the Presbyterian Church enjoyed great gains between 1831 and 1834, an alarming portion of these gains were from the section where the Plan of Union operated so efficiently. Naturally this disturbed the Presbyterians and aroused "the perfectly reasonable fear" that the traditional ways of the church would suffer from those not in sympathy with the Calvinistic system of belief.[57] As the program was extended, it gave to Congregational churches, which never adopted the doctrine of the Presbyterian Church and even opposed the Presbyterian form of government, as much influence in the governing of a particular Presbyterian church as that possessed by an equal number of Presbyterians. The churches functioning under the Plan of Union, according to the contention of the Old School group, were not real Presbyterian churches. This situation naturally caused discussion and dissension.[58] In the years immediately ahead the Presbyterians with their rigid Scotch-Irish background were to see in these changes a threat to the Calvinistic beliefs. Philip Lindsley of Nashville realized the situation clearly in 1833 when he wrote: "There never was a period when the Presbyterian Church in our country exhibited an aspect or stood in an attitude of predicament, so critical and perilous as at this moment:—whether we consider its internal convulsions or its external relations and prospects. [She has been] Threatened with dissolution or schism from agitators and nullifiers within her own bosom—assailed by Christians, politicians, and infidels of every sect . . . denounced as bigots and fanatics, as the enemies of civil and religious liberty, as the ambitious aspirants to universal ecclesiastical dominion, as the insidious plotters and conspirators to effect a union of church and state, with a view to become lords paramount of both. . . ."[59]

Two parties in the church, known as the Old School and the New School, were forming and aligning against each other. A head-on clash of these two groups led in 1837 and 1838 to the division of the Presbyterian Church. In general it is reasonably accurate to call the New School liberal and the Old School conservative. The doctrinal rift between the two parties is usually attributed to a sermon in 1828 by Nathaniel W. Taylor who belonged to the New School; the point of the sermon was directed against the doctrine of original sin.[60] Heresy trials occurred in many sections of the country[61] and rocked the very foundations of the church. The trial of Lyman Beecher of the Lane Theological Seminary at Cincinnati closely touched the church in Kentucky and Tennessee.[62]

The new beliefs found ready reception in east Tennessee, for Hopkinsianism had taken here an early hold under Hezekiah Balch,[63] who believed with a group of New England theologians in "impartial, disinterested good-will, love or benevolence to all beings capable of happiness . . . a benevolent complacency in the moral excellence of all who possess this essential qualification for happiness, and for promoting its diffusion." Balch had accepted the new beliefs largely through personal relations with Samuel Hopkins and Nathanael Emmons.[64] For forty years Balch had preached these beliefs in east Tennessee before they caused so much discussion in the East. Beyond question doctrinal differences contributed to the division, yet only a small number of Presbyterians accepted the doctrines of the new teachings.[65]

A second source of trouble arose from the intense rivalry over the means of conducting benevolent enterprises. Throughout the West there had been numerous local and state organizations before the American Home Missionary Society was formed in 1826. This society was supported by both Congregationalists and Presbyterians under the Plan of Union.[66] Although the Presbyterians had formed a Board of Missions as early as 1816, it had not been effective. Twelve years later, in response to intense Old School pressure, the board was reorganized for the purpose of bringing Presbyterian mission work in the West under exclusive control of the Presbyterians.[67] Fuel was added to the fire by the insistence that the American Home Missionary Society was ambitious in plans and innovations. Until the Presbyterian Church clearly realized that those who controlled the education of the ministers and stationed the missionaries would eventually control the church, this fight was only a trivial clash. In a resolution in the

General Assembly of 1835 the Presbyterians made clear their position in declaring "That it is the first and binding duty of the Presbyterian Church to sustain her own boards."[68]

As has already been pointed out in a previous chapter,[69] there is little doubt that slavery, "although its influence was more incidental than direct," was a third important factor that led to the division of the church. Through the years slavery had been kept in the background by the leaders of both sides; the New School presbyteries and synods were consistently anti-slavery in sentiment. The strength of the Old School was in the Cotton Kingdom and it relied on the support of the solid South. Whenever opinions clashed, "hostility was most openly manifest in those regions where the most liberal interpretations of the symbols prevailed, where revivals were most abundant, and where church government assumed its freest type."[70] By 1836 there were definitely antislavery and proslavery branches of the church. There existed a general and well-founded conviction that the New School represented the abolition element in the church. This opinion is well supported by the fact that the four synods exscinded in 1837 had passed resolutions against slavery.[71] There can be no basis for the belief or contention that slavery was of no consequence in the ultimate division.[72]

When the General Assembly of 1837 met, it was evident to all present that the Old School party was safely in the majority. In rapid succession the Assembly abrogated the Plan of Union; exscinded the four synods of Western Reserve, Utica, Geneva, and Genesee; separated the church from voluntary societies and declared its own boards for education and missions to be the only agents of the church. The commissioners of the four synods appealed to the General Assembly of 1838 for recognition, but the appeal was declared out of order. The New School constituency was organized then into a church representing some four-ninths of the ministry and membership of the entire Presbyterian Church.[73] The Old School party had adopted "harsh, abrupt, and revolutionary" measures to win a "victory of pure doctrine and strict church order,"[74] and, "though perhaps not exactly glorious, [it] was triumphant and irreversible."[75] In an effort to relieve itself of heresy, the church by a party vote had cut away 533 churches and more than 100,000 members. The Old School leaders had not dared to risk their program by referring the question to the presbyteries. Unfortunately the result threw the church on the defensive and forced it to adopt an "apologetic tone."[76]

The division of the Presbyterian Church resulted in establishing practically two denominations, each using the same title, following the same standards, and operating in the same territory. The Old School held to most of the organized churches and their real property in the Old Southwest. In the West especially the results were definitely detrimental to the continued progress of the church because men had lost faith in the organization and its program.[77]

In Kentucky and Tennessee the defections proved to be serious indeed. In the 1838 meeting of the Synod of Kentucky a large majority resolved that the synod concur in the opinion that the Plan of Union was "a violation of the Constitution of the Presbyterian Church." By a vote of seventy-seven to nothing the synod acknowledged that the General Assembly controlled the Old School party.[78] However, eleven ministers and eight elders withheld their approval of the reform measures of the Assemblies of 1837 and 1838. A series of articles in the *Protestant and Herald* on the Assemblies gave much offense to the representatives of this group, the leadership of which was assumed by Joseph C. Stiles.[79] Many Kentucky churches were split asunder by the fight that ensued between the warring parties. A typical example can be found in the New Providence Church, where the conflict continued for years and finally culminated in a division in membership and the organization of a new church.[80] In the northern section of the state Stiles in 1840 called a convention at Versailles, which resulted ultimately in his suspension and deposition from the Presbyterian ministry. Undaunted he drove ahead and called a second convention which resolved itself into a New School synod. By 1842 it contained three presbyteries, fourteen ministers, twenty-one churches, and nearly one thousand members.[81]

The Old School group brought much opposition against the New School preachers in Kentucky if one can judge by the experience of Archer C. Dickerson, who was accepted as a supply minister by the Bowling Green Church. When the Kentucky Synod proceeded to admonish the church, the latter published reasons for its choice and actions. Dickerson said that the Old School party accused him of being a Campbellite and a Unitarian. In order to injure him further, he said, they sent "a flippant, bawling Methodist here from Nashville, who took mortal offense at some instructions I gave . . . went off and preached three days publicly against me, got the public mind all agitated and raised a prodigious to do."[82]

The Synod of Tennessee, meeting in the fall of 1838, by a decisive vote of thirty-two to eight resolved to adhere to the New School Assembly. The synod objected to "the unconstitutional and unrighteous acts of the Assembly in the abrogation of the Plan of Union, the excision of the Synods, etc." Furthermore, the synod expressed its sympathy for the American Home Missionary Society and the American Education Society.[83] The Holston Presbytery of the Tennessee Synod considered "the acts of the last General Assembly as a mournful exhibition of party-spirit . . . a picture of misguided zeal, alarming to every friend of civil, as well as religious, liberty."[84] Difference in the matter of faith seemed of no consequence. On the other hand, an Old School minority of the Holston Presbytery renounced the New School group "to all intents and purposes, seceders from the true Presbyterian Church, and, *as such,* are no longer members of the true Holston Presbytery."[85]

Although the Synod of West Tennessee in 1838 deplored the excision of the four synods as "unconstitutional and unwise," it remained faithful to the Old School.[86] There were evidences, however, of dissatisfaction. Rev. Thomas F. Scott, the commissioner sent by the West Tennessee Presbytery to the General Assembly of 1838, was so disgusted with the New School and Old School Assemblies that he refused to recognize either. So thoroughly was he convinced that no advantage could be derived from connection with either Assembly that he wrote his presbytery: "I am persuaded, moreover, that the parts of the Presbyterian Church separately have suffered . . . [since the General Assembly] has been little else than a theater of the fiercest contention, a fountain of the bitterest waters." A few years later Scott, completely exasperated, became a candidate for orders in the Protestant Episcopal Church.[87]

Strong sentiment in Alabama for the Old School party led to a resolution, introduced in 1838 before the Synod of Alabama, directing each presbytery to examine its churches and to exclude those who did not adhere to the Old School. Fortunately for the peace of the synod, this resolution was indefinitely postponed.[88]

Even in Mississippi there were scattered evidences of dissension. By 1839 the Carmel Church had divided about half and half into a

New School and Old School church. One group took possession of the session book and the other wrote into a new book that "rather than be litigious the session has determined to proceed without [the book]."[89] The action of the Carmel Church was not typical of churches in the Lower Southwest. There slavery was so securely entrenched that the Old School found little opposition and divisions were rare indeed.

In numerous instances members, ministers, and churches who regarded the acts of the General Assembly of 1837 as definitely unconstitutional saw no legitimate reason to withdraw from the Old School party. Some felt satisfied when they had protested against the action.[90] In an effort to meet many of the criticisms, the General Assembly of 1842 ruled that membership in the church did not require the approval of the acts of 1837 and 1838.[91]

Altogether less than one-fourth of the churches in the South cast their lot with the New School. Opposition to abolition and antislavery sentiment in the New School party brought about a policy of co-operation among Southern churches in the face of a "repugnance of the South to the centralization of authority in the national government [which] suggested an opposition to the assumption of authority by the national Assembly of the church."[92] Although the divisions in the churches, presbyteries, and synods in the Old Southwest were relatively few, the effect was a great blow to the onward progress of the church and its work. A general decrease of home missionary work, a loss of heart on the part of men once filled "with hopes inspired by the previous history of the Church," and a general willingness to abandon work against which many prejudices had arisen[93]—these and other results seem to have been the price paid by a religious body which had taken drastic measures to rid itself of heresy.

XII

IN RETROSPECT

THE PRESBYTERIAN CHURCH emerged from the American Revolution as the best organized and the strongest of all Protestant churches in America. From two standpoints it was in a most favorable position for westward expansion and growth. It had been a frontier church from the moment it was introduced to the colonies; and it was essentially missionary in character. Its government was readily adaptable to frontier needs and demands, and, in order to carry forward its program, few adjustments in organization were necessary. Actually its form was that of a republic governed not by prelates but by elders of the people, both clerical and lay elders. By the absence of an overhead authority the local church was a strong unit, and this separateness or individuality appealed to a democratic folk whose spirit was congenial with liberty. By their participation in the American Revolution the Presbyterians indicated their wholehearted devotion to the cause of liberty.

The Presbyterian Church construed religion intelligently, basing it on knowledge and thought; its creed was systematic, and its clergy closely adhered to the creed. The lofty and exalted discourses of the ministers sought to teach people to think, weigh, and decide the vital questions of Christian worship. In order to achieve this goal, the church threw all of its force to the support of academies and colleges, which gave Presbyterians the best educated ministers and members in the Old Southwest and elsewhere on the frontier.

The learned minister studied God's Word as a basis for the preparation for all sermons. He preached a stern doctrine of election, predestination, and limited salvation. His three desires were to glorify God, to bring righteousness among men, and to establish a temperate society. To attain these ends, he needed divine grace and help. Any minister who believed piety and learning inseparable naturally revolted against excesses of revivals and questioned the propriety of worship which seemed to contain extreme enthusiasm, hypocrisy, and even witchcraft.

124

The raw West held a people lustful for speculation, passionate for excitement, and desirous to get ahead. The rapidity with which the land was conquered, populated, and politically organized almost defies comprehensible explanation. Nothing is clearer, however, than that church membership was in inverse ratio to education and in direct ratio to emotional appeal. In these respects the Methodist and Baptist churches had all the advantages over the more formal Presbyterian approach. The Presbyterian Church could not thrive numerically in competition with denominations that took every advantage of the frontiersman's affinity for the miraculous or the spontaneous. The majority preferred the minister who had little or no formal education, a man born among the people, one who preached a simple religion in a vernacular the people understood. Although the Methodist Church had the most autocratic government of the three great democratic churches, its numerical success largely came through its liberal doctrine. On the other hand, the Baptist Church owed much of its success to a combination of democratic ideals and free church ideas, a flexible church administration, and a mild adherence to Calvinism.

By the very nature of the program of his church, the Presbyterian minister was limited in his appeal. He and his church were looking only for Presbyterians or those who would conform rigidly to its discipline and doctrine. Presbyterians usually settled in compact communities in order to enjoy the religious peculiarities of the church. Seldom did a Presbyterian church, unlike the Baptist or Methodist, represent a cross section of Western society. Therefore its appeal was limited in comparison to that of churches which sought the unchurched wherever he could be found and proselyted him without the slightest hesitation. Even Presbyterians removed from the vicinity of their own church often fell prey to the Methodists.

The Presbyterian stress on doctrine made the Calvinistic faith too stern and unbending for the Western mind and the unsteady state of Western morals. Adherence to a rigid formal education for its ministry and to a strict interpretation of its Westminster Confession placed the church in a very unfavorable position when the Baptists and Methodists began their great evangelistic campaigns. Only by letting down the educational bars and admitting unqualified men to the ministry could the Presbyterians hope to compete. This situation led to one of the many divisions in the church and to the formation of the Cumberland Presbyterian branch, which met a distinct need on the frontier. As divisive as the Presbyterians tended to be, many of the divisions were healed by the stronger ties of common agreement on the great fundamental points of Calvinistic faith. The very features which were weaknesses from one point of view were from another angle factors making for unity. Presbyterians possessed a denominational consciousness that other churches had to obtain by a common enterprise, such as Indian missions.

Despite weaknesses and failures, there is much on the credit side of the Presbyterian ledger. The Presbyterian Church restrained uncontrolled behavior among its members and enforced strict rules of social and moral conduct. Through its restraining power the church contributed to the development of law and order and eventually to the stabilization of Western society. The church was naturally less effective in its prohibitions and warnings when the notions of the general populace ran counter to it than when abetted by public opinion. Its attitude on slavery was especially rigid in Kentucky but had little chance of enforcement in the Gulf States. Among the Indians the early efforts were particularly noteworthy and commendable, but the greed for land was overpowering. Although losing many of its goals, the church and its highly trained clergy held tenaciously not only to its rigid theology but also to the means which it considered essential to any achievement—education.

While the Baptist and Methodist churches seemed to expand without plan, the Presbyterian Church refused to budge from its consistency with theology and ecclesiastical tradition. No Protestant church stood more staunchly by its doctrines, and for this no church paid a greater price in membership. In numerical strength it was far in the rear by 1837, yet in several ways it was the most influential religious body on the frontier. Religion, virtue, and knowledge had been the three cardinal possessions of the Scotch-Irish. These qualities the Presbyterian Church succeeded in instilling into many people who led the Old Southwest from the crudity of the backwoods to the stability of an enlightened society.

APPENDIX

APPENDIX

THE FIRST SESSION BOOK OF THE OLDEST
PRESBYTERIAN CHURCH IN MISSISSIPPI

The Presbyterian Church at Pine Ridge, Adams County, Mississippi, is the oldest regularly constituted Presbyterian Church in existence in the state; it is the third oldest with respect to organization.[1] On February 25, 1807, James Smylie[2] organized a Presbyterian church among some Scottish families living near the community of Washington, at that time the capital of the Mississippi Territory. Twenty-two communicants,[3] whose names indicate a dozen families, were on the first roll. The church was given the Biblical name of Salem, which was later changed to Pine Ridge when a new building was located for convenience on the geographical rise of that name,[4] four miles west of Washington. Four clergymen identified with the early history of the Pine Ridge Church were intimately connected with the development of the territory and the expansion of the Presbyterian Church. James Smylie, Joseph Bullen, Jacob Rickhow, and William Montgomery are significant names. All originally came into the territory on a missionary assignment: Bullen was sent in 1799 by the Synod of New York as a missionary to the Chickasaw Nation;[5] Rickhow, apparently supported by some organization, came to Natchez in 1810;[6] Montgomery[7] was sent in 1801 with James Hall and William Bowman on a missionary reconnaissance for the Synod of the Carolinas.[8] At the Pine Ridge Church, Smylie was pastor until 1810; Rickhow supplied the pulpit until Montgomery began his ministry in 1811; Bullen often preached and assisted on sacramental occasions. Closely co-operating over a period of years, these four ministers constituted the Presbytery of Mississippi in 1815.

In the archives of the Historical Foundation of the Presbyterian and Reformed Churches at Montreat, North Carolina, is a small bound volume of the session records of Washington [Pine Ridge] Presbyterian Church, from February 1807 to May 1820. It contains a direct account of the organization of this frontier church and a record of its sessional and congregational meetings. Written in a clear, bold handwriting, the first entries indicate the clerk's acquaintance with formal procedure. Later minutes are recorded with less skill in chirography and orthography, but the recitation continues the story of the expansion of both territory and church. The irregular entries contain almost every distinguishing feature of Presbyterian church government and organization. With scrutiny the vignette grows third-dimensional; with reading, the particular becomes the general.

The Inhabitants of the Toun[9] of Washington and its Vicinity having a desire to promote the glory of God and advance their own spiritual Interest,—

129

held a meting at the Toun of Washington, on 25th of February 1807 for the purpose of organising a Church of the Presbyterian order—After prayer for the blessing of God and direction of Heaven. Robert H. Morrow was chosen, Moderator of the meeting, and the society passed the following resolutions.--------
1st Resolved that this society in future, be known by the name of the Washington Presbyterian Church.--------
2nd Resolved that Mess[rs] John Bolls,[10] John Grafton, and James McKnight, act as elders[11] in transacting the Spiritual concerns of said Church.--------
3rd Resolved that Mess[rs] Thomas Grafton, Alexa[r] Bisland, Robert H. Morrow, Samuel Marshal, Francis Nailor, Abel Miller and Pearson Lewis compose a standing committee,[12] to regulate the Temporal concerns of said Church.--------
4th Resolved that this Committee hold their first meeting at this place on the second Saturday, in March, and afterwards meet upon their own adjournments--------

After passing these resolutions, and imploreing the blessing of the Great Head of the Church upon their attempts, the Society adjourned.

Robert H. Morrow, Mod[tr 13]

Washington March the 14th 1807

The committee appointed by the Washington Presbyterian church to transact the temporal concerns thereof met according to appointment. Present Mess[rs] Robert H. Morrow, Pearson Lewis, Thomas Grafton, Francis Nailor, & Abel Miller.

Abel Miller was chosen chairman, & R. H. Morrow clerk--------

According to a motion made & Seconded Alex[r] Bisland was chosen Standing Clerk of the committee.--------

According to a motion made & Seconded Pearson Lewis was chosen Treasurer.--------

According to a motion made & Seconded Mess[rs] John Bolls, Thomas Grafton, & Francis Nailor were appointed Church collectors.

It was resolved that this committee should hold their Stated meetings on the Second Saturdays of June, September, December & March.

The Committee adjourned to meet at this place on the Second Saturday in June, at 11o-Clock

Alex[r] Bisland, St.[d] Clk.[14]

Washington May 24th 1807

The Sacrament of the Lords Supper was administered at Washington by Rev. James Smylie, & assisted by Rev. Joseph Bullin Pastor of Bethel congregation congregation [sic] & David Woods[15] a Licentiate[16] of the Presbytery of Transylvania Kentucky--------

The Communicants[17] were as follows—John Bolls, John Grafton, James McNight, John Bisland, Thomas Grafton, Samuel Marshal, Henery Cassels, Darius Anderson, Alexander Armstrong, John Griffing, John Henderson, Alexander Bisland, Alex[r] Callender, Mary McEwin, Jannet Grafton, Margaret McNight, Violet Cassels, Martha Bolls, Hepa Cassels, Elizabeth Grafton, Susanna Bisland, Margaret Marshel.

Alx[r] Bisland, Clk.

June the 7th 1807—

Mr. David Woods, being a Licentiate & without a regular charge, The Washington Presbyterian Church, considered it their duty to afford him some pecuniary aid, & therefore contributed twenty nine dollars & seventy five cents, obtained by a publick collection———

Alex^d Bisland St^d Clk.

Washington Septr 22^d 1807

The committee appointed to transact the temporal concern of the Washington Presbyterian Church met at Mr. Lewis's—present Miss^{rs} Pierson Lewis, Francis Naylor, Samuel Marshal and abel Miller—absent Thos Grafton———

The former Chairman being absent Mr. P. Lewis was chosen Chairmen— The Clerk beeing absent and the Revd J. Smiley present, he was chosen Clerk pro. Tempore—Mr. Lewis and Mr. Naylor beeing absent from the last meeting and present at this rendered satisfactory reason for this absence———

A letter of resignation was rec^d from Alexan^r Bisland, and his request assented to———

The Committee proceeded to chose the Revd James Smiley as stated clerk of the committee

Upon a motion beeing made and Seconded Mr. John Bolls was chosen member of the committee in the room of R. H. Morrow resignd and the rev^d James Smiley in the room of Alr. Bisland resig^d———

The Committee ordered that Francis Naylor John Bolls and Thos Grafton use their endeavours to collect the monies due on Subscription by the next meeting of the committee———

The committee ordered that Francis Naylor John Bolls and Thos Grafton obtain a certificate of their being duely authorised to collect the monies.

Monies due by Subscription viz

In the year one thousand eight hundred & seven

Thomas Grafton's List

[27 names—with donations ranging from $5-$30]

Francis Naylor List

[6 names—$5-$10]

John Bolls List

[12 names—$5-$12]

The business of the day beeing finished the Committee adjourned to meete again on the Second Saturday in December at Mr. Lewis Washington 10 o'clock A. M———

James Smiley C. P^{ro} Tem.

Washington Decem^r 12th 1807

The Committee met agreeable to adjournment, but there not beeing a sufficient number of members present to forme a Quorum they adjourned untill notifyed to meete again

Ale^r Bisland S. C.[18]

Washington 19th March 1808

The standing Committee beeing notifyed, they accordingly met, present

John Bolls James Smiley, Pierson Lewis Thos Grafton and Aler Bisland. Mr. John Bolls beeing Chairman,—a motion beeing made and Seconded, 1st That Miss[rs] Thos Grafton John Rhea Stephen Justice John Bisland and William Barland als[o] Sam[l] Marshal be appointed as commissioners to point out a place and contract for the building a meeting House on the Pine Ridg for the Presbyterian Society------

2[d] That Miss[rs] Bolls, Defrance Marshal and Daniel Grafton be nominated to present
present Subscription papers for the Support of the Revd. James Smiley------3[d] That those gentlemen who have Been nominated to present the subscription papers, make their returns on the Second Saturday in June next------4th Res[d] that Mr. John Rhea be appointed a member of the Church Committee in the Stead of Francis Naylor, who has resigned------a motion being made and seconded that the committee adjourn to meet on the 2[d] Saturday of June next at the Government house   10 O'Clock A. M.------

Aler Bisland Clerk

Washington, Government house 11th June 1808
   The committee met agreeable to adjournment, but the Clerk not being present nor the procedings of the last committee, they adjourned to meet, at Washington Meetinghouse on Thoursday 16th June.

Aler Bisland Clerk

Washington 16th June 1808------
   The committee met agreeable to adjournment present Missrs. Bolls, Lewis, Smiley, Marshal, and Thos. Grafton------Mr. Bolls, in the Chair, agreeable to a resolution of the committee of the 19th March last, the subscriptions were presented and the amt on them were $264------

It is agreed by the committee that an alteration be made in the original resolution relative to the meeting of the committee at Washington & is as follows, Resolved that in future the Quarterly meetings of the committee be held alternately at Salem and Washington------

Resolved farther than [that] an intermediate committee be held at Salem the 1st Saturday of July next where said Subscription shall again be presented for further consideration------The committee having gon through the business, they have adjourned to meet at Salem the 2[d] Saturday of September next

Aler Bisland Clerk

Salem 2[d] July 1808
   The committee met agreeable to a resolution of the last meeting—present Missrs Bolls, Lewis, Smiley and Tho[s] Grafton------The subscriptions were presented, nothing was done with them, consequently it was defered untill the next meeting of the committee------

A motion being made and seconded, that Mr. Daniel McCown be a member of the Standing Committee------the committee having done the Business, the [y] adjourned------

Aler Bisland Clerk

Selam March the 19th 1811

this day agreeable to a public notice given by the session of this Congregation Collected at this Church the heads of the families in order to adopt a plan of Calling a Minister of the gospel of the prysbiterian order & making a provision for some to suply in this Congregation as successar to the rev[d] James Smylie[19] till such time as we would have an oppertunity [of] getting a minister Establish in this Church & being limited in a pluarelty of two we proceeded as follows [at] same time------

preceeding our meeting we received information of the rev[d] Mr. Mount-[g] omery Coming to this Country with his family it was good news to us indeed & in order not to be left as a flock wanting a sheepherd we resolved to aply to the rev[d] Jacob Rickhow to take Charge of our Congragation as our Minister for the term of six months & that if Mr. Mountgomery did not arive in that time it was understood that if the rev[d] Mr Rickhow was satisfied that we should Continue him till such further time [until] Mr. Mountgomery Coming[.] accordingly the rev[d] Mr. Rickow acceeded to our requist for the term above mentioned which we embrace him as our Minister & moderator of our Session During his time amongst us------his time comenced the first sabath in April------

N B at the request of the Congreation our Minister the revd Mr. Rickhow administred the Sacrament of the Lords Supper in this Church------on the first day of June assisted by the rev[d] Mr. Mountgomery who took a seat with our session w[h]ere on friday before the solemnity a nomination was made of two aditional Elders in our Congration & made known publickly to the members & Cordialy received as such[.] the nominated is Mr. John Henderson & Mr. Joseph Foreman the session then entred upon the business of the church & first adopted the measure of Distributing the Comunion tokens[20] on saturday after sermon & after Delebration on the Several Duties of the Church there was several aplications made to the Session for Church privalege which after due enquierys obtained the same amongst the rest the privasion was presented with an aplication from Mrs. Pheaby Coghran who had hithertofore applied & not admitted but she Continuing her suit it caused the session to be more Circumspect on the subject in making every necessary enquiery in order to do Justice to the ap[pl]icant & Clear our Conscience the session thought fit to admit her[21] & C. Communicants Names first [in list are] ministers & Elders
The rev[d] Jacob Rickhow
the rev[d] William Mountgomery
[Then follow the names of 6 elders and 33 communicants.]
February the 24th 1810 whereas Jn[o] Grafton gave in his resignation of

elder & membership in this Congragation and demanded a Certificate[22] from the session obtained the same & at the request of said session he hath resumed to his former standing in the Church & acording to order returned his Certificate & it was reported to the Congregation that it might [be] entred on the minutes of the session book his return bears date May the 19th 1811.

The rev[d] Jacob Rickhows pastorel Charge of Salem Congragation ended the second Sabath in October 1811 & the Congregation then remained vaccant till new year at the requist of Congregation.

January the 1st 1812 the first sabath of the present Month this Congregation receved the rev[d] William Mountgomery with unanimus Cordiality as thier Minister & the af[o]resaid day he took the charge of the Congreation & entered upon the functions of his Cap[a]cities in all its various branches as pertains to a Minister of the gospel for the term of one year from the above date & to Continue from year to year according as circumstances will admit & we the members of this Congregation Consider ourselves in duty bound to Suport him for his ministerial Labours according to what part of his time is devouted to us & C--------

March the 21st our rev[d] pastor held a general examination in this Church of the diffrent sects & ages of his Congregation & in order to gratify the people at large to continue thier perceeding made of examination be Complied with the same & issued quieries in writing to the male [?] sect[23] that was of meture age all the young & familes in the shorter Catechism the date above the Congregation Colected------together for the intended purpose & after solemly imploring god for his blessing to Crown his proceedings he began the buiseness of the day--------where he receiv[d] the answers in written form proven by the scriptures every ones answers publickly read & verry lengthy & stands fil[e]d in the Church then entered[24] on the shorter Catechise throughout & Cloased the buisness of the day by prayer & C.

March the 29 the rev[d] William Mountgomery administred the Sacrament of the Lords Supper assisted by the revds Joseph Bullion James Smylie Jacob Rikhow the Communicants name is as follows [list of 50 communicants]

October the 3[d] 1812

The above Date our rev[d] Pastor held a publick exemination in this Church of both sects which Composeth this Congregation according to the Costum our pastor issued written Questions which stands filed in this Church upon the day appointed the people attended & our rev[d] pastor entered on the buisness of the day by solmly imploring the divine blessing to Concor with his endavours where he received the answer in writing from each individual & publick read before the whole audiance each Question proven by various texts of Scripture N B next he entred on the shorter Catechism w[h]ere our young folks answered throughout the book & had it enjoined on them against the next examination to answer the first proof anext to each Question the buisness being ended was closed by exhortation & prayer & C--------

Salem october the 11th 1812 the rev^d William Mont[g]omry administred the Sacrament of the Lords Supper in this Church assisted by the rev^d James Smiley who preached the action sermon[25] from 1st John the 17th & first verse these wor[d]s spoke Jesus & lifted up his eyes to heaven and said father the hour is come glorify theyself that they son allso may glorify thee & C--------

The Comunicants name is as follows first the ministers[21 names—misnumbered 22]

January the 10th 1813
This day Composeth one year of the rev^d William Montgomerys Ministerial services in this Congregation & hath Commenced his second year the date above mentioned-------Salem Church

April the 3^d 1813

This day above written the rev^d William Montgomry Pastor of this Congreation held a publick exemination and the atending who belonged to this Church & the aforesad Pastor began the buisness of the day in his usual manner imploring the blessing of god to Concur with his endavours when finished [he] Cloased the meeting with impressive Exhortation and prayer & C

Salem April the 11th 1813 the rev^d William Montgomry administred the Sacrament of the Lords supper in this Church without any assistant Clargey a verry labouress undertaking indeed but was enabled by divine aid to perform the whole buisness of the solem ocasion to the great satisfaction of his audience which [was] numerous the action sermon he delivered in a verry solemn and impressive manner from 1st John the-------17th Chapter and first vers the Comunicants names as follows rev^d Mountgomery [20 names]

Names in the margine who Deposited Certificates[26] with us[10 names]
Salem Church september the 19th 1813 this day the rev^d William Montgomry administerd the Sacrament of the Lords Supper in the aforesaid Church assisted by the rev^d Joseph Bullion who preached the action sermon from the 4th Chapter and 11th verse of the first epistle general of John the words of the Text-------be[l]oved if god so loved us we ought also to love one an other & C--------
Communicants Names [26 names—numbered 27]
N B No 11 omited which makes the total but 26 & C--------
Salem Congregaion—April the 24th 1814 this day the sacrament of the Lords supper was administred by the rev^d William Montgomry pastor of the above Congregation assisted by the rev^d James Smylie who preached the action sermon from 1st John the 3rd Chapter and 3^d verse. Jesus answered and said unto him virily verily i say unto thee except a man be born again he Cannot see the kingdom of god & C the solemnity began on friday & Closed on Sabath evening--------
[30 names]

Salem Congregation November the 13th--------1814-------this day the Sacrement of the Lords Supper was administred by the rev^d William Montgomry assisted by the rev^d Joseph Bullion who preached the action sermon to a large audiance of peple the Comunicants names as follows [24 names—but numbered 25—#22 omitted]

March the 5th———1815

this day was nominated two aditional Elders to act as such in Salem Congregation & published & received the nominated is Thomas Grafton &
Peter Bisland
rotation of the members[27]
rev^d William Montgomry Mod
Jn° Grafton
Saml Marshell
Thomas Grafton
Peter Bisland

Salem Congregation June the 11th 1815

this day the Sacrement of the Lords supper was aministered by the rev^d William Montgomry assisted by the rev^d Joseph Bullion & the revd Jacob Rickhow and the revd James Smylie. N. B. on saturday the 4th preceding the sacrament——— our pastor held a publick exemanation of All the Congragation in the Church ———[List communicants—first four are preachers—total 37]

Selam Congreation october the 22^d 1815

this day the Sacrement of the Lords Supper was administred by the rev^d William Montgomry assisted by the revd Joseph Bullen the revd Montgomry preached the action sermon from song of soloman 4th Ch. & 8th verse Come with me from lebanon my spouse with me from lebanon look from the top of amana from the top of shenir and hermon from the lion dens from mountains of the lepords———
[31 names, but totaled 32]

Selam Congration March the 19 1816

this day the sacrament of the Lords supper was administred by the rev^d William Montgomry assisted by the revrends Joseph Bullin Jacob Rickhow James Smylie Daniel Smith the revd Smith[28] preached the action sermon———
the minutes of the different Texts on the occation mislead [mislaid]———
[31 names]

Salem Church november the 9th 1816

the sacraments of the Lords was administred in this Church tenth day of the present Month by the rev^d William Montgomry assisted by the rev^d Joseph Bullion who preched on saturday from first kings 8 Chapter & last clause of the 39th verse the action sermon Deliverd by the rev^d William Montgomry from the acts of the Apostles the 10 Chapter and 31^{1st} verse & C

N B on saturday the second of the above present Month our rev^d pastor William Mongomry held a publick exemenation in this Church & wereas he issued a few w[r]itten Quieries on Certain points of doctrines from the holy Scriptures to be answered and proven from the same source agreeable his apointment the people under his Charge atended & delivered thier respective answers in writing which was generaly aprobated him & then he turned his atention to

the shorter Catechism opned the meeting by prayer and Cloased it in like manner manner [sic] with an adition of some excelent observations & advice N B this should have been first on this page
[26 communicants listed and numbered]

Salem Congregation February the 23ᵈ 1817
this day the revd William Montgomry agreeable to the rules laid down for the Decipline of the Church of Scotland as is represented in our American Edition of the Confession of faith pertaining to the above mentioned Church Hath in regulary in Due form and manner ordained the following Persons as Elders of the above Congregation to wit

N B: in the   )
presence of   )
the Congregation)

John Grafton
Samuel Marshel
Peter Bisland & C

Salam Church May the 4
            1817
the Sacremant of the Lords supper was administred by the Revᵈ William Montgomery assisted by the Rev Joseph Bullan who preached the Action sarmon
[22 names]
a publick Exemination was performed preceding the sole[m]nity as usual by the revd Montgomry Pastor said Congregation———Selam Congregation December the 21 1817
this day the revd William Montgomry administred the Sacrament of the Lords Supper assisted by the revd Joseph Bullin who preached of [on] saturday from Genesis the 35ᵗʰ & 2ᵈ verse the revᵈ Montgomry preached the acion sermon from issiah the 55ᵗʰ & first verse & C
[17 names]
First Sabath in Jamuary 1818 this day the revᵈ William Montgomry withdrew his Ministerial labours from Selam Congregation for his Conveniency[29] which renders it at preasant Vacant
March Session of the Mississippi Prsybitry—1818 ordred that the revᵈˢ Messers Bullion & Smylie hold a sacramental occasion in Salem Church Pineridge the first Sabath in June the solemnity to begin of friday which apointment was Complied with & C Selam Congregation June the 7ᵗʰ 1818———
this day the revᵈˢ Messers Joseph Bullen & James Smylie administred the Sacrament of the Lords Supper in this Church revᵈ James Smylie preached the action sermon from first John the 6ᵗʰ Chapter &
[25 names]

Suplies———
the revᵈ James [Smylie] on the 14th June Delivered a descours in this Church

Postiscript

    the aforesaid Suply was by order of Prsybitery——May the 24[th] 1820) after Close of Prysbitry the Sacrament of the Lords Supper was administred by re[v]ds Messrs James Smylie & William Montgomry & Joseph Bullen the Action Sermon was Delivred by the rev[d] Montgomry

---

Communicants Names [28 names]

This book is Transferd From John Grafton to

NOTES

I

THE PRESBYTERIANS REACH TENNESSEE
AND KENTUCKY

1. Constance L. Skinner, *Pioneers of the Old Southwest* (New Haven, 1920), 3-7. For the origins of the Presbyterians in Europe and especially in Great Britain see George P. Hays, *Presbyterians, A Popular Narrative of Their Origin, Progress, Doctrines, and Achievements* (New York, 1892), 25-57. For the beginnings of Presbyterianism in America see Robert E. Thompson, *A History of the Presbyterian Churches in the United States* (New York, 1902), Chaps. II-VI; Ezra H. Gillett, *History of the Presbyterian Church in the United States of America,* 2 vols. (Philadelphia, 1864), I, *passim;* Leonard J. Trinterud, *The Forming of an American Tradition: A Re-examination of Colonial Presbyterianism* (Philadelphia, 1949).

2. The evidence seems irrefutable that emigration from Ulster to America resulted largely from economic causes and not from religious. See Henry J. Ford, *The Scotch-Irish in America* (New York, 1941), 167-71.

3. Thompson, *Presbyterian Churches,* 17.

4. James G. Craighead, *Scotch and Irish Seeds in American Soil: The Early History of the Scotch and Irish Churches, and Their Relations to the Presbyterian Church of America* (Philadelphia, c. 1878), 267-68.

5. Between 1700 and 1730 some twenty thousand people left Ulster and came to America. Colin B. Goodykoontz, *Home Missions on the American Frontier* (Caldwell, Idaho, 1939), 75.

6. Skinner, *Pioneers of the Old Southwest,* 1-2.

7. For the reason which they gave see Goodykoontz, *Home Missions,* 75.

8. William W. Sweet, *The Story of Religions in America* (New York, c. 1930), 173.

9. Charles A. Briggs, *American Presbyterianism, Its Origin and Early History* (New York, 1885), 343. The Presbyterians had 170 ministers in seventeen presbyteries. Leonard W. Bacon, *A History of American Christianity* (New York, 1921), 186.

10. For sketches of Makemie see William H. Foote, *Sketches of Virginia, Historical and Biographical* (Philadelphia, 1850), 40-63; William B. Sprague, *Annals of the American Pulpit,* 9 vols. (New York, 1857-1869), III, 1-4; William F. Finney, "Francis Makemie's Contribution to Presbyterianism in America," *Journal of the Presbyterian Historical Society* (Philadelphia), XV (1930-1931), 335-46.

11. Hays, *Presbyterians,* 67-68; Thompson, *Presbyterian Churches,* 19-20. The minutes of the Philadelphia Presbytery begin with the year 1706.

12. *Records of the Presbyterian Church in the United States of America* (Philadelphia, 1841), 10.

13. Gillett, *Presbyterian Church,* I, 108-109; Henry A. White, *Southern Presbyterian Leaders* (New York, 1911), 32-35.

14. Charles A. Hanna, *The Scotch-Irish; or the Scot in North Britain, North Ireland, and North America,* 2 vols. (New York, 1902), II, 381.

15. White, *Southern Presbyterian Leaders,* 38-40.

16. A Call from the United Congregation of Providence and Timber Ridge in Augusta County to be presented to Mr. John Brown . . . in August 1753. MS., Presbyterian Historical Society, Philadelphia. Hereafter cited as Philadelphia.

17. Robert H. Bishop, *An Outline of the History of the Church in the State of Kentucky, during a Period of Forty Years: Containing the Memoirs of Rev. David Rice* (Lexington, Ky., 1824), 66-67, *passim.* Until shortly before the American Revolution the Presbyterian missionaries had little competition in the Valley of Virginia. Ernest T. Thompson, *Presbyterian Missions in the Southern United States* (Richmond, 1934), 26.

18. William H. Foote, *Sketches of North Carolina, Historical and Biographical* (New York, 1846), 79-80.

19. Ford, *The Scotch-Irish in America,* 401-403.

20. Support for this statement can be found in a large variety of secular and religious sources.

21. George Bancroft, *History of the United States of America,* 6 vols. (New York, 1891), IV, 101.

22. Craighead, *Scotch and Irish Seeds in American Soil,* 324, 343.

23. After inscribing his name, Witherspoon said: "Although these gray hairs must descend soon into a sepulchre, I would infinitely rather that they should descend thither by the hand of a public executioner than desert, at this crisis, the sacred cause of my country." Quoted in *Addresses Delivered at the Celebration of the Centennial of the General Assembly of the Presbyterian Church* (Philadelphia, c. 1888), 12. For sketches of Witherspoon see Ford, *The Scotch-Irish in America,* 438-41; Sprague, *Annals,* III, 288-300.

24. Sweet, *Religions in America,* 260.

25. For a sketch of Blackburn see Sprague, *Annals,* IV, 43-58.

26. Lyman C. Draper, *King's Mountain and Its Heroes* (Cincinnati, 1881), 176.

27. White, *Southern Presbyterian Leaders,* 144-53.

28. Charles L. Thompson, *The Presbyterians* (New York, 1903), 97. After the formation of the General Assembly of the Presbyterian Church in 1789 one of its first acts was to address a letter to President Washington, confirming its faith in his leadership. The letter to Washington and his reply to the Assembly are printed in the *Minutes of the General Assembly of the Presbyterian Church in the United States of America from Its Organization A. D. 1789 to A. D. 1820 inclusive* (Philadelphia, c. 1835), 11-12, 24.

29. Thompson, *The Presbyterians,* 119. War dealt harshly with the churches in Virginia and elsewhere on the frontier. Joseph F. Tuttle, "Presbyterianism on

the Frontiers," *Presbyterian Quarterly and Princeton Review* (New York), VI (1877), 445-69. For a brief essay on the effect of the American Revolution upon religion see Robert Baird, *Religion in America* (New York, 1856), 207-212.

30. John DeWitt, "Characteristics of the Presbyterian Church in the United States of America," *Journal of the Presbyterian Historical Society*, I (1901-1902), 56-71 *passim;* William T. Hanzsche, *The Presbyterians* (Philadelphia, 1934), 88.

31. Thomas P. Abernethy, *From Frontier to Plantation in Tennessee* (Chapel Hill, 1932), 210.

32. Hays, *Presbyterians*, 132-33.

33. *Addresses at the Centennial of the General Assembly,* 104.

34. Thompson, *Presbyterian Churches,* 66. Philip Lindsley called Presbyterian government "as perfect a model of pure democracy or representative thought as can be found in the world." Le Roy J. Halsey (ed.), *The Works of Philip Lindsley, D. D.,* 3 vols. (Philadelphia, 1866), II, 138.

35. One session composed of the minister and a single elder proceeded to suspend a member for intemperance. MS. Session Record, Mount Zion (Kentucky) Church, 1823-1925, January 1842, Historical Foundation of the Presbyterian and Reformed Churches, Montreat, North Carolina. Hereafter cited as Montreat. The manuscript records of the sessions, presbyteries, and synods bear so many different titles, I have arbitrarily used the term "record" for the session and "minutes" for the presbyteries and synods.

36. Samuel J. Baird, *A Collection of the Acts, Deliverances, and Testimonies of the Supreme Judicatory of the Presbyterian Church* (Philadelphia, 1855), 65, 66-80 *passim.*

37. In some cases the membership of the church was so small that satisfactory elders could not be found. Gillett, *Presbyterian Church,* II, 482.

38. Thompson, *Presbyterian Churches,* 230.

39. Guy S. Klett, "Some Aspects of the Presbyterian Church on the American Colonial Frontier," *Journal of the Presbyterian Historical Society,* XIX (1940-1941), 118-19; Baird, *Collection,* 247-49.

40. MS. Session Record, New Providence (Kentucky) Church, 1822-1849, October 12, 1831, Montreat.

41. MS. Session Record, Bethany (Mississippi) Church, 1818-1864, March (?) 1849, *ibid.*

42. MS. Session Record, Brazeau (Missouri) Church, 1833-1851, January 28, 1843, *ibid.* This was a well-known practice in the Presbyterian Church in Scotland.

43. MS. Session Record, New Providence (Kentucky) Church, 1822-1849, December 29, 1833, *ibid.*

44. MS. Session Record, First Presbyterian Church, Louisville, 1819-1823, September and October 1822, *ibid.*

45. For examples see MS. Session Record, Mount Hope Bethel (Tennessee) Church, 1828-1870, *ibid.;* MS. Session Record, Brazeau (Missouri) Church, 1833-1851, *ibid.*

46. Much is often recorded that little concerns the session but is valuable for a study of society. For a complaint on the contents of a session book see MS.

Session Record, New Providence (Kentucky) Church, 1822-1849, February 1, 1830, *ibid.*

47. For the best example found see MS. Session Record, Shiloh (Tennessee) Church, 1834-1858, pp. 98, 99, 103, 107, 108, *ibid.*

48. MS. Session Record, Carmel (Mississippi) Church, 1839-1866, p. 2, Mississippi State Department of Archives and History, Jackson, Mississippi. Hereafter cited as Mississippi Archives.

49. Baird, *Collection,* 64. Often churches had no deacons. More than twenty years elapsed between the organization of a certain Kentucky church and the first election of deacons. MS. Session Record, Walnut Hill (Kentucky) Church, 1818-1854, February 13, 1842, Montreat.

50. MS. Minutes, Tuscaloosa Presbytery, 1835-1843, April 6, 1842, *ibid.*

51. The first presbytery in the United States, formed in 1705 or 1706, was the sole governing body of the Presbyterian Church until 1717, when the presbytery was divided and a synod was organized. Gillett, *Presbyterian Church,* I, 18-32.

52. Examine MS. Minutes, Tuscaloosa Presbytery, 1835-1843, *passim,* Montreat.

53. Hays, *Presbyterians,* 399.

54. MS. Minutes, Tuscaloosa Presbytery, 1835-1843, December 13, 1841, Montreat.

55. MS. Minutes, South Alabama Presbytery, 1833-1835, November 19, 1834, *ibid.*

56. MS. Minutes, Holston Presbytery, 1827-1860, p. 1, *ibid.*

57. MS. (copy) Minutes, Elk Presbytery, 1813-1815, no paging, Tennessee State Library, Nashville. Hereafter cited as Nashville.

58. MS. Minutes, North Alabama Presbytery, 1825-1844, May 7, 1842, Montreat.

59. James W. Marshall, The Presbyterian Church in Alabama, 1813-1898, p. 923. MS., Alabama State Department of Archives and History, Montgomery. Hereafter cited as Alabama Archives.

60. Baird, *Collection,* 263; *Minutes of the General Assembly, 1789 to 1820,* p. 304.

61. Thompson, *Presbyterian Churches,* 67.

62. For the earliest example found see *Rules and Standing Docket of the Synod of Kentucky, Adopted during Their October Session, 1822* (Mayfield, Ky., 1823).

63. Baird, *Collection,* 280, 284, 300-303. For an excellent sketch of the history of the General Assembly from 1789 to 1825 see Gillett, *Presbyterian Church,* I, 268-99, 436-70; II, 213-42.

64. The ascendant element in the westward movement into Tennessee and Kentucky was the Scotch-Irish whose ministers "preached not only the theology of Calvin, but the gospel of the freedom of the individual, and the compact theory of the state. They constituted a new order of Americans." Frederick J. Turner, "Western State-Making in the Revolutionary Era," *American Historical Review* (New York), I (1895-1896), 73.

65. Henry Adams, *History of the United States of America,* 9 vols. (New York, 1921), I, 58-59.

66. MS. Minutes, Hanover Presbytery, 1769-1785, October 18, 1770; April 10, 1771; June 2, 1773, Union Theological Seminary, Richmond, Virginia. Hereafter cited as Richmond. Also see R. R. Preston, "History of Presbyterianism in Southwest Virginia," *Southwest Virginia Enterprise* (Wytheville), July 3, 1923.

67. William H. Foote, *Sketches of Virginia, Historical and Biographical* (2nd. series, Philadelphia, 1855), 115-17, 123-25.

68. Foote, *Sketches of North Carolina,* 309; "Presbyterianism in Tennessee," *Christian Observer and Presbyterian Witness* (Richmond), October 11, 1866.

69. Gillett, *Presbyterian Church,* I, 425.

70. For sketches of Doak see Sprague, *Annals,* III, 392-97; C. W. Sommerville, "Samuel Doak," *Union Seminary Review* (Richmond), XL (1928-1929), 193-205.

71. James Phelan, *History of Tennessee* (Boston, 1889), 218.

72. Theodore Roosevelt, *The Winning of the West,* 4 vols. (New York, 1889-1896), II, 222.

73. Sprague, *Annals,* III, 308-319.

74. See Goodridge A. Wilson, *History of Abingdon Presbytery* (Pulaski, Va., c. 1936).

75. Gillett, *Presbyterian Church,* I, 422-35.

76. *The First Presbyterian Church, Nashville, Tennessee: The Addresses Delivered in Connection with the Observance of the One Hundredth Anniversary* (Nashville, 1915), 47-48, 73-76.

77. Thomas C. Pears (ed.), "First Formal History of Transylvania Presbytery," *Journal of the Presbyterian Historical Society,* XIX (1940), 147-48; Robert Davidson, *History of the Presbyterian Church in the State of Kentucky* (New York, 1847), 80-81.

78. Bishop, *Outline of the Church in Kentucky,* 66-69, 152; Davidson, *Presbyterian Church in Kentucky,* 64-67, 73.

79. Craighead, *Scotch and Irish Seeds in American Soil,* 284.

80. Examine Daniel Drake, *Pioneer Life in Kentucky, 1785-1800* (ed. by Emmet F. Horine, New York, 1948), *passim.*

81. Pears, "Transylvania Presbytery," *loc. cit.,* 157.

82. R. A. Johnstone, *An Historical Sketch of the Presbytery of Transylvania* (Louisville, 1876), *passim;* Davidson, *Presbyterian Church in Kentucky,* 81-82. Also examine MS. (copy) Minutes, Transylvania Presbytery, 1786-1837, Montreat.

83. William W. Sweet, *Religion on the American Frontier: The Presbyterians, 1783-1840* (New York, 1936), 32.

84. *One Hundred Years of Presbyteriansim in the Ohio Valley* (Cincinnati, 1890), 7-9; Gillett, *Presbyterian Church,* II, 123-24; "Historical Sketch of the First Presbyterian Church, Cincinnati," *Presbyterian Magazine* (Philadelphia), II (1852), 264-68.

85. *Addresses at the Centennial of the General Assembly,* 11.

86. John G. Jones, *A Concise History of the Introduction of Protestantism into Mississippi and the Southwest* (St. Louis, 1866), 225-31.

87. Of the 256 signers of the Cumberland Compact in Tennessee in 1780, only one had to sign with a mark. Albigence W. Putnam, *History of Middle Tennessee; or, Life and Times of Gen. James Robertson* (Nashville, 1859), 100-102; Abernethy, *From Frontier to Plantation,* 160-61.

88. Of the first fifteen Presbyterian ministers in Illinois between 1816 and 1836, fourteen were graduates of the best colleges and universities in the United States. H. D. Jenkins, "The History of Presbyterianism in Illinois," Illinois State Historical Society, *Transactions* (Springfield), 1913, p. 63.

89. Phelan, *History of Tennessee,* 215.

90. Charles A. Beard and Mary R. Beard, *The Rise of American Civilization,* 2 vols. (New York, 1927), I, 529.

91. Merrill E. Gaddis, "Religious Ideas and Attitudes in the Early Frontier," *Church History* (Chicago), II (1933), 169-70.

92. Roosevelt, *Winning of the West,* III, 18-24; Peter Cartwright, *Autobiography of Peter Cartwright the Backwoods Preacher* (ed. by William P. Strickland, New York, 1857), 25; Davidson, *Presbyterian Church in Kentucky,* 63-65, 99-103.

93. Bishop, *Outline of the Church in Kentucky,* 79. Also see Niels Sonne, *Liberal Kentucky, 1780-1828* (New York, 1939), 11-13.

94. *Minutes of the General Assembly, 1789-1820,* pp. 152-53. For an explanation of the failure of Presbyterianism to appeal widely to the common people see Hanzsche, *The Presbyterians,* 88-99.

95. Grover C. Loud, *Evangelized America* (New York, 1928), 98; Benjamin R. Lacy, Jr., *Revivals in the Midst of the Years* (Richmond, 1943), 73-74. For a lengthy sketch of McGready see Foote, *Sketches of North Carolina,* 367-413.

II

THE PRESBYTERIANS AND THE CAMP MEETINGS

1. See Catherine C. Cleveland, *The Great Revival in the West, 1797-1805* (Chicago, 1916), Chap. I.

2. Davidson, *Presbyterian Church in Kentucky,* Chap II; Sweet, *The Presbyterians,* Chaps. I-II.

3. Zachariah F. Smith, "The Great Revival of 1800," Kentucky State Historical Society *Register* (Frankfort), VII (1909), 21-22.

4. Bishop, *Outline of the Church in Kentucky,* 79.

5. James Smith, "Tours into Kentucky and the Northwest Territory, 1783, 1795, 1797," *Ohio Archeological and Historical Quarterly* (Columbus), XVI (1907), 384.

6. Francis Asbury, *The Journal of Rev. Francis Asbury,* 3 vols. (New York, 1852), II, 342.

7. See *Minutes of the General Assembly, 1789-1820*, pp. 146-47, 152-53.

8. See Chap. IV, "The Presbyterian Minister."

9. William W. Sweet, *Revivalism in America: Its Origin, Growth and Decline* (New York, 1944), 120-21.

10. Bishop, *Outline of the Church in Kentucky*, 69-71.

11. For sketches of McGready see Foote, *Sketches of North Carolina*, Chap. XXVII; John Rogers, *The Biography of Eld. Barton Warren Stone, Written by Himself: with Additions and Reflections* (Cincinnati, 1847), 7-8; Loud, *Evangelized America*, Chap. VIII.

12. It is a noticeable fact that Hampden-Sydney and Washington colleges, both in Virginia, furnished the Presbyterians with a large number of the ministers who participated in the revival movement in the West. Sweet, *Revivalism in America*, 119.

13. See Cartwright, *Autobiography*, 24-55, *passim*.

14. Foote, *Sketches of North Carolina*, 376.

15. See Cleveland, *The Great Revival*, Chap. III; Walter B. Posey, *The Development of Methodism in the Old Southwest, 1783-1824* (Tuscaloosa, Ala., 1933), Chap. II.

16. Frederick M. Davenport, *Primitive Traits in Religious Revivals* (New York, 1906), 66-67.

17. James Smith, *History of the Christian Church from its Origin to the Present Time* (Nashville, 1835), 583.

18. Phelan, *History of Tennessee*, 222.

19. Rogers, *Barton Warren Stone*, 8.

20. Loud, *Evangelized America*, 97.

21. Davenport, *Primitive Traits*, 67-69.

22. Davidson, *Presbyterian Church in Kentucky*, 132.

23. Cleveland, *The Great Revival*, 51.

24. Davidson, *Presbyterian Church in Kentucky*, 136.

25. Loud, *Evangelized America*, 106.

26. "In this deranged state of things, some of the friends of religion, hoping to remedy a share of the evils which prevailed, encouraged men to come forward as exhorters under the direction of the Presbytery." MS. Minutes, West Tennessee Presbytery, 1810-1836, April 7, 1812, Montreat.

27. Davidson (*Presbyterian Church in Kentucky*, 140) holds the Methodists responsible, while Cartwright (*Autobiography*, 46) contends that the Presbyterians "went into great extremes and downright wildness."

28. James R. Rogers, *The Cane Ridge Meeting House* (Cincinnati, 1910), 157; Richard McNemar, *The Kentucky Revival* (New York, 1846), 26-36. Also see the account of the Cane Ridge meeting by John Lyle, a Presbyterian minister. Cleveland, *The Great Revival*, 183-89.

29. *Methodist Magazine* (New York), III (1820), 191.

30. By 1803 the revival movement had also spread through the Northern and Eastern presbyteries (*Minutes of the General Assembly, 1789-1820*, p. 274), though there was definite indication that the zeal was dying. By 1805 the fires were almost extinguished, despite sporadic revivals for years.

31. Posey, *Methodism in the Old Southwest,* Chap. II.

32. Smith, *Christian Church,* 580.

33. Smith, "Great Revival of 1800," *loc. cit.,* 35.

34. See Chap. III, "A Sequel to the Revivals."

35. In practically all instances in history, revivals have started at the bottom stratum of social life.

36. Cleveland, *The Great Revival,* 121-22.

37. Sonne, *Liberal Kentucky,* 22.

38. Kenneth W. Dean, *Social and Economic Conditions in Kentucky as Reflected in the Newspapers, 1788-1804* (M. A. thesis, University of Chicago, 1925), 28-29. The manuscript records of the sessions contain very few references to the revivals.

39. Baird, *Collection,* 215-21. If the Methodist Church had followed such admonitions, its membership increase would have been slight indeed.

40. Reprinted in Bishop, *Outline of the Church in Kentucky,* 340-84.

41. *Ibid.,* 367.

42. See Franceway R. Cossitt, *The Life and Times of Rev. Finis Ewing* (Louisville, 1853), 409-416.

43. Sprague, *Annals,* IV, 179.

44. See Chap. III, "A Sequel to the Revivals." There is much reason to believe that Lyle was unfair in his evaluation of the exercises and extravagances of the revivals.

45. A seventy-page booklet, privately printed in 1803. This was answered by David Thomas (*The Observer Trying the Great Reformation in this State, and Proving It to Have Been a Work of Divine Power,* Lexington, Ky., c. 1803, pp. 32-42), who contended that the revival was "pure sterling gold" and that much good had resulted therefrom.

46. Adam Rankin, *A Review of the Noted Revival in Kentucky* (n.p, 1803), 10-11.

47. Davis to ? Patterson, Philadelphia.

48. Charles C. Ware, *Barton Warren Stone, Pathfinder of Christian Union* (St. Louis, 1932), 119.

49. James Gallaher, *The Western Sketch-Book* (Boston, 1852), 40, 48-49.

50. Davidson, *Presbyterian Church in Kentucky,* 185 n.

51. McNemar, *The Kentucky Revival,* 27.

52. Sweet, *The Presbyterians,* 46-47.

53. And also liberalism. See Sonne, *Liberal Kentucky,* 18-21, *passim.*

54. Gillett, *Presbyterian Church,* II, 196.

55. See Posey, *Methodism in the Old Southwest,* 122; Posey, "The Early Baptist Church in the Lower Southwest," *Journal of Southern History* (Baton Rouge), X (1944), 161-73.

III

A SEQUEL TO THE REVIVALS

1. See "The Rankin Schism," Chap. III, Davidson, *Presbyterian Church in Kentucky.*

2. "Extracts from the Minutes of the Transylvania Presbytery, 1786-1837," April 26, October 4, 1792, in Sweet, *The Presbyterians,* 138-39.

3. Robert Marshall to James Welch, August 27, 1792, Philadelphia; Johnstone, *Presbytery of Transylvania,* 32-34; William O. Shewmaker, *The Pisgah Book, 1784-1909* (n.p., 1909), 13-15. Also see Adam Rankin, *A Process in the Transilvania Presbytery* (Lexington, Ky., c. 1793), *passim;* Rankin, *A Reply to A Narrative of Mr. Adam Rankin's Trial* (Lexington, 1794), *passim.*

4. For a sketch of Balch see Sprague, *Annals,* III, 308-319.

5. Balch's Hopkinsian doctrines are explained clearly in John E. Alexander, The Presbyterian Church of Greeneville, Tenn., 1876. MS., Philadelphia.

6. Sprague, *Annals,* III, 314.

7. See MS. Minutes, Synod of the Carolinas, 1788-1800, Richmond. Of the 190 pages in these minutes, nearly all of them are devoted to the Balch trial.

8. *Minutes of the General Assembly, 1789-1820,* pp. 151-57. Also see Baird, *Collection,* 629-34.

9. *Christian Observer and Presbyterian Witness,* October 25, 1866; Thompson, *Presbyterian Churches,* 78.

10. Edward Crawford to James Crawford, September 18, 1797, Philadelphia.

11. Johnstone, *Presbytery of Transylvania,* 43.

12. Richard McNemar, *The Kentucky Revival, passim;* Davidson, *Presbyterian Church in Kentucky,* Chap. VIII; Rogers, *Barton Warren Stone, passim; A Serious Address, from the Synod of Kentucky, to the Churches under Their Care* (Lexington, 1804).

13. See comment by William Thomson to James Dickey, June 2, 1820, Philadelphia.

14. Cleveland, *The Great Revival,* 136-41.

15. See Foote, *Sketches of North Carolina,* Chap. XXVII, *passim.*

16. MS. letter, December 11, 1807, Philadelphia.

17. Cleveland, *The Great Revival,* 134-35.

18. Bacon, *American Christianity,* 241.

19. *Christian Observer,* January 3, 1867.

20. "Minutes of the Transylvania Presbytery, 1786-1837," October 9, 1801, in Sweet, *The Presbyterians,* 186-87. For a later comment on this action see pastoral letter, MS. Minutes, West Tennessee Presbytery, 1810-1836, April 7, 1812, Montreat.

21. Originally this idea is supposed to have come from David Rice, who, impressed with great need, encouraged young men of intelligence and character to exhort. Smith, *Christian Church,* 580; Davidson, *Presbyterian Church in Kentucky,* 224.

22. "Minutes of the Transylvania Presbytery, 1786-1837," October 6-7, 1802, in Sweet, *The Presbyterians*, 187-89.

23. "Minutes of the Synod of Kentucky, 1802-1811," October 15, 1802, *ibid.*, 310-11.

24. Davidson, *Presbyterian Church in Kentucky*, 229. Note the type of examination given by the Cumberland Presbytery. "The Minutes of the Cumberland Presbytery, 1803-1806," October 5, 1803, in Sweet, *The Presbyterians*, 286-87; *Presbyterian Magazine*, IV (1854), 226.

25. Baird, *Collection*, 81.

26. John V. Stephens, "Was Education the Cause of Separation from the Mother Church?" *Cumberland Presbyterian* (Nashville), February 1, 1900.

27. Cossitt, *Finis Ewing*, 352; Thaddeus C. Blake, *The Old Log House, A History and Defense of the Cumberland Presbyterian Church* (Nashville, 1897), 65-68. As early as 1729 the Synod of Philadelphia passed the adopting act by which a candidate for the ministry was required to subscribe only to "the essential and necessary articles." *Records of the Presbyterian Church*, 92.

28. Barton W. Stone left the Presbyterian Church largely on the question of Calvinism. See Rogers, *Barton Warren Stone*, 33-34.

29. Gaddis, "Religious Ideas and Attitudes in the Early Frontier," *loc. cit.*, 162-63.

30. Benjamin W. McDonnold, *History of the Cumberland Presbyterian Church* (Nashville, 1888), Chap. XII.

31. A name of derision often used by the "orthodox" group. Ware, *Barton Warren Stone*, 125-26.

32. Cartwright, *Autobiography*, 47-48.

33. "Minutes of the Synod of Kentucky, 1802-1811," October 22, 1804, in Sweet, *The Presbyterians*, 328-30.

34. Davidson, *Presbyterian Church in Kentucky*, 231; Cossitt, *Finis Ewing*, 124.

35. "Minutes of the Synod of Kentucky, 1802-1811," October 17, 18, 1805, in Sweet, *The Presbyterians*, 331-35.

36. See Gillett, *Presbyterian Church*, II, 181-85.

37. A Narrative of Rev. John Lyle's Mission in the Bounds of the Cumberland Presbytery (1805), 20-21, 40, 57. MS., Kentucky Historical Society, Frankfort. Hereafter cited as Frankfort.

38. Cossitt, *Finis Ewing*, 133-50; McDonnold, *Cumberland Presbyterian Church*, 80-81.

39. Davidson, *Presbyterian Church in Kentucky*, 236. For Chap. XIV of the Form of Government see *The Constitution of the Presbyterian Church in the United States of America* (Utica, 1822), 368-74. This chapter has the title, "Of Licensing Candidates or Probationers to Preach the Gospel."

40. "Minutes of the Synod of Kentucky, 1802-1811," December 9, 1805, in Sweet, *The Presbyterians*, 341-43.

41. Cossitt, *Finis Ewing*, 159-60; McDonnold, *Cumberland Presbyterian Church*, 82.

42. "Minutes of the Synod of Kentucky, 1802-1811," October 27, 28, 1806, in Sweet, *The Presbyterians,* 351-54.

43. *Minutes of the General Assembly, 1789-1820,* pp. 378-83.

44. Reprinted in Cossitt, *Finis Ewing,* 479-86.

45. *Minutes of the General Assembly, 1789-1820,* pp. 389-90, 392-93, 406, 408-409.

46. *Ibid.,* 416. See Cossitt's caustic charge against the Synod of Kentucky. *Finis Ewing,* 157-58.

47. Davidson, *Presbyterian Church in Kentucky,* 119, 250.

48. Hays, *Presbyterians,* 465. For an interesting summary see *A Brief History of the Rise, Progress, and Termination of the Proceedings of the Synod of Kentucky, Relative to the Late Cumberland Presbytery* (Lexington, 1823).

49. E. B. Crisman, *Origin and Doctrines of the Cumberland Presbyterian Church* (St. Louis, 1858), 68-69; McDonnold, *Cumberland Presbyterian Church,* 83-84.

50. Hays, *Presbyterians,* 466-67.

51. See *A Circular Letter Addressed to the Societies and Brethren of the Presbyterian Church, Recently under the Care of the Council by the Late Cumberland Presbytery* (Russellville, Ky., 1810), *passim;* Robert V. Foster, "A Sketch of the History of the Cumberland Presbyterian Church," *American Church History,* 13 vols. (New York, 1893-1897), XI, 268-70.

52. Davidson, *Presbyterian Church in Kentucky,* 253.

53. November 6, 1811, Philadelphia.

54. MS. Minutes, West Tennessee Presbytery, 1810-1836, September 17, 1811, Montreat. In the fall of the same year, Blackburn arbitrarily suspended, without trial, four elders of his Columbia, Tennessee, congregation for participating in a Communion service held in a Cumberland Presbyterian church. Two confessed the wrong and were restored. W. A. Provine, Early History of the Cumberland Presbyterian Church in Maury County, Tennessee, 6. MS., Nashville.

55. For title see n. 51 above.

56. McDonnold, *Cumberland Presbyterian Church,* Chap. XII; Foster, "Cumberland Presbyterian Church," *loc. cit.,* 287-88. See *The Constitution of the Cumberland Presbyterian Church in the United States of America* (Russellville, Ky., 1821).

57. At the same time the Presbyterian Church had only 2,700. It is quite likely, however, that in 1820 not more than one-tenth of the population of the state were members of any church. Bishop, *Outline of the Church in Kentucky,* 307.

58. James H. B. Hall, *The History of the Cumberland Presbyterian Church in Alabama prior to 1826* (Montgomery, 1904), 11.

59. John A. McKamy, *The Development of the Cumberland Presbyterian Church* (Nashville, 1903), 19. In 1823 the new church had some 2,500 members, most of whom were in Kentucky and Tennessee. *Bishop, Outline of the Church in Kentucky,* 126.

60. Thomas J. Simpson, *History of the Cumberland Presbyterian Church*

(Jefferson City, Mo., 1844), Chap. V, *passim;* McKamy, *Cumberland Presbyterian Church,* 20.

61. J. Berrien Lindsley, "Sources and Sketches of Cumberland Presbyterian History," *Theological Medium* (Nashville), VI (1876), 33.

62. See James B. Finley, *Autobiography of Rev. James B. Finley: or, Pioneer Life in the West* (Cincinnati, 1854).

63. Since only four ordained Cumberland Presbyterian ministers came from the Presbyterian Church, the word "schism" is misleading. McDonnold, *Cumberland Presbyterian Church,* 85-86.

64. John M. Gaut, *Cumberland, the Story of a Name* (Nashville, 1904), 40-41; McKamy, *Cumberland Presbyterian Church,* 5-6.

65. *Addresses at the Centennial of the General Assembly,* 16.

66. Cossitt, *Finis Ewing,* 166.

67. Davidson, *Presbyterian Church in Kentucky,* 261.

68. MS. Minutes, Alabama Presbytery, 1821-1826, April 2, 1824, Montreat.

69. An interdenominational paper printed in Lexington, Kentucky, by Thomas T. Skillman, a Presbyterian minister.

70. Issues of December 24, 1828, and July 1, 1829.

71. Gallaher, *Western Sketch-Book,* 61. Many of the Cumberland Presbyterian ministers lived on small farms from which they earned most of their living. See Richard Beard, *Brief Biographical Sketches of Some of the Early Ministers of the Cumberland Presbyterian Church* (Nashville, 1867); *ibid.,* 2nd series (Nashville, 1874).

72. See A. G. Bergen, "Ministerial Equipment," *Cumberland Presbyterian Review* (Nashville), IV (1892), 257-68.

73. Lindsley, "Sources and Sketches of Cumberland Presbyterian History," *loc. cit.,* VI, 34. In 1905 more than half of the ministers and one-third of the members of the Cumberland Presbyterian Church united with the Presbyterian Church, U. S. A. Later another third of the members were lost to other denominations. Thomas H. Campbell, *Studies in Cumberland Presbyterian History* (Nashville, 1944), 283-84.

IV

THE PRESBYTERIAN MINISTER

1. See "The Circuit Rider Among Frontier Folk," Posey, *Methodism in the Old Southwest,* Chap. III.

2. Bishop, *Outline of the Church in Kentucky,* 66-67, *passim;* Sprague, *Annals,* III, 247-48.

3. Edward Crawford to James Crawford, September 29, 1786, Philadelphia.

4. See various manuscripts in Shane Papers, *ibid.*

5. See Joseph P. Howe Papers, *ibid.* As a rule the Presbyterian ministers in the West rarely served more than two or three churches, in contrast to the Methodist itinerant, who sometimes traveled a circuit as much as four hundred

miles in circumference. For an example see Oscar P. Fitzgerald, *John B. McFerrin* (Nashville, 1888), 62-69.

6. MS. Session Record, Louisville First Presbyterian Church, 1819-1828, pp. 3-5, Montreat.

7. McDonnold, *Cumberland Presbyterian Church,* 147-48.

8. For good general descriptions of various aspects of the frontier see Frederick L. Paxson, *History of the American Frontier, 1763-1893* (Boston, 1924); James Hall, *Sketches of History, Life, and Manners in the West,* 2 vols. (Philadelphia, 1835); Cartwright, *Autobiography.*

9. Sprague, *Annals,* III, 392. Also see John E. Alexander, *A Historical Sketch of Washington College* (n.p., 1902), 8.

10. McDonnold, *Cumberland Presbyterian Church,* 162.

11. See William W. Sweet, "The Churches as Moral Courts of the Frontier," *Church History,* II (1933), 3-21.

12. Davidson, *Presbyterian Church in Kentucky,* 129-30.

13. MS. Minutes, Shiloh Presbytery, 1815-1830, April 14, May 18, 1821, Montreat.

14. MS. Session Record, Pine Ridge (Mississippi) Church, 1823-1838, November 24, 1827, *ibid.*

15. MS. Minutes, Tuscaloosa Presbytery, 1835-1843, October 16, 1841; *ibid.* For other cases of intemperance see History of the Presbyterian Church in Sommerville, Tennessee, 1-2. MS., Philadelphia; "Extracts from the Minutes of the Transylvania Presbytery, 1786-1837," February 18, 19, 1795; October 2, 1804, in Sweet, *The Presbyterians,* 149-52, 193-97.

16. Noted criminal lawyer and politician from Tennessee. See Joseph H. Parks, *Felix Grundy, Champion of Democracy* (University, La., 1940).

17. Governor of Tennessee from 1821 to 1827 and from 1829 to 1835. See sketch in *Dictionary of American Biography,* V, 529-30.

18. MS. Minutes, West Tennessee Presbytery, 1810-1836, April 8-14, 1825, Montreat.

19. MS. Minutes, South Alabama Presbytery, 1833-1835, March 3, 1834, *ibid.*

20. "Minutes of the Transylvania Presbytery, 1786-1837," October 11, November 19, 1824; April 29, 1825; October 10, 1826, in Sweet, *The Presbyterians,* 250-57.

21. MS. Minutes, Arkansas Presbytery, 1835-1848, April 10, August 20, 1847; April 15, 1848, Montreat.

22. MS. Session Record, Louisville First Presbyterian Church, 1828-1839, December 30, 1829; February 22, April 16, 1830, *ibid.*

23. On this point see Walter B. Posey, "The Frontier Baptist Ministry," East Tennessee Historical Society's *Publications* (Knoxville), No. 14 (1942), 7-9; Posey, *Methodism in the Old Southwest,* 45-46.

24. Davidson, *Presbyterian Church in Kentucky,* 123-24 n.

25. MS. Session Record, Washington (Mississippi) Church, 1807-1820, June 7, 1807, Montreat.

26. Lindsley, "Cumberland Presbyterian History," *loc. cit.,* VI, 421.

27. MS. Session Record, First Presbyterian Church, Nashville, 1833-1853, April 29, 1833, church vault, Nashville.

28. Horace E. Orr, "One Hundred Years of New Prospect Presbyterian Church, Knox County, Tennessee, 1834-1934," East Tennessee Historical Society's *Publications*, No. 7 (1935), 53.

29. An Account of Money Received as a Preacher from Different Places, 1812-1832. MS., Marshall Papers, Philadelphia.

30. L. R. Janes, The Presbyterian Church of Strawberry Plains, Tennessee, 32-33. MS., *ibid*. Also see A. A. Hogue, *An Historical Discourse* (Louisville, 1859), 5.

31. See David Nelson Papers, Philadelphia; Davidson, *Presbyterian Church in Kentucky,* 112.

32. Beard, *Biographical Sketches,* 124-26; *ibid.,* 2nd. series, 187-88.

33. For example see Jesse Herrmann, *James McChord—A Portrait* (Lexington, Ky., 1940), 64-65.

34. Bishop, *Outline of the Church in Kentucky,* 110.

35. MS. Minutes, Cabbin Creek (Kentucky) Church, August 15, 1825, Philadelphia.

36. Sweet, "The Churches as Moral Courts," *loc. cit.,* 19.

37. Beard, *Biographical Sketches,* 223.

38. See Baird, *Collection,* 80-84.

39. MS. Minutes, Alabama Presbytery, 1821-1826, December, 1823, Montreat.

40. MS. Minutes, South Alabama Presbytery, 1828-1832, October, 1828, *ibid*.

41. MS. Minutes, North Alabama Presbytery, 1825-1844, July 14, 1827, *ibid*.

42. For an example see Sweet, *The Presbyterians,* 703.

43. See "Church Officers," Baird, *Collection,* Book I, Chap. II.

44. Although a candidate held an M.A. degree, he was not excused from an examination in sciences. See ruling in MS. Minutes, Tuscaloosa Presbytery, 1835-1843, April 2, 1840, Montreat.

45. James K. Hall, Biographical Sketch of Richard H. King, *passim*. MS., Philadelphia.

46. MS. Minutes, West Tennessee Presbytery, 1810-1836, September 17, 1811, Montreat.

47. MS. Minutes, Cumberland Presbytery, 1810-1813, July 27, 1810, Philadelphia.

48. MS. Minutes, South Alabama Presbytery, 1828-1832, April 3, 1829, Montreat. For a similar case see MS. Minutes, North Alabama Presbytery, 1825-1844, May 29, 1828, *ibid*.

49. Examine Sprague, *Annals,* III and IV.

50. Edward P. Humphrey and Thomas H. Cleland, *Memoirs of the Rev. Thomas H. Cleland, D.D.* (Cincinnati, 1859), 132-33.

51. Bishop, *Outline of the Church in Kentucky,* 97-98.

52. *Christian Spectator* (New Haven), II (1820), 297-300.

53. John Lyle to James Dickey, c. 1812, Philadelphia.

54. *Ibid.,* February 18, 1812, *ibid*. Also see "How to Preach," *Watchman of the South* (Richmond), April 19, 1838.

55. John Carr's comment on Craighead is true of many other Presbyterian preachers. See *Early Times in Middle Tennessee* (Nashville, 1857), 66. For another example of "cold and monotonous" preaching see T. C. Anderson, *Life of Rev. George Donnell* (Nashville, 1858), 102.

56. Hays, *Presbyterians,* 453.

57. Davidson, *Presbyterian Church in Kentucky,* 129.

58. "President Young's Address," *Home Missionary* (New York), January 1, 1835.

59. See V. Alton Moody, "Early Religious Efforts in the Lower Mississippi Valley," *Mississippi Valley Historical Review* (Cedar Rapids), XXII (1935-1936), 176. For examples of excellent Presbyterian sermons see *Original Sermons; by Presbyterian Ministers, in the Mississippi Valley* (Cincinnati, 1833). An examination of Methodist and Baptist preaching will clearly reveal a deliberate purpose to preach in a style essentially suited to the rugged frontier. See Luther A. Weigle, *American Idealism* (New Haven, 1928), 150; Posey, "Early Baptist Church," *loc. cit.,* 165.

60. E. H. Green, A Brief History of Portersville Church, Tipton County, Tennessee, 1855, p. 3. MS., Philadelphia.

61. Coffin to editor, *Family Visitor* (Richmond), April 20, 1822.

62. Diary of the Rev. John Lyle, 1801-1803, p. 50. MS., University of Chicago.

63. Isaac Anderson to W. H. Parks, April 21, 1824. MS., Philadelphia.

64. "The Oldest Church," *Daily American* (Nashville), February 16, 1890.

65. James G. M. Ramsey, *History of Lebanon Presbyterian Church 'In the Fork,' Five Miles East of Knoxville, Tenn.* (n.p., c. 1918), 7.

66. On this point examine the scholarly Charles Hodge, *The Constitutional History of the Presbyterian Church,* 2 vols. in 1 (Philadelphia, 1839-1840), *passim.*

67. William W. Sweet, *Religion in Colonial America* (New York, 1943), 266.

68. Blythe to William Williamson, c. 1810, Philadelphia.

69. "Minutes of the Transylvania Presbytery, 1786-1837," in Sweet, *The Presbyterians,* 233-45.

70. Todd to James Lapsley, April 8, 1815, Philadelphia. This letter, in a small handwriting, covers twenty large pages. Also examine letter from John Todd to Andrew Todd, May 22, 1813, *ibid.*

71. Herrmann, *James McChord,* 31.

72. See "Plan of Union of 1801" between Presbyterians and Congregationalists. Henry Woods, *The History of the Presbyterian Controversy* (Louisville, 1843), Chap. V.

73. Timothy Flint to John Roche, July 13, 1830, Philadelphia. In 1839, after having visited the South, Harriet Martineau called Presbyterian preaching "a hard, ascetic, persecuting religion." *Society in America,* 3 vols. (London, 1839), III, 279.

74. Roosevelt, *Winning of the West,* II, 223-24.

75. William E. Dodd, *The Cotton Kingdom* (New Haven, 1920), 102. Also see Rogers, *Barton Warren Stone,* 30-34.

V

PRESBYTERIAN INTEREST IN EDUCATION

1. Jeremiah L. Diman, "Religion in America, 1776-1876," *North American Review* (Boston), CXXII (1876), 19-20.

2. Compare the Presbyterian requirements with those of the Baptists and the Methodists. See Posey, "The Frontier Baptist Ministry," *loc. cit.,* 3-10; Posey, *Methodism in the Old Southwest,* Chap. III.

3. Baird, *Collection,* 80-84; *Records of the Presbyterian Church,* 144; C. Harve Geiger, *The Program of Higher Education of the Presbyterian Church in the United States of America* (Cedar Rapids, 1940), 26-27, 81-82, *passim.*

4. *Records of the Presbyterian Church,* 7, 26.

5. See Archibald Alexander (ed.), *Biographical Sketches of the Founder and Principal Alumni of the Log College* (Philadelphia, 1851), *passim.*

6. This, in turn, became Washington College and finally the present Washington and Lee University.

7. Note the expense of a Kentucky student at Princeton in 1819. James Marshall to Robert Marshall, November 11, 1819, Philadelphia.

8. Peter G. Mode, *The Frontier Spirit in American Christianity* (New York, 1923), 64-65.

9. In his *Book of Discipline for the Scottish Church* (1560), John Knox proposed: "That everie severall churche have a schoolmaister appointed, such a one as is able at least to teach Grammar and the Latin tung, yf the Town be of any reputation." Quoted in Elwood P. Cubberley, *The History of Education* (New York, 1920), 335.

10. John J. Robinson, *Memoir of Rev. Isaac Anderson, D.D.* (Knoxville, 1860), ix-x.

11. Holland Thompson, "Some 'Log Colleges' in Western North Carolina," *Presbyterian Quarterly* (Richmond), XIV (1900), 67-68. For subjects taught in elementary schools see Howe Papers, Philadelphia.

12. Dodd, *Cotton Kingdom,* 100.

13. Articles of Agreement between Robert Marshall and Undersigned Subscribers, 1808. MS., Philadelphia.

14. Many of the Baptist preachers and some of the Methodist earned their living by cultivating farms.

15. The College of New Jersey, established in 1746, was finally located at Princeton in 1757.

16. Contrary to belief, the early settlers in Tennessee were not as ignorant as supposed. In 1776 when they sent a petition to North Carolina asking for incorporation into a state, only two of the 108 could not sign their names. Putnam, *Middle Tennessee,* 100-102.

17. Edward T. Sanford, *Blount College and the University of Tennessee* (Knoxville ? 1894 ?), 9.

18. Roosevelt, *Winning of the West,* II, 222.

19. Early school life in Tennessee is described in Phelan, *History of Tennessee,* Chap. XXIV; William T. Hale and Dixon L. Merritt, *A History of Tennessee and Tennesseans,* 8 vols. (Chicago, 1913), Vol. II, Chap. XXV.

20. James G. M. Ramsey, *The Annals of Tennessee* (Charleston, 1853), 294.

21. See Lucius S. Merriam, *Higher Education in Tennessee* (Washington, 1893), 227.

22. Quoted in Sprague, *Annals,* III, 395.

23. A commencement, "the only gala-day in the year," was a great occasion. All display possible was used to celebrate the event. Doak was in wig, shoes with buckles, short breeches, and long stockings. John E. Alexander, *A Brief History of the Synod of Tennessee, from 1817 to 1887* (Philadelphia, 1890), 65-66.

24. See sketch of Doak in *Dictionary of American Biography,* V, 332-33.

25. Alexander, *Synod of Tennessee,* 66.

26. John E. Alexander, A Centennial Sketch of Greeneville and Tusculum Colleges, *passim.* MS., Philadelphia; Charles W. Dabney, *Universal Education in the South,* 2 vols. (Chapel Hill, 1936), I, 282; Allen E. Ragan, *A History of Tusculum College, 1794-1844* (Greeneville, Tenn., 1945), 36-42.

27. See sketches of Balch in Sprague, *Annals,* III, 308-319.

28. Geiger, *Higher Education of the Presbyterian Church,* 35.

29. Alexander, *Synod of Tennessee,* 69.

30. See sketches of Coffin in Sprague, *Annals,* IV, 246-56.

31. The Journal of Charles Coffin, 1800-1822 (typed copy, Philadelphia) is an interesting account of the day by day life of an early Tennessee preacher-educator. In 1868 Greeneville College was combined with Tusculum. See also Ragan, *Tusculum College,* 27-28.

32. Sprague, *Annals,* III, 433-35.

33. *Dictionary of American Biography,* III, 520.

34. Sanford, *Blount College,* 13.

35. Dabney, *Universal Education,* I, 283.

36. Stanley J. Folmsbee, "Blount College and East Tennessee College, 1794-1840," East Tennessee Historical Society's *Publications,* No. 17 (1945), 22-50.

37. See "Sketch of the Life and Character of Rev. Isaac Anderson, D.D.," *Presbyterian Quarterly Review* (Philadelphia), VI (1858), 194-210.

38. *Maryville College Bulletin* (Maryville, Tenn., 1946), 19.

39. For sketches of Anderson see Gillett, *Presbyterian Church,* II, 206-209; Samuel T. Wilson, *Isaac Anderson, Founder and First President of Maryville College* (Maryville, Tenn., 1932), *passim.*

40. Robinson, *Isaac Anderson,* 52-55; Wilson, *Isaac Anderson,* 83.

41. In 1825 the General Assembly clearly stated the value of establishing seminaries in the West. After "taking into consideration the numerous and rapidly increasing population . . . in the great valley of the Mississippi; and believing that the interests of the Presbyterian Church imperiously require it, and that the Redeemer's kingdom will be thereby promoted, [we] do resolve, that it is expedient forthwith to establish a theological Seminary in the West, under the supervision of the General Assembly." *Minutes of the General Assembly*

of the Presbyterian Church in the United States of America from A.D. 1821 to A.D. 1835 inclusive (Philadelphia, c. 1835), 144.

42. Alexander, *Synod of Tennessee*, 18-19.

43. *First Presbyterian Church, Nashville*, 47.

44. Phelan, *History of Tennessee*, 234-35, 238-39; Albert C. Holt, *The Economic and Social Beginnings of Tennessee* (Nashville ? 1923 ?), 138-42.

45. See Halsey, *Works of Philip Lindsley, passim.*

46. At one time twenty-eight members of the lower house of Congress had graduated under Lindsley. Dabney, *Universal Education*, I, 287. For Lindsley's dignified address to the graduating class of 1826 see *Visitor and Telegraph* (Richmond), January 6, 1827.

47. Sprague, *Annals,* IV, 45, 51.

48. MS. Minutes, Synod of West Tennessee, 1826-1849, October 13, 15, 19, 1829, Montreat.

49. MS. Minutes, West Tennessee Presbytery, 1810-1836, April 4, 1835, *ibid.*

50. Robert Peter and Joanna Peter, *Transylvania University, Its Origin, Rise, Decline, and Fall* (Louisville, 1896), 18-20.

51. William H. Whitsitt, *Life and Times of Judge Caleb Wallace* (Louisville, 1888), 122-30.

52. See sketches in Sprague, *Annals,* III, 246-49.

53. Bishop, *Outline of the Church in Kentucky,* 96-97.

54. Davidson, *Presbyterian Church in Kentucky,* 289-90.

55. Peter and Peter, *Transylvania University,* 43-55 *passim;* Thomas D. Clark, *A History of Kentucky* (New York, 1937), 325-26.

56. See two subscription papers, May 1794, circulated in behalf of a seminary to be under the control of this presbytery. MSS., Philadelphia.

57. See address To the People of the Atlantic States of America, March 11, 1795, concerning the plans of the board of trustees of the Kentucky Academy. MS., Philadelphia; Davidson, *Presbyterian Church in Kentucky,* 292; "Subscription Lists for Kentucky Academy, 1794-1797," in Sweet, *The Presbyterians,* 583-89.

58. Ware, *Barton Warren Stone,* 71-72.

59. MS. Minutes of Kentucky Academy, March 11, 1797, Philadelphia.

60. *Ibid., passim.* For a list of books recommended for the use of this school see "Extracts from the Minutes of the Transylvania Presbytery, 1786-1837," February 17, 1795, in Sweet, *The Presbyterians,* 148-49.

61. L. G. Barbour, "The Relation of the Presbyterian Church to Education in Kentucky," in *Centennial of Presbyterianism in Kentucky* (Harrodsburgh, Ky., 1883), 57; Peter and Peter, *Transylvania University,* 71.

62. F. Garvin Davenport, *Ante-Bellum Kentucky: A Social History, 1800-1860* (Oxford, Ohio, 1943), 39-40.

63. *Presbyterian Church in Kentucky,* 298. Davidson is generally regarded as biased.

64. The best source for Holley is Charles Caldwell, *A Discourse on the Genius and Character of the Rev. Horace Holley* (Boston, 1828). Also see an excellent study by Sonne, *Liberal Kentucky, passim.*

65. Peter and Peter, *Transylvania University, passim;* Davenport, *Ante-Bellum Kentucky,* 41-45.

66. One of Holley's critics charged that "his fine preaching" and sermons were "everything but what they ought to be—the plain preaching of the gospel—the doctrine of the cross." John P. Cunningham to James L. Marshall, no date, Philadelphia.

67. Clark, *History of Kentucky,* 329-30.

68. Some Presbyterians wished success to Methodist educational efforts in Kentucky, hoping that this would aid in forcing the removal of Holley. For an example see W. L. Maccalla to Archibald Cameron, February 24, 1824, Philadelphia. For a scathing indictment of Holley see S. V. Marshall to his father, Robert Marshall, September 23, 1823, *ibid.*

69. Sonne, *Liberal Kentucky,* 260. For a very different view of Holley see Davidson, *Presbyterian Church in Kentucky,* 300-318.

70. James H. Hewlett, "Centre College of Kentucky, 1819-1830," *Filson Club Historical Quarterly* (Louisville), XVIII (1944), 173-91. Also see Peter and Peter, *Transylvania University,* 140; MS. (copy), Minutes of the Synod of Kentucky, 1822-1845, October 15, 17, 1824, Montreat.

71. Davenport, *Ante-Bellum Kentucky,* 49-51.

72. MS. (copy) Minutes, Synod of Kentucky, 1822-1845, October 18, 1841, Montreat.

73. John V. Stephens, "A Historical Sketch of the Educational Spirit and Interests of the Cumberland Presbyterian Church," *Cumberland Presbyterian,* April 5, 1900.

74. Lindsley, "Cumberland Presbyterian History," *loc. cit.,* VII, 132-48; Campbell, *Cumberland Presbyterian History,* 232.

75. MS. Minutes of the General Assembly of the Cumberland Presbyterian Church, 1829-1840, p. 52, Philadelphia.

76. McDonnold, *Cumberland Presbyterian Church,* 201.

77. MS. Minutes of the General Assembly of the Cumberland Presbyterian Church, 1829-1840, p. 11, Philadelphia.

78. Lindsley, "Cumberland Presbyterian History," *loc. cit.,* VII, 141.

79. See McDonnold, *Cumberland Presbyterian Church,* 216-17; Campbell, *Cumberland Presbyterian History,* 232-33.

80. Lindsley, "Cumberland Presbyterian History," *loc. cit.,* VII, 158-71 *passim.* This institution should not be confused with Cumberland College founded in Nashville in 1806 nor with Cumberland University established by the Cumberland Presbyterians in Lebanon, Tennessee, in 1842. See Winstead P. Bone, *A History of Cumberland University* (Lebanon, Tenn., 1935).

81. Sonne, *Liberal Kentucky,* 261.

82. J. R. Burgett, "The Presbyterian Church in Alabama," in *First Presbyterian Church, Montgomery, Ala.* (n.p., c. 1897), 34.

83. MS. Minutes, South Alabama Presbytery, 1833-1835, October 30, 1833; November 21, 1833, Montreat.

84. MS. Minutes, South Alabama Presbytery, 1835-1840, September 29, 1837,

ibid. In some manner the early Presbyterians in Alabama were connected with other educational institutions such as the Pleasant Ridge Academy in Greene County and the Florence Female College.

85. John R. Hutchison, *Reminiscences, Sketches and Addresses* (Houston, 1874), 22-25; Sprague, *Annals,* IV, 590-95.

86. "An Appeal to the Public in Behalf of the Uneducated Children of Our Country," *Western Presbyterian Herald* (Louisville), August 25, 1836.

87. Sweet, *The Presbyterians,* 75-76.

88. Gaddis, "Religious Ideas and Attitudes in the Early Frontier," *loc. cit.,* 159.

89. Clarence E. Hix, *The Conflict between Presbyterianism and Free-Thought in the South, 1776-1838* (Chicago, 1940), 151-56, believes that new ideas were not welcomed by the Presbyterians, since to them the Westminster Confession of Faith contained "the entire body of truth" and any deviation from it served only to warp the truth. On this point see Sonne, *Liberal Kentucky, passim.*

90. Thompson, *Presbyterian Churches,* 68-71.

VI

THE PRESBYTERIAN CHURCH AMONG THE INDIANS

1. *Records of the Presbyterian Church,* 160.

2. For sketches of Brainerd see Sprague, *Annals,* III, 113-17; *Dictionary of American Biography,* II, 591-92.

3. *Records of the Presbyterian Church,* 244.

4. John M. Linn, "The Relation of the Church to the Indian Question," *Presbyterian Review* (New York), I (1880), 682.

5. Goodykoontz, *Home Missions,* 78. Also see Thompson, *Presbyterian Missions,* 42-48, *passim.*

6. Gillett, *Presbyterian Church,* I, 436; II, 203, 367-69.

7. *Minutes of the General Assembly, 1789-1820,* pp. 195, 197, 278, 333.

8. See J. W. M. Breazeale, *Life As It Is; or, Matters and Things in General* (Knoxville, 1842), 249-50, for an interesting description of Blackburn.

9. Robert S. Walker, *Torchlights to the Cherokees: The Brainerd Mission* (New York, 1931), 1.

10. *Minutes of the General Assembly, 1789-1820,* pp. 280-81; Sweet, *The Presbyterians,* 58.

11. "An Account of the Origin and Progress of the Mission to the Cherokee Indians; in a Series of Letters from the Rev. Gideon Blackburn, to the Rev. Dr. Morse," *Panoplist* (Boston), III (1807-1808), 84-86.

12. *Ibid.,* 84-86, 322-23, 416-18.

13. *Ibid.,* 418.

14. *Minutes of the General Assembly, 1789-1820,* pp. 362, 368, 391, 406, 428; Sherman H. Doyle, *Presbyterian Home Missions* (Philadelphia, 1902), 19-21.

15. "Origin and Progress of the Mission," *loc. cit.*, 475-76.

16. Sprague, *Annals*, IV, 45.

17. Joseph Tracy, *History of the American Board of Commissioners for Foreign Missions* (New York, 1842), 68. Also see Henry T. Malone, *Cherokee Civilization in the Southern Appalachians before 1830* (M.A. thesis, Emory University, 1949).

18. Alexander, *Synod of Tennessee*, 44.

19. Jacob H. Patton, *A Popular History of the Presbyterian Church* (New York, 1900), 328.

20. *Records of the Presbyterian Church*, 257-58. Fourteen years later this committee was enlarged into a Board of Missions. *Ibid.*, 633. Also see "Missions and Church Boards," Hays, *Presbyterians*, Chap. XIV.

21. Usually called the American Board or the A. B. C. F. M.

22. See Tracy, *American Board*, Chaps. II-IV; *Memorial Volume of the First Fifty Years of the American Board of Commissioners for Foreign Missions* (Boston, 1861), Chaps. I-V.

23. William W. Sweet, *Religion on the American Frontier: The Congregationalists* (Chicago, 1939), 51.

24. Bacon, *American Christianity*, 255.

25. For the preparatory efforts in 1816 to establish this school see Tracy, *American Board*, 63-64.

26. Walker, *Torchlights to the Cherokees*, Chaps. II, VIII; Tracy, *American Board*, 69-70.

27. Walker, *Torchlights to the Cherokees*, 69.

28. Tracy, *American Board*, 150, 166-67, 236.

29. *Western Luminary* (Lexington, Ky.), October 15, 1828.

30. MS. Minutes, North Alabama Presbytery, 1825-1844, April 14, 15, 1831, Montreat. Two years later Huss was ordained after having given correct answers to thirty-four questions and then preaching a sermon on Matthew 7: 13-14. *Ibid.*, July 19, 1833.

31. *Ibid.*, May 29, 1828.

32. William B. Morrison, *The Red Man's Trail* (Richmond, 1932), 45-50; Tracy, *American Board*, 76, 85, 93, 109-110.

33. *View of the Missions* (n. p., 1828), 10-11.

34. Morrison, *The Red Man's Trail*, 48, 51.

35. Tracy, *American Board*, 208-209, 223.

36. *Abstract of the Twenty-Second Annual Report of the American Board of Commissioners for Foreign Missions* (n. p., c. 1831), 20.

37. John F. H. Claiborne, *Mississippi as a Province, Territory and State* (Jackson, Miss., 1880), 504. Undoubtedly Claiborne exaggerates the Indian fervor for the white man's religion.

38. Tracy, *American Board*, 132-33, 193.

39. Howe, *Presbyterian Church in South Carolina*, II, 405-406, 429-31.

40. *Ibid.*, II, 432; [Sarah Tuttle], *Letters on the Chickasaw and Osage Missions* (Boston, 1831), 6-8.

41. This money usually came from Indian annuities and treaties. Although

the federal government made donations to the schools for Indians, the amount was only a small part of the total received from private contributions. Between 1823-1825 the ratio was probably one to ten or fifteen. See George D. Harmon, *Sixty Years of Indian Affairs Political, Economic, and Diplomatic, 1789-1850* (Chapel Hill, 1941), 163-64.

42. Howe, *Presbyterian Church in South Carolina,* II, 432-33.

43. For the conditions under which the transfer was made see Tracy, *American Board,* 197.

44. Howe, *Presbyterian Church in South Carolina,* II, 433.

45. *Twenty-Second Annual Report of the American Board,* 19.

46. [Tuttle], *Letters,* 10. For a summary of the work of the American Board among the American Indians in 1830 see Sweet, *The Congregationalists,* 54.

47. Sweet, *The Presbyterians,* 641, 646. Byington readily mastered the Choctaw language. In one year he preached 176 sermons in Choctaw, wrote thirty sermons, and translated ten hymns. Morrison, *The Red Man's Trail,* 53.

48. McDonnold, *Cumberland Presbyterian Church,* 129-37; Beard, *Biographical Sketches,* 2nd series, 99-102; Campbell, *Cumberland Presbyterian History,* 193-95. Subscription lists pledging aid to the school revealed contributions from twenty-five cents to ten dollars and from a pair of socks to a jean coat.

49. Beard, *Biographical Sketches,* 2nd series, 105-106.

50. McDonnold, *Cumberland Presbyterian Church,* 139-41.

51. See Harmon, *Sixty Years of Indian Affairs,* Chaps. XIV-XVII, *passim;* John S. Bassett, *The Life of Andrew Jackson,* 2 vols. in 1 (New York, 1916), 684-92.

52. *Extracts from the Records of the Synod of Mississippi and South Alabama, from 1829 to 1835* (Princeton, N. J., 1835), 5-6, 11, 17.

53. H. S. Halbert, "Story of the Treaty of Dancing Rabbit," Mississippi Historical Society, *Publications,* VI (1902), 377-78.

54. Grant Foreman, *The Five Civilized Tribes* (Norman, Okla., 1934), 22, 99, *passim.*

55. Althea Bass, *Cherokee Messenger* (Norman, 1936), 137-60; Walker, *Torchlights to the Cherokees,* Chaps. XIX, XX.

56. For this tragic removal see Grant Foreman, *Indian Removal: The Emigration of the Five Civilized Tribes* (Norman, 1932), 229-312; Ralph H. Gabriel, *Elias Boudinot: Cherokee and His America* (Norman, 1941), Chap. XXIII.

57. Formed in New York City in 1817 by a joint committee of the Presbyterian, Reformed Dutch, and Associate Reformed churches, this society was amalgamated with the American Board in 1825. *First Fifty Years of the American Board,* 90.

58. E. E. Stringfield, *Presbyterianism in the Ozarks, 1834-1907* (n. p., 1909), 16-17.

59. Tracy, *American Board,* 85, 94-95, 133, 400. Cephas Washburn, *Reminiscences of the Indians* (Richmond, 1869), Chaps. I-IV.

60. *Christian Intelligencer* (New York), October 15, December 24, 1831; January 28, 1832.

61. Stringfield, *Presbyterianism in the Ozarks,* 17.

62. Timothy Flint, *Recollections of the Last Ten Years* (Boston, 1826), 144-46.

63. Quoted by E. Merton Coulter, *Georgia: A Short History* (Chapel Hill, 1947), 231-32.

64. Foreman, *Five Civilized Tribes,* 18-20, 82-85. Also see T. C. Stuart's estimation of the results attained by the Chickasaw Mission before it was dissolved in Mississippi and after its removal farther west. Howe, *Presbyterian Church in South Carolina,* II, 435-38.

65. For example, four of the most prominent missionaries among the Choctaws in Mississippi were Cyrus Kingsbury, a native of New Hampshire, Cyrus Byington and Ebenezer Hotchkin from Massachusetts, and Alfred Wright from Connecticut.

66. For the very pregnant comment on the Westerner's lack of interest in religion and his greed for land see Asbury, *Journal,* II, 342.

VII

THE SLAVERY QUESTION

1. Martineau, *Society in America,* III, 230-31.

2. Stephen S. Foster, *The Brotherhood of Thieves, or, A True Picture of the American Church and Clergy* (New London, Conn., 1843), 45.

3. William Goodell, *Slavery and Anti-Slavery* (New York, 1852), 154-55.

4. Quoted in William S. Jenkins, *Pro-Slavery Thought in the Old South* (Chapel Hill, 1935), 214-15, 240.

5. For a study of slavery in the Methodist Church see Walter B. Posey, "Influence of Slavery upon the Methodist Church in the Early South and Southwest," *Mississippi Valley Historical Review,* XVII (1930-1931), 530-42.

6. *Records of the Presbyterian Church in the United States of America,* 540.

7. Davidson, *Presbyterian Church in Kentucky,* 66-68; Bishop, *Outline of the Church in Kentucky, passim.*

8. David Rice, *Slavery, Inconsistent with Justice and Good Policy* (Philadelphia, 1792), 21.

9. "Extracts from the Minutes of the Transylvania Presbytery, 1786-1837," October 13, 1794, in Sweet, *The Presbyterians,* 147. Also see Pears (ed.), "Transylvania Presbytery," *loc. cit.,* 145-63.

10. *Minutes of the General Assembly, 1789-1920,* p. 104 n.

11. Quoted in Davidson, *Presbyterian Church in Kentucky,* 336.

12. "Minutes of the Transylvania Presbytery, 1786-1837," October 5, 1797, in Sweet, *The Presbyterians,* 169-70.

13. Rice to James Blythe, December 11, 1799, Philadelphia.

14. Bishop, *Outline of the Church in Kentucky,* 83.

15. MS. (copy) David Rice's will, March 22, 1816, Philadelphia.

16. MS. Journal of James Blythe, 1792-1793, *ibid.*

17. Rogers, *Barton Warren Stone,* 27-28, 79, 288-93.

18. *Minutes of the General Assembly, 1789-1820*, pp. 692-93.

19. Albert Barnes, *The Church and Slavery* (Philadelphia, 1857), 54-66.

20. Goodell, *Slavery and Anti-Slavery*, 152.

21. Henry K. Rowe, *The History of Religion in the United States* (New York, 1924), 99-100.

22. Bacon, *American Christianity*, 270.

23. James Smylie, *Minority Report of a Committee of the General Association of Connecticut, on the Sin of Slavery* (Salisbury, Conn., c. 1849), 4. Carter G. Woodson, *The History of the Negro Church* (Washington, 1921), 97, believes there were less than twenty thousand Negroes in the Presbyterian Church at any time before the Civil War.

24. Edward Channing, *A History of the United States*, 7 vols. (New York, 1907-1932), V, 409, 433.

25. For South Carolina see William A. Schaper, "Sectionalism and Representation in South Carolina," American Historical Association, *Annual Report*, 1900, 2 vols. (Washington, 1901), I, 237-463.

26. Isaac V. Brown, *Memoirs of the Rev. Robert Finley, D.D.* (New Brunswick, 1819), 127-29.

27. John Robinson, *The Testimony and Practice of the Presbyterian Church in Reference to American Slavery* (Cincinnati, 1852), 53; "Minutes of the Synod of Kentucky, 1802-1811," October 12, 1809, in Sweet, *The Presbyterians*, 378-79.

28. MS. Session Record, Paris (Kentucky) Presbyterian Church, 1820-1824, pp. 89-90, Frankfort.

29. MS. Session Record, Pisgah (Mississippi) Presbyterian Church, 1823-1874, December 22, 1827, Montreat.

30. William H. Smith, *A Political History of Slavery*, 2 vols. (New York, 1903), I, 18-19. Also see Early L. Fox, *The American Colonization Society, 1817-1840* (Baltimore, 1919), *passim*.

31. Davidson, *Presbyterian Church in Kentucky*, 337.

32. MS. Session Record, Louisville First Presbyterian Church, 1819-1828, July 9, 1826, Montreat.

33. MS. Session Record, New Providence (Kentucky) Presbyterian Church, 1822-1849, October 1, 1826; July 1, 1827; July 21, 1828, *ibid.*

34. MS. Minutes, North Alabama Presbytery, 1825-1844, October 8, 1830, *ibid.*

35. MS. Minutes, Synod of West Tennessee, 1826-1849, October 18, 1833, *ibid.*

36. New Orleans *Observer*, April 9, 1836.

37. For an excellent discussion of the antislavery efforts in Tennessee see Asa E. Martin, "The Anti-Slavery Societies of Tennessee," *Tennessee Historical Magazine* (Nashville), I (1915), 261-81. For Kentucky see Asa E. Martin, *The Anti-Slavery Movement in Kentucky prior to 1850* (Louisville, 1918), *passim*.

38. Martin, *Anti-Slavery Movement in Kentucky*, 64.

39. Quoted *ibid.*, 84.

40. Quoted in Bacon, *American Christianity*, 281-82, from *Biblical Repertory*, July 1833.

41. MS. Minutes, Synod of West Tennessee, 1826-1849, October 18, 1833, Montreat.

42. McDonnold, *Cumberland Presbyterian Church,* 410.

43. Quoted in Lindsley, "Cumberland Presbyterian History," *loc. cit.,* VII, 11.

44. Cossitt, *Finis Ewing,* 273.

45. Sweet, *The Presbyterians,* 280 n.

46. Will Breckinridge to Sam D. Blythe, May 11, 1830, Philadelphia.

47. Raymond L. Hightower, "Joshua L. Wilson, Frontier Controversialist," *Church History,* III (1934), 314-15. For Wilson's views on slavery see Sweet, *The Presbyterians,* 744-48.

48. Bacon, *American Christianity,* 277-78.

49. "Extract from the Minutes of the Synod of Mississippi," *Journal of the Presbyterian Historical Society,* XXI (1943), 200-205.

50. *A Review of a Letter, from the Presbytery of Chillicothe, to the Presbytery of Mississippi, on the Subject of Slavery* (Woodville, Miss., 1836), *passim.* Also see Jones, *Protestantism and the Southwest,* 240-42.

51. Bacon, *American Christianity,* 278.

52. "Extract from the Minutes of the Synod of Mississippi," *loc. cit.,* 205.

53. For the evolution of a philosophy of "positive good" in contrast to an earlier one of "necessary evil" see Arthur Y. Lloyd, *The Slavery Controversy, 1831-1860* (Chapel Hill, 1939).

54. MS. Minutes, South Alabama Presbytery, 1835-1840, September 26, 1835, Montreat.

55. MS. Minutes, Synod of West Tennessee, 1826-1849, October 9, 1835, *ibid.*

56. MS. Minutes, Tuscaloosa Presbytery, 1835-1843, October 2, 1835, *ibid.*

57. For a series of resolutions on slavery presented to the Synod of Kentucky in 1834 see MS. (copy) Minutes, Synod of Kentucky, 1822-1845, October 11, 1834, *ibid.*

58. *Address on Slavery* (Newburyport, Mass., c. 1836). The chief features of the report are found in Louisville *Western Presbyterian Herald,* May 26, 1836.

59. Davidson, *Presbyterian Church in Kentucky,* 340-41.

60. Robinson, *Testimony and Practice,* 54-62.

61. For the action of the Transylvania Presbytery see "Minutes of the Transylvania Presbytery, 1786-1837," April 2, 1836, in Sweet, *The Presbyterians,* 278.

62. New Orleans *Observer,* December 12, 1835.

63. MS. Minutes, South Alabama Presbytery, 1835-1840, April 10, 1837, Montreat. For a similar resolution see *Synod of South Carolina and Georgia on the State of the Church* (n. p., c. 1836), 4.

64. *Minutes of the General Assembly of the Presbyterian Church . . . 1836* (Philadelphia, 1836), *passim.*

65. *Ibid.,* 247-48, 250.

66. Goodell, *Slavery and Anti-Slavery,* 154.

67. *Minutes of the General Assembly, 1836,* pp. 272-73.

68. See Chap. XI. For explanations of this division see Gillett, *Presbyterian Church,* Vol. II, Chaps. XL-XLIII; Sweet, *The Presbyterians,* Chap. V; Henry Woods, *The History of the Presbyterian Controversy* (Louisville, 1843); Zebulon Crocker, *The Catastrophe of the Presbyterian Church in 1837* (New Haven, 1838).

69. *Minutes of the General Assembly of the Presbyterian Church* . . . *1837* (Philadelphia, 1837), 421-22, 439-40, 444-45.

70. In general Presbyterians in the slave states belonged to the Old School. Even in Kentucky slavery was a vital force in encouraging most of the Presbyterians in the state to adhere to the Old School.

71. Gillett, *Presbyterian Church,* II, 526. For others who support the emphasis on slavery see Edward D. Morris, *The Presbyterian Church: New School, 1837-1867* (Columbus, Ohio, 1905), 59-61; James H. Johnston, *A Ministry of Forty Years in Indiana* (Indianapolis, 1865), 18-19.

72. Patton, *Presbyterian Church,* 437-39. Thomas C. Johnson, an excellent historian of Presbyterianism, believes that the Old School was the victor "only by virtue of an almost 'solid South.' " See "History of the Southern Presbyterian Church," *American Church History,* XI, 359.

73. When a proslavery element in the New School formed the United Synod of the Presbyterian Church in 1857, the New School virtually disappeared in the South.

74. Gilbert H. Barnes, *The Antislavery Impulse, 1830-1844* (New York, 1933), 94.

75. See "The Moral Philosophy of Slavery," Jenkins, *Pro-Slavery Thought,* 200-241.

76. Note the position of Dr. N. L. Rice, the "fencewalker," whose famous report to the General Assembly of 1845 served largely as the standard of the church until the Civil War. Sweet, *Religions in America,* 442-43.

77. Bacon, *American Christianity,* 292.

78. On this point see Henry Wilson, *History of the Rise and Fall of the Slave Power in America,* 3 vols. (Boston, 1877), III, 697-724; Robert L. Stanton, *The Church and the Rebellion* (New York, 1864), *passim.*

VIII

THE NEGRO SLAVE IN THE PRESBYTERIAN CHURCH

1. See William P. Harrison (ed.), *The Gospel Among the Slaves* (Nashville, 1893), *passim.*

2. *Records of the Presbyterian Church,* 540.

3. "Extracts from the Minutes of the Transylvania Presbytery, 1786-1837," October 13, 1794, in Sweet, *The Presbyterians,* 147.

4. *Records of the Presbyterian Church,* 275.

5. "Minutes of the Synod of Kentucky, 1802-1811," October 18, 1809, in Sweet, *The Presbyterians,* 382. Also see MS. (copy) Minutes, Synod of Kentucky, 1802-1822, October 10, 1811, Montreat.

6. "Minutes of the Transylvania Presbytery, 1786-1837," April 9, 1811, in Sweet, *The Presbyterians,* 232.

7. See *Records of the Presbyterian Church,* 632-33.

8. *Extracts from the Report of the Board of Missions of the General Assembly of the Presbyterian Church for the Year 1820* (Philadelphia, 1821), 10.

9. Charles E. Hedrick, *Social and Economic Aspects of Slavery in the Transmontane prior to 1850* (Nashville, 1927), 132.

10. Baird, *Collection,* 822.

11. MS. (copy) Minutes, Synod of Kentucky, 1822-1845, October 16, 1825, Montreat.

12. Davidson, *Presbyterian Church in Kentucky,* 338.

13. Baird, *Collection,* 827.

14. Woodson, *The Negro Church,* 153-54. See also Charles C. Jones, *The Religious Instruction of the Negroes in the United States* (Savannah, 1842), *passim.*

15. MS. Minutes, North Alabama Presbytery, 1825-1844, October 10, 1829, Montreat.

16. Harrison, *Gospel Among the Slaves,* 79-80.

17. MS. Minutes, South Alabama Presbytery, 1828-1832, October 15, 1832, Montreat.

18. *Synod of Mississippi and South Alabama, 1829-1835,* pp. 40-41.

19. MS. Minutes, South Alabama Presbytery, 1833-1835, September 27, 1834, Montreat.

20. *Address on Slavery,* 5.

21. "Minutes of the Transylvania Presbytery, 1786-1837," April 2, 1836, in Sweet, *The Presbyterians,* 278.

22. MS. Minutes, West Tennessee Presbytery (Old School), 1837-1849, October 9, 1837, Montreat.

23. Harrison, *Gospel Among the Slaves,* 84; Robinson, *Testimony and Practice,* 154.

24. William West to Robert Marshall, December 9, 1817, Philadelphia.

25. Robert Marshall to William West, December 9, 1817, *ibid.*

26. James Blythe to Samuel D. Blythe, February 3, 1830, *ibid.*

27. MS. Minutes, South Alabama Presbytery, 1844-1848, April 6, 1845, Montreat.

28. *Report of the Committee to Which Was Referred the Subject of the Religious Instruction of the Colored Population of the Synod of South Carolina and Georgia* (Charleston, 1834), 9. Also see Charles S. Sydnor, *Slavery in Mississippi* (New York, 1933), 56.

29. Bishop, *Outline of the Church in Kentucky,* 205.

30. Robinson, *Testimony and Practice,* 151.

31. MS. Minutes, South Alabama Presbytery, 1844-1848, April 6, 1846, Montreat.

32. Sydnor, *Slavery in Mississippi,* 57. For a plan by which one minister could take care of about nine plantations see a letter, September 4, 1831, from B. W. Williams, a Presbyterian minister, to General John A. Quitman, a Mississippi planter. Sydnor, *Slavery in Mississippi,* 58. There is much evidence that more ministers became planters than planters became ministers.

33. MS. Session Record, Pine Ridge (Mississippi) Church, 1823-1838, December 10, 16, 1832, Montreat.

34. George G. M'Afee to editor, *Home Missionary,* March 1, 1835.

35. *Report of the Committee,* 4.

36. Richard C. Reed, "A Sketch of the Religious History of the Negroes in the South," *Papers of the American Society of Church History* (Chicago), IV (1914), 189.

37. Jones, *Religious Instruction of Negroes,* 78.

38. *Synod of Mississippi and South Alabama, 1829-1835,* pp. 40-41.

39. Jones, *Religious Instruction of Negroes,* 95-96.

40. *Western Luminary,* March 11, 1829.

41. See MS. Minutes, Synod of Alabama, 1837-1847, January 23, October 20, 1843; October 24, 1844; October 23, 1846; October 22, 1847, Montreat; MS. Minutes, Tuscaloosa Presbytery, 1843-1850, September 25, 28, October 25, 1846, *ibid.*

42. Gillett, *Presbyterian Church,* I, 486-87.

43. Haven P. Perkins, "Religion for Slaves: Difficulties and Methods," *Church History,* X (1941), 236.

44. Dodd, *Cotton Kingdom,* 117; Ulrich B. Phillips, *Life and Labor in the Old South* (Boston, 1929), 202.

45. Sydnor, *Slavery in Mississippi,* 60.

46. Perkins, "Religion for Slaves," *loc. cit.,* 243.

47. *Report of the Committee,* 15-16.

48. Perkins, "Religion for Slaves," *loc. cit.,* 236.

49. For examples see entries during 1820 to 1840 in MS. Minutes, Monroe (Chickasaw Nation, Mississippi) Church, 1823-1898, Montreat.

50. MS. Session Record, Ebenezer (Alabama) Church, 1827-1848, June 23, July 5, 1840; April 25, 1845, *ibid.*

51. MS. (copy) Session Record, Bethany (Mississippi) Church, 1818-1864, April 19, May 3, 1846; January 1, 1847; October 1, 1848, *ibid.*

52. MS. Session Record, New Providence (Kentucky) Church, 1822-1849, October 24, 1832, *ibid.*

53. *Ibid.,* April 19, 1823.

54. MS. Session Record, Paris (Kentucky) Church, 1820-1824, June 2, 1822, *ibid.*

55. MS. Session Record, Monroe (Chickasaw Nation, Mississippi), Church, 1823-1898, December 20, 1830, *ibid.*

56. MS. (copy) Session Record, Bethany (Mississippi) Church, 1818-1864, May 9, 1823, *ibid.*

57. MS. Session Record, Paris (Kentucky) Church, 1820-1824, December 10, 1823, *ibid.*

58. For an example see MS. Session Record, Pisgah (Mississippi) Church, 1823-1874, December 22, 1827, *ibid.*

59. For a complete omission of Negroes and slavery examine the MS. Session Record, Baton Rouge (Louisiana) Church, 1833-1850, *ibid.*

60. Goodell, *Slavery and Anti-Slavery,* 152-53.

61. The Negroes brought the large sum of $8,566. MS. Journal of Joseph L. Howe, 1816-1826, Philadelphia.

62. McDonnold, *Cumberland Presbyterian Church,* 412-13.

63. Goodell, *Slavery and Anti-Slavery,* 154 n.

64. *Minority Report of a Committee of the General Association, on the Sin of Slavery* (Salisbury, Conn., c. 1849), 4.

65. For a similar course in the Methodist Church see Posey, "Influence of Slavery upon the Methodist Church," *loc. cit.,* 530-42.

66. Typed copy, Journal of Dr. Charles Coffin, 1800-1822, p. 361, Philadelphia.

67. For excellent examples see John C. Young, *The Duty of Masters; A Sermon Preached in the Presbyterian Church in Danville, Ky.* (n.p., c. 1846); William T. Hamilton, *The Duties of Masters and Slaves Respectively: or Domestic Servitude As Sanctioned by the Bible. A Discourse Delivered in the Government-Street Church, Mobile, Alabama* (Mobile, 1845).

68. *Religious Instruction of Slaves: Suggestions on the Religious Instruction of the Negroes in the Southern States* (Philadelphia, 1847).

69. Robinson, *Testimony and Practices,* 154.

70. For titles see Harrison, *Gospel Among the Slaves,* 76.

71. Quoted by Woodson, *The Negro Church,* 97-98.

72. Albert H. Newman, *A History of the Baptist Churches in the United States* (New York, 1900), 338.

73. Reed, "Religious History of the Negroes," *loc. cit.,* 189. Of course no financial contributions were expected from the colored members. It must have been surprising, however, when fifteen Negro members of the Ebenezer (Alabama) Church in 1839 pledged sums ranging from twenty-five cents to one dollar. MS. Session Record, Ebenezer (Alabama) Church, 1827-1848, pp. 45-46, Montreat.

74. Quoted by Mrs. Bennett D. Bell, "History of Shiloh Presbyterian Church," *Sumner County News* (Gallatin, Tenn.), May 22, 1930. In 1830 the Shiloh Church had 123 white members and thirty-eight colored. The first two names on the colored list were Michael Blythe, exhorter, and Jack Kilpatrick, Sunday school teacher. *Ibid.,* May 15, 1930. Session records for some Presbyterian churches show a rather steady addition of Negroes to the church rolls. For example, see MS. Session Record, Oak Grove (Alabama) Presbyterian Church, 1837-1845, *passim,* Montreat.

75. Beard, *Biographical Sketches,* 290.

76. *Minutes of the General Assembly, 1789-1820,* p. 617.

77. MS. Session Record, Louisville First Presbyterian Church, 1819-1828, Montreat.

78. MS. Session Record, Pine Ridge (Mississippi) 1823-1838, February 23, 1833, *ibid.*

79. MS. Session Record, Plum-Creek (Kentucky) Church, 1835-1845, December 11, 1837, Presbyterian Theological Seminary, Louisville. Hereafter cited as Louisville.

80. MS. Minutes, West Tennessee Presbytery, 1810-1836, September 6, 1814, Montreat.

81. Josephine P. Snapp, *The Development of Religion in Kentucky to 1830* (M.A. thesis, University of Chicago, 1916), 67.

82. Robinson, *Testimony and Practice,* 255-56.

83. Woodson, *The Negro Church,* 97.

IX

THE CHURCH ELEVATES WESTERN MORALS

1. Gaddis, "Religious Ideas and Attitudes in the Early Frontier," *loc. cit.,* 154.

2. For examples see MS. Session Record, Monroe (Mississippi) Church, 1823-1898, Montreat. Sweet has written a revealing paper on "The Churches as Moral Courts of the Frontier," *loc. cit.,* 3-21.

3. Baird, *Collection,* 65-99, 247-49. The duties of the deacons were limited largely to collecting and distributing the charities of the church.

4. MS. Session Record, Washington (Mississippi) Church, 1807-1820, March 21, 1812, Montreat.

5. Mary M. Tenney, *Communion Tokens, Their Origin, History, and Use* (Grand Rapids, Mich., c. 1936), *passim;* James Park, *The Centennial Anniversary of the First Presbyterian Church of Knoxville, Tennessee* (Knoxville, 1897), 21; McDonnold, *Cumberland Presbyterian Church,* 19, 109-110.

6. MS. Session Record, Apple Creek (Missouri) Church, 1839-1857, March 28, 1847; September 29, November 29, 1848, Montreat.

7. Hardly a session record fails to note one or more cases of drunkenness.

8. MS. Session Record, New Providence (Kentucky) Church, 1822-1849, July 18, August 10, 1827; March 10, 1828, Montreat.

9. MS. Session Record, Shiloh (Tennessee) Church, 1834-1858, October 28, November 10, 26, 1845; January 11, 1847, *ibid.* The terms fornication and adultery were often used interchangeably in the citations.

10. MS. Session Record, Mount Pisgah (Alabama) Cumberland Presbyterian Church, 1834-1847, May 14, 1842, Alabama Archives.

11. Baird, *Collection,* 802-803.

12. *Minutes of the General Assembly, 1789-1820,* p. 690.

13. MS. Minutes, North Alabama Presbytery, 1825-1844, September ? 1837; April 8, 1841, Montreat; MS. Minutes, West Tennessee Presbytery, 1810-1836, April 9, 1817, *ibid.*

14. "Session Record of the First Presbyterian Church of Murfreesboro, Tennessee, 1812-1829," June 23, 1829, in Sweet, *The Presbyterians,* 459.

15. MS. Minutes, West Tennessee Presbytery, 1810-1836, April 9, 1817, Montreat.

16. MS. Minutes, North Alabama Presbytery, 1825-1844, April 8, 1841, *ibid.*

17. "Duck Creek Church, Ohio, 1815-1847," March 30, 1837; January 1, 1838, in Sweet, *The Presbyterians,* 424, 428.

18. MS. Session Record, Murfreesboro (Tennessee) Church, 1812-1860, February 7, April 11, 27, 31, 1831, Montreat.

19. Baird, *Collection,* 805.

20. Theodore Clapp, *Autobiographical Sketches and Recollections during a Thirty-Five Years' Residence in New Orleans* (Boston, 1857), 94.

21. Joseph D. Shields, *Natchez, Its Early History* (Louisville, 1930), 247.

22. Baird, *Collection,* 805.

23. Among the many church records examined for this study, the writer did not find one censure for participating in lotteries.

24. MS. Session Record, Baton Rouge (Louisiana) Church, 1833-1850, August 10, 1842, Montreat.

25. *Christian Observer and Presbyterian Witness,* November 1, 1866.

26. Baird, *Collection,* 802-803.

27. *Western Luminary,* January 30, 1828; March 18, 1829.

28. MS. Session Record, New Providence (Kentucky) Church, 1822-1849, January 20, 1838, Montreat.

29. MS. Minutes, Synod of Kentucky, 1822-1845, October 16, 1835, *ibid.*

30. MS. Session Record, Shiloh (Tennessee) Church, 1834-1858, October 28, November 10, 26, 1845, *ibid.*

31. MS. Session Record, Pisgah (Kentucky) Church, 1820-1824, July ? August 11, 1820; February 21, March 2, 1821; January 31, 1824, Frankfort. This session record contains more space devoted to moral infractions than any that I have examined.

32. MS. Session Record, New Providence (Kentucky) Church, 1822-1849, July 18, August 10, 1827; March 20, 1828, Montreat.

33. MS. Session Record, Mount Bethel (Tennessee) Church, 1828-1870, April 27, 1834, *ibid.*

34. MS. Session Record, First Presbyterian Church, Nashville, 1833-1853, October 8, 1849, church vault.

35. MS. Session Record, Shiloh (Tennessee) Church, 1834-1858, November 26, 1845; January 11, 1847, Montreat.

36. "Excerpts from the Records of Kentucky Presbytery, Associate Reformed Presbyterian Church, Touching the Case of Mr. John Snodgrass, 1801-1802," in Sweet, *The Presbyterians,* 576-78.

37. "Minutes of the Synod of Kentucky, 1802-1811," October 26, 1807, *ibid.,* 362.

38. "Extracts from the Minutes of the Transylvania Presbytery, 1786-1837," October 4, 1798, *ibid.,* 181-83.

39. MS. Session Record, Pisgah (Alabama) Church, 1834-1846, August 2, 21, 1841, Alabama Archives.

40. See Chap. IV, "The Presbyterian Minister."

41. MS. Session Record, Lasting Hope (Tennessee) Cumberland Presbyterian Church, 1834-1855, March 25, 1843, Vanderbilt University.

42. MS. Session Record, Apple Creek (Missouri) Church, 1833-1841, August 7, 13, 1833, Montreat.

43. MS. Session Record, Baton Rouge (Louisiana) Church, 1833-1850, September 14, 1844; January 25, March 6, July 16, 1845; January 30, 1846, *ibid*.

44. MS. Session Record, Plum Creek (Kentucky) Church, 1835-1845, June 15, November 12, 1839, Louisville. In addition to the above references, many pages of this session record are devoted to the fighting of J. N. Allen.

45. MS. Session Record, Bethany (Mississippi) Church, 1818-1864, July 27, August 24, November 5, 1823, Montreat.

46. MS. Session Record, Paris (Kentucky) Church, 1830-1841, March 27, April 22, 1833, Frankfort.

47. Session Record, Zion (Tennessee) Church, 1809-1939, August ? 1811, on microfilm, Vanderbilt University.

48. Edward Crawford to James Crawford, September 18, 1797, Philadelphia.

49. MS. Session Record, Apple Creek (Missouri) Church, 1839-1857, March 28, 1847, Montreat.

50. MS. Session Record, Murfreesboro (Tennessee) Church, 1812-1860, August 7, 22, 23, 24, 1836, *ibid*.

51. Session Record, Zion (Tennessee) Church, 1809-1939, September 11, 1811, on microfilm, Vanderbilt University.

52. Orr, "New Prospect Church," *loc. cit.*, 54.

53. MS. Session Record, Brazeau (Missouri) Church, 1833-1851, May 17, 1836, Montreat.

54. MS. Minutes, Holston Presbytery, 1837-1849, April 7, October 6, 1838, *ibid*.

55. "Extracts from the Minutes of the Transylvania Presbytery, 1786-1837," February 11, 1807, in Sweet, *The Presbyterians,* 217.

56. Joseph Smith, *Old Redstone, or Historical Sketches of Western Presbyterianism and its Early Ministers* (Philadelphia, 1854), 251-65; Finley, *Autobiography,* 248-51; Drake, *Pioneer Life in Kentucky,* 27, 55, 184, 193. One writer says that in Kentucky on election days "whiskey and apple toddy flowed through the streets of every town and village like Euphrates through ancient Babylon." Davenport, *Ante-Bellum Kentucky,* 22.

57. Channing, *History of the United States,* IV, 138-39; V, 175 n.

58. "The Cause of Temperance," *Home Missionary and American Pastor's Journal* (New York), VII (1834-1835), 117.

59. John H. DeWitt (ed.), "Journal of John Sevier," *Tennessee Historical Magazine,* VI (1920-1921), 59. Also see Claiborne, *Mississippi,* 528; William G. Brownlow, *Helps to the Study of Presbyterianism* (Knoxville, 1834), 101.

60. "Personal Recollections of M. W. Trimble" (typed copy of articles printed in *The Witness,* October 13-November 17, 1860), 16-18, Philadelphia.

61. The frontier Methodist ministry fought liquor more vigorously than did the Presbyterian clergy. See "Efforts for a Temperate Social Order," Posey, *Methodism in the Old Southwest,* Chap. VIII.

62. *Minutes of the General Assembly, 1789-1820,* pp. 493, 511. Francis Asbury, noted Methodist bishop, declared that whisky and brandy were "the two great

potentates of the Western World" and if unchecked they would eventually lead to "the ruin of all that is excellent in morals and government." Asbury, *Journal* II, 481.

63. MS. Minutes, Synod of West Tennessee, 1826-1849, October 5, 1827, Montreat; *Synod of Mississippi and South Alabama,* 30.

64. MS. Minutes, Elyton Cumberland Presbyterian Presbytery, 1832-1869, April 13, 1832, Alabama Archives.

65. "Extracts from the Minutes of the Transylvania Presbytery, 1786-1837," October 10, 1829, in Sweet, *The Presbyterians,* 262. Unfortunately too many of the resolutions had the famous phrase "except for medicinal purposes" which provided a convenient escape for many who, otherwise, might have suffered punishment. For a typical example, see *Synod of Mississippi and South Alabama,* 30.

66. For an example see Sweet, "The Churches as Moral Courts," *loc. cit.,* 19.

67. MS. Minutes, Cumberland Presbytery, 1803-1805, October 2, 1805, Montreat.

68. "Extracts from the Minutes of the Transylvania Presbytery, 1786-1837," October 2, 1804, in Sweet, *The Presbyterians,* 193-97.

69. R. E. Sherrill, History of the Presbyterian Church, in Somerville, Tennessee, 1-2. MS. (c. 1885), Philadelphia.

70. MS. Session Record, First Presbyterian Church (Nashville) 1833-1853, January 27, 1845, church vault; MS. Session Record, Franklin (Tennessee) Church, 1810-1848, October 19, 1844, Montreat.

71. MS. Session Record, Baton Rouge (Louisiana) Church, 1833-1850, August 10, 1842, *ibid.*

72. MS. Session Record, Pisgah (Alabama) Church, 1834-1846, July 5, 1839, Alabama Archives.

73. MS. Session Record, Bethany (Mississippi) Church, 1818-1864, April ? 1830, Montreat.

74. MS. Session Record, First Presbyterian Church, Nashville, 1833-1853, January 27, 1845, church vault.

75. "Extracts from the Minutes of the Transylvania Presbytery, 1786-1837," April 17, 1807, in Sweet, *The Presbyterians,* 203.

76. MS. Session Record, Murfreesboro (Tennessee) Church, 1812-1860, November 2, 18, 1833, Montreat.

77. Lindsley, "Cumberland Presbyterian History," *loc. cit.,* VII, 2-3.

78. Baird, *Collection,* 808, 809.

79. MS. Session Record, First Presbyterian Church, Louisville, 1828-1839, April 18, 1834, Montreat.

80. MS. Minutes, West Tennessee Presbytery, 1810-1836, April 2, 1816, *ibid.*

81. Baird, *Collection,* 57.

82. MS. Session Record, Shiloh (Tennessee) Church, 1834-1858, January 3, 1847, Montreat.

83. MS. Session Record, New Providence (Kentucky) Church, 1822-1849, July 18, 1829, *ibid.*

84. MS. Minutes, South Alabama Presbytery, 1844-1848, October 22, 1844, *ibid.*

85. MS. Minutes, Synod of West Tennessee, 1826-1849, October 6, 1827, *ibid.;* MS. Minutes, North Alabama Presbytery, 1825-1844, September 13, 1828, *ibid.*

86. MS. Minutes, Synod of West Tennessee, 1826-1849, October 6, 1827, *ibid.*

87. MS. Minutes, South Alabama Presbytery, 1833-1835, November 19, 1834, *ibid.*

88. MS. Minutes, North Alabama Presbytery, 1825-1844, September 13, 1829, *ibid.*

89. December 3, 1828.

90. *Minutes of the General Assembly, 1789-1820,* pp. 513-14, 565-66, 601, 634; *Western Luminary,* March 4, 11, 18, 1829; MS. Minutes, Synod of Kentucky, 1802-1822, October 11, 1811, Montreat.

X

THE LOCAL CHURCH: ITS PHYSICAL STRUCTURE AND SOCIAL SERVICES

1. *Pioneer Presbyterianism in Tennessee* (Richmond, 1898), 21; "Old Gaspar River Meeting-House. The Birthplace of Cumberland Presbyterianism," *Cumberland Presbyterian,* February 10, 1876.

2. L. T. Chiles, *et al., Centennial Celebration of the First Presbyterian Church, Mt. Sterling, Ky.* (n.p., c. 1895), 5; Will A. McTeer, *History of New Providence Church, Maryville, Tennessee, 1786-1821* (Maryville, 1921), 79-81; Katherine S. Battle, *History of Valley Creek Presbyterian Church, Selma, Alabama* (n.p., n.d.), 12; Oliver Taylor, *Historic Sullivan* (Bristol, Tenn., 1909), 179.

3. Before the building of churches in the West, courthouses, "meeting sheds," and open fields were used instead of churches. See Park, *Presbyterian Church of Knoxville,* 17; Orr, "New Prospect Church," *loc. cit.,* 52; "Sketch of the Life and Character of Rev. Isaac Anderson, D.D.," *Presbyterian Quarterly Review,* VI (1858), 201.

4. W. T. Knott, *History of the Presbyterian Church in What Is Now Marion County and City of Lebanon, Kentucky* (n.p., c. 1895), 9-12. As early as 1807, while traveling in Kentucky, Fortescue Cuming found the Presbyterians in Lexington, Kentucky, a town of three thousand people, erecting a church costing eight thousand dollars. Fortescue Cuming, *Sketches of a Tour to the Western Country* (Reuben G. Thwaites, *Early Western Travels,* IV, Cleveland, 1904), 185-87.

5. MS. Session Record, Pine Ridge (Mississippi) Church, 1823-1838, January 15, 29, March 13, 1827; January 14, March 28, 1828, Montreat.

6. MS. Session Record, New Providence (Kentucky) Church, 1822-1849, September 24, 1830, *ibid.*

7. Knott, *Presbyterian Church,* 9.

8. McTeer, *New Providence Presbyterian Church,* 67.

9. *Pioneer Presbyterianism*, 22.

10. John D. Paxton, *A Memoir of J. D. Paxton, D.D., Late of Princeton, Indiana* (Philadelphia, 1870), 305.

11. Robinson, *Isaac Anderson*, 44.

12. Paxton, *Memoir*, 306.

13. Once Jeremiah Chamberlain in Mobile used his silk hat for a pulpit on which he laid his notes. Louis Voss (comp.), *Presbyterianism in New Orleans and Adjacent Points* (New Orleans, 1931), 21.

14. L. R. Janes, The Presbyterian Church of New Market, Tennessee, 19. MS., Philadelphia.

15. Battle, *Valley Creek Presbyterian Church*, 10; Park, *Presbyterian Church of Knoxville*, 21. The Methodists used the term "mourners bench." In 1829 some fifteen or twenty persons "were on the anxious seats" at the New Providence (Kentucky) Church, while at a meeting five years later nearly forty took the seats. MS. Session Record, New Providence (Kentucky) Church, 1822-1849, January 18, 1829; July 20, 1834, Montreat.

16. Rev. Mr. Cunningham to editor, *Visitor and Telegraph*, September 18, 1828.

17. Some members of the churches came from considerable distances—even a dozen miles or more. As early as 1793, the Transylvania Presbytery ordered that, unless specific permission be secured, no congregation should be formed within ten miles of an older congregation. "Extracts from the Minutes of the Transylvania Presbytery, 1786-1837," April 24, 1793, in Sweet, *The Presbyterians*, 141.

18. "[Session Record], Duck Creek Church, Ohio, 1815-1847," April 18, 1845, *ibid.*, 437-38.

19. "Sessional Record of the First Presbyterian Church of Murfreesboro, Tennessee, 1812-1829," October 2, 1826, *ibid.*, 450.

20. MS. Session Record, Franklin (Tennessee) Church, 1810-1848, February 13, 1835, Montreat.

21. MS. Session Record, Mount Zion (Kentucky) Church, 1823-1925, December 7, 1845, *ibid.*

22. Shields, *Natchez*, 247.

23. Clapp, *Autobiographical Sketches*, 93-94; Voss, *Presbyterianism in New Orleans*, 43.

24. Herrmann, *James McChord*, 58.

25. MS. Session Record, New Providence (Kentucky) Church, 1822-1849, p. 4, Montreat.

26. [Charles B. Verner], *One Hundred Years of Presbyterianism in Tuscaloosa, Alabama* (n.p., c. 1927), 6-7. See receipts for pew rent given by various churches in the West. McDowell Papers, Philadelphia.

27. *First Presbyterian Church, Nashville*, 114-19. This was the only sale of pews in the history of this church.

28. MS. Minutes, Cabbin Creek Church, August 15, 1825, Philadelphia.

29. MS. Session Record, Washington (Mississippi) Church, 1807-1820, September 22, 1807, Montreat.

30. MS. Session Record, New Providence (Kentucky) Church, 1822-1849, November 8, 1829; Annual Report for 1829-1830, p. 96; August 7, October 5, 1831, *ibid*.

31. MS. Session Record, Pine Ridge (Mississippi) Church, 1823-1838, February 15, 1829, *ibid*.

32. MS. Session Record, First Presbyterian Church, Louisville, 1828-1839, April 1 ?, 1839, *ibid*.

33. MS. Minutes, Tuscaloosa Presbytery, 1835-1843, October 5, 1839, *ibid*.

34. MS. Session Record, Plum Creek (Kentucky) Church, 1835-1845, April 1, 1839, Louisville.

35. MS. Session Record, Baton Rouge (Louisiana) Church, 1833-1850, November 15, 1841, Montreat.

36. See William J. Hinke, "The Early German Hymn Books of the Reformed Church in the United States," *Journal of the Presbyterian Historical Society*, IV (1907-1908), 147-61.

37. Thompson, *Presbyterian Churches*, 146.

38. Battle, *Valley Creek Presbyterian Church*, 10.

39. Park, *Presbyterian Church of Knoxville*, 21; McTeer, *New Providence Presbyterian Church*, 54.

40. Lacy, *Revivals*, 85.

41. MS. Session Record, Murfreesboro (Tennessee) Church, 1812-1860, October 21, 1832, Montreat.

42. MS. Session Record, First Presbyterian Church, Nashville, 1833-1853, September 1, 1851, church vault.

43. See Chap. III, "A Sequel to the Revivals." Despite Rankin's efforts, Theodore Dwight's revision and enlargement of Watts' collection was adopted by the General Assembly of 1802, with the statement that permission to use the new collection of hymns and psalms "is hereby cheerfully allowed, in such congregations and churches as may think it for edification to adopt and use the same." *Minutes of the General Assembly, 1789-1820*, p. 249.

44. MS. Minutes, Tuscaloosa Presbytery, 1835-1843, October 17, 1842, Montreat.

45. Beard, *Biographical Sketches*, 51; *ibid.*, 2nd series, 144.

46. Stringfield, *Presbyterianism in the Ozarks*, 3-4.

47. *One Hundred and Fifty Years of Presbyterianism in the Ohio Valley, 1740-1890* (Cincinnati, 1941), 14. In Kentucky and Tennessee one Communion service each quarter seems to have been the rule.

48. When strictly enforced, fencing was a more rigid method of controlling Communion than that practiced by the Baptist church in "close" Communion. Most Presbyterian churches, however, did not limit the table to its members, as found in an entry of the Pisgah (Kentucky) Church which stated that "a great many Christians belonging to other denominations partook and seemed to have a refreshing season. . . ." MS. Session Record, Pisgah (Kentucky) Church, 1828-1865, January 22, 1841, Montreat. Also see MS. Session Record, Franklin (Tennessee) Church, 1810-1848, February (?) 1811, *ibid*.

49. MS. Session Record, Pine Ridge (Mississippi) Church, 1823-1838, August 6, 1825, *ibid.*

50. The session of the Ebenezer (Alabama) Church ordered "Nathaniel Cameron to stand back from the Communion this day, & untill certain rumors against him is examined into." MS. Session Record, Ebenezer (Alabama) Church, 1827-1849, March 25, 1849, *ibid.*

51. A table and benches once used by the Salem River (South Carolina) Church are preserved at Montreat. The table is approximately nine feet in length and nine inches in width.

52. The material on Communion is rather extensive. One of the most satisfactory books was written by Tenney, *Communion Tokens.*

53. Davidson, *Presbyterian Church in Kentucky,* 103-104. The "sacramental season," like the Methodist camp meeting, offered golden opportunities for news gathering, courting, and marrying. They were occasions of mixed emotions that tended to brighten the dreariness of frontier life. Sweet, *The Presbyterians,* 62-63. For some interesting sacramental experiences see the Diary of Rev. John Lyle, June 14, 1801-July 22, 1803, *passim.* MS., Frankfort.

54. See the contract. Shane Collection, Philadelphia.

55. Adriaan J. V. Wyck, *The Rise of the Sunday School in Kentucky* (Th. M. thesis, Louisville Presbyterian Seminary, 1945), 5.

56. W. H. Averill, *A History of the First Presbyterian Church, Frankfort, Kentucky* (Cincinnati, 1902), 198-209.

57. Some of the ministers believed curiously that teaching on the Sabbath was a profanation of the day, so they objected to the Sunday schools. *One Hundred Years of Presbyterianism in the Ohio Valley,* 30-31.

58. Gillett, *Presbyterian Church,* II, 237-38.

59. Baird, *Collection,* 185.

60. Gillett, *Presbyterian Church,* II, 334.

61. Alexander, *Synod of Tennessee,* 53. The American Sunday School Union, established in 1824, gave much aid to Western efforts. The Transylvania Presbytery in 1829 requested the union to send an agent to promote Sabbath schools and Bible classes in its bounds. "Extracts from the Minutes of the Transylvania Presbytery, 1786-1837," October 10, 1829, in Sweet, *The Presbyterians,* 262-63.

62. MS. Minutes, South Alabama Presbytery, 1826-1828, March 10, 1827, Montreat.

63. MS. Minutes, South Alabama Presbytery, 1828-1832, October 23, 1830, *ibid.* Also see Marshall, Presbyterian Church in Alabama. MS., Alabama Archives.

64. Alexander, *Synod of Tennessee,* 53.

65. Alexander Bartlett, *The History of New Providence Church* (Maryville, Tenn., 1876), 7. In 1839 Rev. John McCullagh, probably the most successful promoter of Sabbath schools the West ever had, settled in Kentucky and remained there through his long and active life. See Joseph H. McCullagh, *The Sunday-School Man of the South* (Philadelphia, 1889), *passim.*

66. *One Hundred Years of Presbyterianism in the Ohio Valley,* 35-36.

67. Averill, *First Presbyterian Church, Frankfort,* 204.

68. McTeer, *New Providence Presbyterian Church,* 87.

69. MS. Session Record, Baton Rouge (Louisiana), Church, 1833-1850, ? 1833, Montreat.

70. "Minutes of the Synod of Kentucky, 1802-1811," September ? 1803; October 17, 1805, in Sweet, *The Presbyterians,* 320, 332-33.

71. "Minutes of the Transylvania Presbytery, 1786-1837," October 15, 1806, *ibid.,* 202.

72. *Minutes of the General Assembly, 1798-1820,* pp. 196, 317, 450-51, 478.

73. Thompson, *Presbyterian Churches,* 131.

74. Alexander, *Synod of Tennessee,* 62-63.

75. Thomas H. Spence, "Southern Presbyterian Reviews," *Union Seminary Review, LVI* (1945), 2.

76. Lindsley, "Sources and Sketches of Cumberland Presbyterian History," *loc. cit.,* VI, 26, 386.

XI

EXPANSION AND DIVISION

1. For the origin and adoption of the Plan of Union see Sweet, *The Presbyterians,* 41-45; Woods, *Presbyterian Controversy,* 41-44; Baird, *Collection,* 570-74.

2. Bacon, *American Christianity,* 219-21.

3. J. Van Vecten, "Address," *Home Missionary and American Pastor's Journal, II* (1829), 21.

4. Baird, *Collection,* 857.

5. See Myron L. Fuller, "The New Madrid Earthquake," *United States Geological Survey Bulletin,* 1912, No. 404. For a bibliography of original source material of the New Madrid earthquakes see Frances A. Sampson, "The New Madrid and Other Earthquakes in Missouri," Mississippi Valley Historical Association, *Proceedings* (Cedar Rapids), VI (1912-1913), 218-38.

6. "Earthquakes," *Evangelical Record and Western Review* (Lexington), I (1812), 16.

7. Henry Howe, *Historical Collections of the Great West,* 2 vols. in 1 (Cincinnati, 1854), 236. See an interesting account by William C. Love, a boy of thirteen years at the time of the earthquakes. Beard, *Biographical Sketches,* 2nd. series, 359-60.

8. "Extracts from the Autobiography of J. Allan," in Sweet, *The Presbyterians,* 819-21. Allan himself was converted and joined the Presbyterian Church during the earthquake period.

9. MS. Minutes, Synod of Kentucky, 1811-1818, October 21, 1812, Louisville.

10. Susan L. Martin to Polly Dickey, August 2, 1812, Philadelphia.

11. W. C. Humphrey, *Historical Sketch of the Synod of Kentucky, 1802-1902* (n. p., c. 1902), 25.

12. Davidson, *Presbyterian Church in Kentucky,* 283-84.

13. *Minutes of the General Assembly, 1789-1820,* p. 619.

14. Isaac Reed, *The Christian Traveller* (New York, 1828), 55-72 *passim*.

15. Bishop, *Outline of the Church in Kentucky,* 256. For a comment on poor church attendance in Kentucky, as late as 1832, see a letter from Samuel Steele to S. D. Blythe, March 2, 1832, Philadelphia. A letter written to the *Western Presbyterian Herald,* April 21, 1836, declared that more than half of the Presbyterian pulpits in the state were vacant or partially supplied. For Presbyterian membership in Kentucky in 1830 and 1835 see *Home Missionary,* II (1830), 188; VII (1835), 152-54.

16. "Annual Meeting of the Massachusetts Missionary Society. Report of the Trustees," *Panoplist,* X (1814), 283.

17. William S. Jacobs (comp.), *Presbyterianism in Nashville* (Nashville, 1904), 13-14; *First Presbyterian Church, Nashville,* 47-52.

18. *Board of Missions for 1820,* p. 9.

19. Letter to editor, *Home Missionary,* III (1830), 60, 80.

20. Samuel C. Williams, *Beginnings of West Tennessee, 1541-1841* (Johnson City, Tenn., 1930), 191.

21. Robert H. McCaslin, *Presbyterianism in Memphis, Tennessee* (Memphis, n.d.), 26-27; History of First Church, Memphis, Tennessee, 1-2. Unsigned MS., Philadelphia; A. B. Curry, *Historic Churches of West Tennessee* (Memphis, c. 1923), *passim*.

22. Robert Latham, *History of the Associate Reformed Synod of the South, to Which Is Prefixed A History of the Associate Presbyterian and Reformed Presbyterian Churches* (Harrisburg, Pa., 1882), 386.

23. MS. Minutes, Synod of West Tennessee, 1826-1849, October 15, 1830, Montreat.

24. Quoted by Lindsley, "Sources and Sketches of Cumberland Presbyterian History," *loc. cit.,* VII, 3.

25. The West Tennessee Presbytery was formed in 1810 by dividing the Transylvania Presbytery. In 1815 the West Tennessee was divided to form the Mississippi.

26. Marshall, Presbyterian Church in Alabama, 1-5. MS., Alabama Archives.

27. David Lowry, *Life and Labors of the Late Rev. Robert Donnell* (Alton, Ill., 1867), 102.

28. Burgett, "The Presbyterian Church in Alabama," *loc. cit.,* 22-23.

29. Information from miscellaneous material on churches copied from the *Mobile Register* of 1894, Alabama Archives.

30. John B. Warren, *A Discourse Delivered in the City of Mobile, May 1829. Commemorative of the Dedication of Government-Street Church* (New York, 1829). For a survey of Presbyterian ministers and churches in Alabama in 1834 see *Home Missionary, VII* (1834), 46-47.

31. *Annual Report of the Board of Missions of the General Assembly of the Presbyterian Church in the United States* (Philadelphia, 1836), 32.

32. Letter to editor, *Western Luminary,* August 20, 1828. Also see *Visitor and Telegraph,* September 18, 1828.

33. "Annual Meeting of the Massachusetts Missionary Society," *loc. cit.,* X (1814), 283. Politics, land, cotton, and Negroes so completely occupied the

minds of all classes in Mississippi that many Presbyterian ministers and missionaries became deeply discouraged. For examples see letters to *Home Missionary,* IX (1836), 99, 107, 108.

34. *Minutes of the General Assembly of the Presbyterian Church 1826-1829* (Philadelphia, n.d.), 42. In 1835 the Presbyterian church in Jackson, Mississippi, was in an "unfinished state," had no pastor but depended on "gratuitous supply" of occasional ministers. Joel Parker to *New Orleans Observer,* October 20, 1835.

35. Gideon Blackburn to editor, *Religious Remembrancer* (Philadelphia). July 6, 1816. Buttrick Evans visited New Orleans in 1818 and commented that "There is, perhaps, no place in the world, where the influence of the gospel is more needed. . . ." See *A Pedestrious Tour of Four Thousand Miles* (Thwaites, *Early Western Travels,* VIII, Cleveland, 1904), 345-46. As late as 1833 a Presbyterian missionary found between Baton Rouge and New Orleans people who had never seen a Bible. *Home Missionary,* VI (1833), 104.

36. Gillett, *Presbyterian Church,* II, 374-75.

37. For a sketch of Larned see Sprague, *Annals,* IV, 556-71.

38. Voss, *Presbyterianism in New Orleans,* 23. For a description of the interesting ceremony that accompanied the laying of the cornerstone of this church see *New Orleans Chronicle,* March 11, 1819.

39. See Ralph R. Gurley, *Life and Eloquence of the Rev. Sylvester Larned* (New York, 1844), *passim.*

40. Clapp, *Autobiographical Sketches* should be examined with care. Also see his *Theological Views* (Boston, 1859); *Reasons for the Decision of the Mississippi Presbytery in the case of Mr. Theodore Clapp* (Natchez, 1833); Elma Kalman, *The History of the Presbyterian Church in New Orleans, 1817-1860* (M.A. thesis, Tulane, 1939), *passim;* John K. Bettersworth, "Protestant Beginnings in New Orleans," *Louisiana Historical Quarterly* (New Orleans), XXI (1938), 823-45. About four years before Clapp's dismissal, a missionary reported that New Orleans, a city of about fifty thousand people, had fewer than one hundred members of Protestant churches. *Visitor and Telegraph,* September 26, 1829.

41. Timothy Flint, *Recollections of the Last Ten Years* (edited by C. Hartley Grattan, New York, 1932), 289. Also see Patton, *Presbyterian Church,* 340.

42. Gillett, *Presbyterian Church,* II, 380.

43. Letter from D. D. Chesnut to editor, *Home Missionary,* III (1830), 81.

44. McDonnold, *Cumberland Presbyterian Church,* 189-90.

45. Benjamin Chase to James Smylie, July 9, 1825, Mississippi Archives.

46. Moody, "Religious Efforts in the Mississippi Valley," *loc. cit.,* 171; James Moore, "Presbyterianism in Arkansas," *Journal of the Presbyterian Historical Society,* III (1905-1906), 58-59; *The History of Presbyterianism in Arkansas, 1828-1902* (n.p., n.d.), 9-13.

47. Lindsley, "Sketches of Cumberland Presbyterian History," *loc. cit.,* VII, 418.

48. Hervey Woods to editor, *Home Missionary,* VIII (1835), 52-53. For another description of the type of minister needed in Arkansas see a letter from William S. Woodruff to the American Home Missionary Society, July 15, 1826, in Sweet, *The Presbyterians,* 657. No Presbyterian church was organized in the

southwestern part of Arkansas until 1845. Asa S. Morgan, "Founding of Presbyterianism in Southwest Arkansas," *Publications of the Arkansas Historical Association* (Fayetteville), II (1908), 237-53.

49. McDonnold, *Cumberland Presbyterian Church*, 263-66. In 1834 Milton Estill, a Cumberland Presbyterian minister from Tennessee, organized a church near Clarksville which may have been the first Protestant church organized on Texas soil. See The Biography of Rev. Richard Overton Watkins, 6-7. Unsigned MS., Montreat.

50. D. S. Southmayd to editor, *Home Missionary*, VIII (1835), 50-52.

51. William S. Red, *A History of the Presbyterian Church in Texas* (Austin, c. 1936), 3; Edward M. Browder, *Rev. Peter H. Fullinwider: the First Presbyterian Minister to Visit and Preach in Texas* (Dallas, 1916), *passim*.

52. Red, *Presbyterian Church in Texas*, 12.

53. L. Tenney, *History of the Presbytery of Central Texas* (Austin, 1895), 3, 17; Hutchison, *Reminiscences*, 214; Edward M. Browder, *A Pioneer Preacher in Texas: the Rev. Hugh Wilson, D. D.* (Dallas, 1916), *passim;* Robert F. Miller, "Early Presbyterianism in Texas as Seen by Rev. James Weston Miller, D. D.," *Southwestern Historical Quarterly* (Austin), XIX (1915-1916), 159-83.

54. William M. Baker, *The Life and Labours of the Rev. Daniel Baker, D. D.* (Philadelphia, 1858), *passim;* Hutchison, *Reminiscences*, 214.

55. Lacy, *Revivals*, 105-106.

56. Gillett, *Presbyterian Church*, II, 443-44; Baird, *Collection*, 858.

57. Bacon, *American Christianity*, 292-93.

58. Baird, *Religion in America*, 482; Sweet, *Religions in America*, 377. Davidson contends (*Presbyterian Church in Kentucky*, 345) that of 139 churches in the Western Reserve Synod (Ohio) only nine had been organized with the Presbyterian form of government. The others were either Congregational or mixed.

59. Halsey, *Works of Philip Lindsley*, II, 370.

60. Gillett, *Presbyterian Church*, II, 446-52; Bacon, *American Christianity*, 294; Thompson, *Presbyterian Churches*, 105.

61. The most notable trial was conducted against Albert Barnes of Philadelphia who had published a disturbing sermon on "The Way of Salvation." See Baird, *Collection*, 661-66, 694-705.

62. The charges of heresy, slander, and hypocrisy were brought against Beecher by the very influential Rev. Joshua L. Wilson of Cincinnati. Gillett, *Presbyterian Church*, II, 462-65; Thompson, *Presbyterian Churches*, 108-109.

63. For estimates of Balch see Sprague, *Annals*, III, 308-319; "Presbyterianism in Tennessee," *Christian Observer and Presbyterian Witness*, October 25, 1866.

64. For sketches of Hopkins and Emmons see *Dictionary of American Biography*, VI, 150-51; IX, 217-18.

65. Alexander, *Synod of Tennessee*, 32. Balch acknowledged before the General Assembly of 1798 that he had made certain errors and swore that henceforth he would not preach or teach what the Assembly had declared erroneous. Baird, *Collection*, 633. Nearly all of the 190 pages of the MS. Minutes, Synod of the Carolinas, 1788-1800, Vol. I, are devoted to the trial and charges against

Balch. For an interesting comment on the Tennessee brand of Hopkinsianism see James Blythe to Samuel D. Blythe, June 8, 1828, Philadelphia. Although earnestly and vigorously opposed to the Cumberland Presbyterian Church, Thomas B. Craighead preached Pelagianism in middle Tennessee, especially at Nashville, for many years. One person exaggeratingly called him "the parent of all the New Lightism, schism, and Shakerism, which has cursed our country." Quoted by Davidson, *Presbyterian Church in Kentucky,* 272 n. Probably Craighead's preaching had little to do with the Old School and New School division, yet it contributed much to the general disturbance of the church in the West. See a letter from James Blythe to William Williamson, c. 1810, Philadelphia.

66. Baird, *Religion in America,* 282-87.

67. Sweet, *The Presbyterians,* 103; Gillett, *Presbyterian Church,* II, 444-45; A. Alexander to James H. Dickey, February 25, 1830, Philadelphia.

68. Patton, *Presbyterian Church,* 418-19, 425.

69. Chapter VII, "The Slavery Question."

70. Morris, *The New School,* 61-62.

71. Sweet, *The Presbyterians,* 118-19.

72. Johnston, *Forty Years in Indiana,* 19; Edmund A Moore, "Robert J. Breckinridge and the Slavery Aspect of the Presbyterian Schism of 1837," *Church History,* IV (1935), 282-94. The contribution of abolitionism to the division has been covered adequately in an excellent article by C. Bruce Staiger, "Abolitionism and the Presbyterian Schism of 1837-1838," *Mississippi Valley Historical Review,* XXXVI (1949-1950), 391-414.

73. For this controversy see Woods, *Presbyterian Controversy;* Crocker, *The Catastrophe of the Presbyterian Church;* Baird, *Collection,* 705-791.

74. Baird, *Religion in America,* 485.

75. Bacon, *American Christianity,* 297.

76. Thompson, *Presbyterian Churches,* 117-18.

77. Gillett, *Presbyterian Church,* II, 552.

78. MS. (copy) Minutes, Synod of Kentucky, 1822-1845, October 12, 1838, Montreat.

79. Davidson, *Presbyterian Church in Kentucky,* 350-61. See six letters from Stiles to Thomas Porter, n.d., Philadelphia; Samuel Y. Garrison to Thomas P. Smith, April 13, 1841, *ibid.*

80. Examine MS. Session Record, New Providence (Kentucky) Church, April 1, 1841-March 15, 1846, *passim,* Montreat.

81. Gillett, *Presbyterian Church,* II, 541.

82. Archer C. Dickerson to T. P. Smith, November 5, 1839, Philadelphia. Also see Gillett, *Presbyterian Church,* II, 538-41.

83. Alexander, *Synod of Tennessee,* 32.

84. "Action of the Holston Presbytery Declaring the Exscinding Acts of the General Assembly of 1837 Unconstitutional," in Sweet, *The Presbyterians,* 864.

85. "Action of the Old School Minority of the Holston Presbytery Relative to the Division of the Presbytery into Old School and New School Bodies," *ibid.,* 867. Some divided churches sought to reunite by means of ministers who "took

moderate ground." For an example see letter from Orville Bradley to James Gallaher, December 2, 1839, Philadelphia.

86. MS. Minutes, Synod of West Tennessee, 1826-1849, October 17, 1837, Montreat.

87. MS. Minutes, West Tennessee Presbytery, 1837-1849, October 4, 1838; March 31, 1843, *ibid*. Also see D. D. Little, *History of the Presbytery of Columbia, Tennessee* (Columbia, 1928), 13-14.

88. MS. Minutes, Synod of Alabama, 1837-1847, October 27, 1838, Montreat. See a resolution by an Alabama presbytery supporting the action of the Old School assembly. MS. Minutes, North Alabama Presbytery, 1825-1849, October 6, 1838, *ibid*.

89. MS. Session Record, Carmel (Mississippi) Church, 1839-1866, ? 1839, Mississippi Archives.

90 Gillett, *Presbyterian Church*, II, 551.

91. Baird, *Collection*, 787-88.

92. Thompson, *Presbyterian Churches*, 122.

93. Gillett, *Presbyterian Church*, II, 552.

APPENDIX

THE FIRST SESSION BOOK OF THE OLDEST
PRESBYTERIAN CHURCH IN MISSISSIPPI

1. Bethel Presbyterian Church near Uniontown, in Jefferson County, was formed by Joseph Bullen in 1804 and was retained as a place of worship until 1822. According to most authorities, the Bayou Pierre Presbyterian Church, near Port Gibson, was also organized by Bullen, early in the year 1807, and deserves to be called the second oldest. Jones, *Protestantism and the Southwest*, 231-32, 234; Hutchison, *Reminiscences*, 234-35; Dunbar Rowland, *History of Mississippi*, 2 vols. (Chicago, 1925), II, 600; Thomas L. Haman, "Beginnings of Presbyterianism in Mississippi," Mississippi Historical Society, *Publications*, X (1909), 216-18.

2. Smylie was born and educated in North Carolina. As a Presbyterian missionary sent by the Synod of the Carolinas to Mississippi in 1805, he soon settled

in Washington, where he supported himself by establishing a classical academy. Although not distinguished for his eloquence, he was recognized as a sound theological scholar. He organized four of the eight churches which became members of the Mississippi Presbytery when it was formed in 1815. Jones, *Protestanism and the Southwest*, 239-42; Hutchison, *Reminiscences*, 226-28; "An Account of the Work of the Reverend James Smylie in the Mississippi Territory," *Journal of the Presbyterian Historical Society*, XXI (1943), 200-201.

3. Those who are eligible to partake of the sacrament of the Lord's Supper.

4. From this period, the church has been generally known as the Pine Ridge Church, which now worships in its third building constructed more than a hundred years ago. Nearby stands the uninhabited manse of the same period. C. W. Grafton, "Rededication of Pine Ridge Church in the Presbytery of Mississippi," *Christian Observer* (Louisville), November 11, 1931; *Mississippi; A Guide to the Magnolia State* (New York, 1938), 335. Now supplied by a minister from nearby Natchez, the church had in 1949 two elders, two deacons, and twelve members. *Minutes of the Ninetieth General Assembly of the Presbyterian Church in the United States* (Richmond, 1950), 210.

5. Bullen was born in Massachusetts, educated at Yale, and spent twenty years as a Presbyterian minister in Vermont. In 1799, accompanied by his son, he started for the Mississippi Territory, which he reached after a hard and arduous journey. After some time in the Chickasaw Nation, he returned to Vermont for his family. By 1803 he had settled about twenty miles northeast of Natchez, where he cultivated a small farm, taught school, and preached in various neighborhoods. Jones, *Protestantism and the Southwest*, 226-32; Gillett, *Presbyterian Church*, II, 367-70; Haman, "Presbyterianism in Mississippi," *loc. cit.,* 212-13.

6. Rickhow, a native of New York, was once a minister in the Methodist Church, but he withdrew because of his dissatisfaction with Methodist doctrine. Although lacking in education, he became a great missionary to the "piney wood" counties of eastern Mississippi, especially in the Pearl River region. Jones, *Protestanism and the Southwest*, 235-36; Hutchison, *Reminiscences*, 228-30.

7. Montgomery was born in Pennsylvania and was educated in North Carolina, probably at Chapel Hill. After the completion of the duty for which he was commissioned, he left the territory and did not return until 1811, when he became president of Jefferson College at Washington. For thirty-seven years he served as the pastor of Ebenezer and Union. Montgomery was a fluent speaker and the finest scholar among the early Presbyterian ministers in the territory. Jones, *Protestantism and the Southwest*, 242-47; Hutchison, *Reminiscences*, 237-40.

8. The best account of this endeavor is found in James Hall, *A Brief History of the Mississippi Territory, to which is Prefixed a Summary View of the Country between the Settlements on Cumberland River, & the Territory* (Salisbury, N. C., 1801). Also see "Documentary Material Relating to the Early History of the Presbyterian Church in Mississippi," *Journal of the Presbyterian Historical Society*, XXI (1943), 186-92; Howe, *Presbyterian Church in South Carolina*, II, 173-79.

9. Except where necessary for clarity or understanding, I have made no addi-

tions whatever to the manuscript.

10. See Hutchison, *Reminiscences,* 234.

11. The session.

12. The deacons.

13. Moderator.

14. Stated Clerk.

15. In March 1809 the Transylvania Presbytery, in Kentucky, "thought proper to cite Mr. Wood . . . to attend the next session to show cause of his long absence." "Extracts from the Minutes of the Transylvania Presbytery, 1786-1837," March 22, 1809, in Sweet, *The Presbyterians,* 221.

16. One licensed to preach as a probationer for the ministry.

17. Those partaking of the Lord's Supper.

18. For some reason Bisland countermanded his resignation of the previous meeting.

19. In this year he moved to Amite County. Rowland, *Mississippi,* II, 600.

20. At Pine Ridge, according to the general custom, the tokens were distributed on Saturday to those who were permitted to participate in the Communion on the following day. See Tenney, *Communion Tokens, passim.* Throughout the country the use of tokens was generally declining by 1825.

21. It is quite evident that this church strictly enforced compliance with doctrine and discipline.

22. A certificate of good standing permits a transfer to another church.

23. Presumably both sexes were included.

24. Asked questions.

25. A sermon immediately preceding the Lord's Supper.

26. Of new members.

27. Some sessions followed a scheme by which its members by taking turns represented the church in the higher judicatories.

28. A Presbyterian minister in North Carolina who was sent by the General Assembly, in 1815, as a missionary to the Natchez district. Smith probably graduated from Yale in 1791. In regard to his mission see a letter from Smith, June 9, 1816, in *Journal of the Presbyterian Historical Society,* XXI (1943), 197-200.

29. Montgomery settled in Jefferson County and, henceforth, devoted full time to the two churches of Ebenezer and Union. For a sketch of the latter see C. W. Grafton, "A Sketch of the Old Scotch Settlement at Union Church," Mississippi Historical Society, *Publications,* IX (1906), 263-71.

INDEX

Act of 1705, 47.
Adams, John, 55.
Adopting Act, 47, 150 n.
African Methodist Episcopal Church, 90.
Alabama, Perry County, 58; Huntsville, 114; Mobile, 114; expansion of church in, 114-15; Tuscaloosa, 104, 115; division of 1837 in, 122.
Alabama churches, Concord, 17; Courtland, 94; Ebenezer, 169 n.; Huntsville, 114; Mobile, 86, 114; Pisgah, 97, 100; Tuscaloosa, 104, 105, 115.
Alabama presbyteries, Alabama, 38, 44, 108, 114; North Alabama, 58, 65, 77, 84, 101; South Alabama, 17, 41, 44, 45, 58, 80, 81, 84, 85, 86, 101, 108; Tuscaloosa, 16, 80, 87, 105, 106.
Allan, John, 112.
American Bible Society, 109, 113.
American Board of Commissioners for Foreign Missions, 64, 66, 68, 71, 72.
American Colonization Society, 77.
American Education Society, 105, 122.
American Home Missionary Society, 111, 119, 122.
American Revolutionary War, Presbyterians in, 13; Synod of Philadelphia, 1775, aids, 13; Battle of King's Mountain in, 14; condition of Presbyterians at close of, 14-15, 124.
American Sunday School Union, 177 n.
American Tract Society, 109.
Anderson, Alexander, 32.
Anderson, Isaac, 50, 53, 87.
Andrews, Jedediah, 49.
Antislavery societies, 77-78.
Anxious seats, 175 n.
Arkansas, expansion of church in, 116-17, 181 n.
Arkansas presbytery, New Harmony, 71.
Arminianism, 32, 33.
Arthur, Michael, 107.
Asbury, Francis, 22-23, 163 n.
Associate Reformed Presbyterian Church, 48, 96, 114.

Bacon, Leonard, 79.
Bacon, Sumner, 117.
Baker, Daniel, 105, 117.
Balch, Hezekiah, 19, 30-31, 50, 51-52, 119, 149 n., 181-82 n.
Banks, Daniel C., 39-40.
Baptism of slaves, 91.
Baptist Church, 23, 24, 81, 90, 91, 105, 114, 125, 126, 155 n.

Barnes, James C., 79.
Bass, Hugh, 79.
Bates, Issachar, 32.
Baxter, George A., 28.
Bean, William, 18.
Beard, Richard, 113.
Beecher, Lyman, 119.
Bell, Robert, 68-69.
Bisland, William, 86.
Blackburn, Gideon, 14, 37, 47, 54, 61, 62-64, 87, 99, 101, 113, 114, 115, 151 n.
Blair, John, 12.
Blount College, 52.
Blythe, James, 45, 48, 55, 56, 58, 59-60, 75, 85.
Board of Missions, Presbyterian, 115, 119.
Books, distribution of, 108-109.
Boone, Daniel, 18.
Bowman, William, 129.
Boyd, John, 49.
Brainerd, David, 61.
Breckinridge, Robert J., 78.
Breckinridge, Will, 79.
Brown, John, 12.
Brown, Mrs. John, 107.
Bullen, Joseph, 20, 61, 129 ff.
Burroughs, William, 46.
Butler, Elizur, 70-71.
Byington, Cyrus, 68, 72, 162 n., 163 n.

Cahoon, Thomas, 45.
Calhoun, John C., 67.
Call, ministerial, 39-40, 133.
Calvin, John, 48.
Calvinism, too cold for Westerner, 23; modified, 31; opposition to, 48, 116; conflict with liberalism, 56; New School vs. Old School, 118 ff.
Calvinistic Magazine, 109.
Cameron, Archibald, 32, 36.
Camp meeting, 24-25, 114, 115. See revivals.
Campbell, Alexander, 32.
Cane Ridge camp meeting, 25.
Carnahan, John, 116.
Carrick, Samuel, 19, 47, 50, 52.
Carroll, William, 41, 47.
Cartwright, Peter, 33, 37, 147 n.
Caruthers, I. N., 44.
Catawba Indians, 13, 62.
Catechisms, for Negroes, 90; examination on, 134.
Catechists, 32, 62.
Centre College, 57, 105.
Certificate of membership, 134.
Chamberlain, Jeremiah, 59.

187

Charity Hall, 69.

Chase, Benjamin, 116.

Cherokee Indian missions, at Hiwassee, 62-63; at Brainerd, 64, 65; at Carmel, 65; at Creek Path, 65; at Haweis, 65; at Hightower, 65; at Willstown, 65; in Arkansas, 71; in Tennessee, 101.

Chickamauga Mission, 64.

Chickasaw Indians, visited by Joseph Bullen, 20, 61; mission at Monroe, 67-68; at Tokshish, 67-68; at Pigeon Roost Creek, 68; formation of Tombigbee Presbytery for, 68; treaty by, 70.

Choctaw Indians, missions in Mississippi, 65-67; formation of Tombigbee Presbytery for, 68; Treaty of Dancing Rabbit Creek by, 70; missionary to, 105.

Christian Spectator, 45.

Christian, William, 19.

Church, government of, 15-18; support of, 105; hymns and singing in, 105-106; Communion service of, 106-107; Sunday school movement in, 107-108; distribution of Bibles and catechisms to, 108-109; religious papers of, 109-110; expansion and division of, 111 ff.; effect of earthquakes on, 111-13; Old School and New School in, 118-23.

Church building, early type of construction, 102; interior of, 102-103; raising money for, 103-104.

Church membership, request for, 133.

Cincinnati, Ohio, 20, 43.

Civil War, 73, 92.

Clapp, Theodore, 104, 115-16.

Cleland, Thomas, 45.

Coffin, Charles, 46-47, 52, 90.

Colbert, James, 67.

Colbert, Levi, 67, 69.

Colleges, advantages of Western, 49-50.

Communion, tokens, 93, 107, 133; sacrament, 107, 176 n.

Confession of Faith, 15, 28, 32, 33, 34, 36, 47, 93, 109, 137, 160 n.

Congregational Church, 64, 111, 118, 119, 181 n.

Connecticut Missionary Society, 115.

Constitutional Convention, 14.

Cornelius, Elias, 115.

Cossitt, Franceway R., 57, 151 n.

Craig, John, 12.

Craighead, Thomas, 19, 48, 50, 53, 182 n.

Crawford, Edward, 39.

Crawford, James, 20.

Creek Indians, 67, 99.

Cumberland College, in Tennessee, 53, 159 n.; in Kentucky, 57-58.

Cumberland Compact, 146 n.

Cumberland Presbyterian Church, formation of, 32-36, 125-26; Cumberland Presbytery of, 33 ff.; first General Assembly of, 37; attitude of Presbyterians toward, 36-37; growth of, 37; ministers of, 40, 43, 91, 150 n., 152 n.; Cumberland Synod of, 57; attitude toward education, 57-58; missions to Indians, 68-69, 71; on slavery question, 78-79; Lasting Hope Church in, 97; hymns, 106; *Religious and Literary Intelligencer* of, 109; revivals of, 114; missionary of, 116-17; Arkansas Presbytery of, 117; Louisiana Presbytery of, 117; in Kentucky and Tennessee, 151 n.

Cumberland Schism, 29, 32-36, 117.

Cummings, Charles, 18-19.

Dancing, 94.

Davidson Academy, 53.

Davidson College, 53.

Davis, William C., 27.

Deacon, office, 16, 130, 144 n., 170 n.

Declaration of Independence, signers, 13.

Dickerson, Archer C., 121.

Division of church, Cumberland Schism, 32-36; Old and New Schools, 118-123.

Doak, John, 51.

Doak, Samuel, 19, 40, 50-51.

Doak, Samuel W., 51.

Doctor of Divinity degree, 45.

Doctrine, stern and unbending, 47-48.

Dodd, William E., 48.

Dress, 38, 58, 95, 157 n.

Dunlavy, John, 31, 32.

Earthquakes, 111-12, 178 n.

East Tennessee College, 52.

Edgar, John T., 42.

Education, Presbyterian respect for, 49; colleges, 49-50, 51 ff.; elementary schools, 50; influential teachers, 50 ff.; manual labor schools, 54, 58-59; academy, 55; liberalism and Calvinism in, 56; general influence of, 60.

Elder, office, 15, 130; unable to find, 143 n.; suspended without trial, 151 n.

Ellis, a slave, 87.

Emmons, Nathanael, 119.

Erskine, George M., 83, 87.

Evangelical Intelligencer, 109.

Evans, David, 49.

Ewing, Finis, 32, 34, 36, 37, 38, 78-79.

Exhorters, 27, 32, 116, 147 n., 149 n.

Expansion of church, in Alabama, 114-15; in Mississippi, 115; in Louisiana, 115-16; in Arkansas, 116-17; in Texas, 117.

Field, Richard, house of, 63.

Finley, James B., 37.

Finley, John Evans, 20.

Finley, Robert, 76.

Finney, Alfred, 71.

Flint, Timothy, 48, 71, 116.

Foster, Stephen S., 73.

Franklin College, 76.

Franklin, state of, 18, 51.

French Huguenots in South Carolina, 11.

Fullenwider, Peter H., 117.

Gaines, Edmund P., General and Mrs., 64.
Gallaher, James, 38, 106.
Gambling, 94-95.
Garrison, William Lloyd, 78.
General Assembly, 17, 25-26, 99, 120; of 1789, 17, 21; of 1795, 74; of 1798, 23, 31; of 1800, 62, 108; of 1803, 26, 62, 83; of 1804, 109; of 1805, 26, 63; of 1806, 26; of 1807, 35; of 1808, 35-36; of 1811, 109; of 1816, 83, 91, 113; of 1818, 75, 84, 94; of 1819, 18, 101; of 1820, 83; of 1824, 108; of 1825, 84; of 1826, 18, 115; of 1828, 100; of 1830, 94; of 1832, 58; of 1833, 16; of 1835, 89, 120; of 1836, 73, 81; of 1837, 81, 100, 120, 121, 123; of 1838, 120, 121, 123; of 1842, 123.
George Peabody College, 54.
Gloucester, John, 87.
Goodell, William, 76.
Green, Ashbel, 27.
Greeneville College, 46, 51-52.
Grundy, Felix, 41, 47.

Hall, James, 129.
Hall, N. H., 45.
Hampden-Sydney College, 23, 49, 50, 147 n.
Harpeth Academy, 54.
Henderson, Richard, 18.
Henderson, Robert, 94-95, 101, 114.
Hodge, Archibald A., 73.
Hodge, Samuel, 36.
Hodge, William, 36.
Holley, Horace, 56, 159 n.
Holmes, James, 65.
Hopkins, Samuel, 119.
Hopkinsianism, 30-31, 119.
Horton, Azariah, 61.
Hotchkin, Ebenezer, 163 n.
Houston, Samuel, 19, 32.
Howe, Joseph L., 89.
Howe, Joseph P., 39.
Hume, William, 19.
Humphreys, Daniel, 67.
Hunley, John, 91.
Huss, John, 65, 161 n.

Immorality, 95-97.
Independent Academy, 54.
Indian Removal Bill, 69, 70.
Indians, work initiated among, 61 ff.; schools among Cherokee, 62-65; Chickamauga mission to, 64; missions to Choctaw, 66-67; missions to Chickasaw, 67-69; cession of lands by, 69-71; trans-Mississippi work among, 71; appraisal of work for, 71-72; federal aid to schools of, 161-62 n.
Intemperance. See whisky.

Jackson, Andrew, 53, 70, 95, 101.
Jackson College, 54.
Jones, Charles C., 84, 85, 88, 90.

Kentucky, Boonesborough, 18; Presbyterians in, 19-20, 151 n.; census of 1800, 20; conditions in 1800 in, 20-21; Logan County, 21, 23, 32, 34; Frankfort, 107, 113; division of 1837 in, 121; vacant pulpits in, 179 n.
Kentucky Academy, 55-56.
Kentucky churches, Bethel, 43; Bowling Green, 121; Cabbin Creek, 104; Cave Run, 20; Concord, 76; Danville, 19-20; Forks of Dick's River, 20; Gasper River, 23, 32, 34; Henderson, 86; Honey Creek, 96; Lexington, 20, 104; Little Mountain, 39; Louisville, 39, 42, 77, 91, 105; Marion County, 102; Mount Zion, 20, 104; Muddy River, 23; New Providence, 77, 88, 96, 103, 104, 105, 121; Paris, 88, 89, 95, 96; Plum Creek, 98, 105; Red River, 23; Springfield, 39; Woodford, 43.
Kentucky papers, Western Luminary, 38, 78, 95, 101, 109; The Temperance Herald of the Mississippi Valley, 100; Presbyterian Advocate, 109; Religious and Literary Intelligencer, 109.
Kentucky presbyteries, Cumberland, 33-38; Elk, 17; Muhlenberg, 46; Springfield, 31; Transylvania, 20, 30, 31, 32, 33, 35, 42, 55, 74, 79, 83, 85, 97, 109, 175 n.; Washington, 20; West Lexington, 20, 76.
King, Richard H., 44.
King, Samuel, 32, 36, 68.
Kingsbury, Cyrus, 64, 65, 66-67, 163 n.
Knox, John, 50, 156 n.
Knoxville Gazette, 25.

Lane Theological Seminary, 119.
Larned, Sylvester, 115.
Liberator, 78.
Liberty Hall Academy, 19, 49, 52, 53.
Licentiates, 45, 130.
Lindsley, Philip, 54, 118, 143 n., 158 n.
Lindsley, Stephen, 43.
"Log College," 49.
Lotteries, church, 94, 104, 115, 171 n.
Louisiana, Purchase of 1803, 111; expansion of church in, 115-16; little religion in New Orleans, 180 n.
Louisiana churches, Baton Rouge, 94, 97-98, 105; New Orleans, 94, 104, 114, 115.
Lundy, Benjamin, 78.
Lyle, John, 25-26, 27, 34, 36, 46, 47.

McAden, Hugh, 13.
McAdow, Samuel, 36.
M'Afee, George G., 86.
McChord, James, 48.
McClure, Andrew, 20.
McGready, James, 21, 23-24, 28, 32, 35, 36, 38, 98.
McMurray, Samuel, 91.
McNemar, Richard, 28, 31, 32.
Makemie, Francis, 12.
Manse, 104.

Manual Labor Institute, in Tennessee, 54; in Alabama, 58-59.

Marriage, of slaves, 91-92; of relatives, 95.

Marshall, Robert, 31, 32, 43, 50, 85.

Marshallites, 31.

Martin, Susan L., 112-13.

Martin Academy, 51.

Martineau, Harriet, 73, 155 n.

Maryville College, 53.

Membership in Presbyterian Church, Negro, 92; in 1812, 111; in 1816, 111; in Kentucky in 1820, 113; in Tennessee in 1814, 113-14; in Louisiana and Mississippi in 1825, 116; in 1831-37, 118; in 1837-38, 120, 121.

Methodist Episcopal Church, 105, 114, 115, 121-22; Francis Asbury, 22-23; revivals in, 24, 33; Peter Cartwright, 33, 37; James B. Finley, 37; slavery, 81; preaching in, 90; Benjamin T. Tanner, 90-91; expansion of, 125-26; itinerants in, 152-53 n.

Miller, Samuel, 27.

Mills, Samuel J., 113.

Ministerial education, Presbyterian requirement, 43-44, 49ff., 154 n., 156 n.; Cumberland Presbyterian requirement, 44-45.

Ministers, migrate to West, 22; foresaw Western expansion, 39; contracts of, 39, 43, 50; hardships of, 40-41; tried for various offenses, 41-42; salaries paid to, 42-43, 99, 104-105; sermons by, 45-46; varied roles, 48; indiscretions of, 99-100; scarcity of, 113, 115, 116; on plantations, 167 n.

Missionaries to Indians, Blackburn, Gideon, 62-64; Brainerd, David, 61; Butler, Elizur, 70-71; Finney, Alfred, 71; Holmes, James, 65; Humphreys, Daniel, 67; Huss, John, 65; Kingsbury, Cyrus, 64, 65; Stuart, T. C., 67; Washburn, Cephas, 71; Wayne, John, 65; Worcester, Samuel A., 70-71.

Mississippi, effects of division of 1837 in, 122-23; oldest church in, 129 ff.

Mississippi churches, Bethany, 89, 100; Bethel, 59, 130; Carmel, 122-23; Jackson, 180 n.; Natchez, 86, 94, 104; Pine Ridge, 41, 86, 102, 105, 129 ff.; Pisgah, 77; Port Gibson, 79; Salem, 91, 129 ff.; Washington, 42, 105, 129 ff.

Mississippi Colonization Society, 77.

Mississippi presbyteries, Mississippi, 59, 79, 115, 116, 117; Tombigbee, 68.

Missouri, Apple Creek Church, 97, 98; Caruthersville, 112; New Madrid, 112.

Missouri Compromise bill, 76.

Monroe, James, 64, 69.

Montgomery, John L., 85.

Montgomery, William, 129 ff.

Moore, James, 54-55, 56.

Moore, James W., 116.

Moore, William, 40, 68.

Morals. See various infractions of accepted code.

Morgan, John, 91.

Morris, Robert, 55.

Negroes, early urge to educate, 83; interest of synods and presbyteries in religious instruction of, 83-85; generosity toward, 85-86; preaching services for, 86-87; preachers and missionaries, 87; sermons to, 88, 90-91; moral charges against, 88-89; sale of, 89-90; baptism of, 91; marriage of, 91-92; membership in church of, 91-92, 164 n.; Sunday schools for, 107-108; financial contribution of, 169 n.

Nelson, David, 106.

Nelson, Thomas, 36.

New Echota, treaty of, 71.

New Lights, 31, 47.

New Orleans *Observer*, 77.

New School, 81, 118 ff., 166 n.

New York Evangelist, 28.

New York Missionary Society, 61.

New York Presbytery, 61.

New York Young Men's Home Missionary Society, 117.

North Carolina, 11, 13, 23, 27.

Oakland College, 59.

Ohio presbytery, Chillicothe, 79.

Old School, 81, 118 ff., 166 n.

Osage Indians, 71.

Palmer, Benjamin M., 73-74.

Pew sales, 104, 175 n.

Philadelphia, First African Church, 87.

Plan of Union, 64, 111, 118 ff.

Precentor, 106.

Presbyterian Advocate, 109.

Presbyterian minister-teacher, importance, 49 ff., 60; contracts, 50.

Presbyterian Missionary Board of New York, 20.

Presbyterian Theological Seminary, 73.

Presbytery, first in America, 1705, 12, 49, 144 n.; body and duty, 16-17.

Princeton College, 115.

Princeton Repertory, 73.

Princeton Theological Seminary, 50, 53, 73, 156 n.

Protestant and Herald, 121.

Protracted meeting, 114, 115.

Pulpits, construction of, 103.

Quakers, 78.

Ramsey, James G. M., 51.

Rankin, Adam, 20, 27, 30, 32, 106.

Reed, Isaac, 113.

Religious and Literary Intelligencer, 109.

Revivals, in preparation, 21; background of, 22; in Virginia, 23; under leadership of McGready, 23; co-operation of Baptists and Methodists, 24; in North Carolina, 23, 27; adopt camp meeting tactics, 24; spread through Kentucky and Tennessee, 24-25; little effect on upper classes, 25; attitude of General Assembly, 25-26; attitude of Presbyterians, 25-27, 28-29, 31-32, 36; favorable reports, 27-28; excesses, 28; not adapted to Presbyterians, 29; spread and decline of, 147 n.

Rice, David, 12-13, 19, 20, 25-26, 39, 43, 45, 54, 55, 74, 75, 149 n.

Rice, N. L., 166 n.

Rickhow, Jacob, 129 ff.

Robertson, James, 18, 53.

Roosevelt, Theodore, 48.

Sabbath Day violations, 100-101, 113.

Sawtell, Eli N., 42.

Schools, established by Presbyterians, 49 ff.; curriculum of, 50, 52.

Scotch-Irish, first settlement in America, 11; seize lands in Virginia and the Carolinas, 11-12; ascendant element in westward movement, 144 n.

Scott, Thomas F., 122.

Sermons, preparation, 45-46; delivery, 46-47; length, 47.

Session, body and duty, 15-16; book of, 16, 129 ff.

Sevier, John, 40, 63, 99.

Shakers, 29, 32.

Shorter Catechism, 62, 109, 134, 137.

Singing, psalms and hymns, 105-106; Cumberland Presbyterian hymns, 106.

Skillman, Thomas T., 78, 109.

Slavery, critics of church attitude toward, 73; leading ministers on, 73-74; first official resolution on, 74; opponents in Kentucky, 74-76, 78, 80; action of General Assembly of 1818, 75-76; effects of cotton expansion on, 76; leniency of church forces on, 76; interest in colonization, 77; emancipation limited, 77-78; attitude of Cumberland Presbyterian ministers on, 78-79; many ministers emigrate because of, 79; apologists for, 79-80; fear of abolition, 80; action of General Assembly of 1836 and of 1837 toward, 81; church compromises with, 81-82.

Smith, Daniel, 86, 113.

Smith, James, 22, 58.

Smylie, James, 76, 79-80, 85, 129 ff.

Snoddy, Robert H., 43.

South Carolina, 11, 13, 84.

Southern and Western Theological Seminary, 53.

Southampton Insurrection, 84.

Southmayd, D. S., 117.

Stiles, Joseph C., 121.

Stone, Barton W., 31, 32, 55, 75, 150 n.

Stoneites, 29, 31.

Stuart, T. C., 67, 163 n.

Subscription papers, 19, 131 ff., 158 n.

Sunday schools, 107-108.

Synod, body and duty, 17.

Synod of Alabama, 87, 122.

Synod of the Carolinas, 31, 62.

Synod of Genesee, 120.

Synod of Geneva, 120.

Synod of Kentucky, 20, 31, 33, 34, 35, 36, 37, 56-57, 76, 77, 78, 80, 83, 84, 85, 87, 89, 92, 108, 112, 115, 121.

Synod of Mississippi, 80, 81, 84, 85, 87.

Synod of Mississippi and South Alabama, 70, 84, 87, 99.

Synod of Missouri, 71.

Synod of New York, 61, 129.

Synod of New York and Philadelphia, 74, 83.

Synod of Philadelphia, 13, 14, 47, 61.

Synod of Pittsburgh, 62.

Synod of South Carolina and Georgia, 67, 68, 86-87, 88.

Synod of Tennessee, 53, 87, 108, 109, 122.

Synod of Utica, 120.

Synod of West Tennessee, 16, 54, 77, 78, 79, 80, 87, 99, 101, 114, 122.

Synod of Western Reserve, 120.

Tanner, Benjamin T., 90-91.

Taylor, Nathaniel W., 119.

Temperance Herald of the Mississippi Valley, 100.

Temperance societies, 100.

Templin, Terah, 19.

Tennent, William, 49.

Tennessee, Nashville, 18, 19; early settlers, 18 ff., 156; census of 1800, 20; conditions in 1800, 20-21; church losses in, 30-31; Wilson County, 114; Humboldt, 114; effect of division in 1837 in, 122.

Tennessee churches, Bethel, 31; Bethesda, 91; Cabbin Creek, 43; Grassy Valley, 53; Lasting Hope, 97; Maryville, 53; Memphis, 114; Murfreesboro, 94, 98, 100; Mount Bethel, 96; Nashville, 19, 42, 43, 94, 96, 104, 113; Shiloh, 91, 96, 114, 169 n.; Springhill, 53.

Tennessee papers, Knoxville Gazette, 25; Theological Medium, 78, 114; Calvinistic Magazine, 109.

Tennessee presbyteries, Abingdon, 19, 31; Elk, 17; Holston, 122; Shiloh, 41; Union, 65; West Tennessee, 37, 41, 44, 85, 94, 98, 114, 122.

Texas, expansion of church in, 117; first Protestant church in, 181 n.

Theater, 95.

Theft, 98.

Theological Medium, 78, 114.

Theological seminaries, need in the West, 157 n.

Theological Seminary of the Synod of South Carolina and Georgia, 90.

Thompson, John, 31, 32.

Thornwell, James H., 73.

Todd, John, 48, 155 n.

Tokens, Communion, 93, 107, 133.

Toulmin, Harry, 55.

Touro, Judah, 115-16.

Transylvania, state of, 18.
Transylvania College, 45.
Transylvania Seminary, 54, 55-56.
Transylvania University, 55-57.
Treaty of Pontotoc, 69.
Trimble, M. W., 99.
Tusculum Academy, 51.

Ulster Presbyterians, emigrate to America, 11, 141 n.
Union Academy, 53.
United Foreign Missionary Society, 71, 162 n.
University of Nashville, 53-54.
University of Tennessee, 52.

Van Vecten, J., 111.
Virginia, 12, 13, 23.
Virginia churches, Ebbing Spring, 18; New Monmouth, 12; New Providence, 12; Sinking Spring, 18; Timber Ridge, 12.

Wallace, Caleb, 54.
War of 1812, 64, 69, 111, 112.
Washburn, Cephas, 71.
Washington and Lee University, 156 n.

Washington, George, 14, 55, 142 n.
Washington College, in Virginia, 28, 147 n., 156 n.; in Tennessee, 51.
Watauga, state of, 18.
Watt's Psalms, 30, 176 n.
Wayne, John, 65.
Wesley, Charles, 105.
West, the, conditions, 20-21, 115; state of religion, 22, 93, 112-13, 114, 115, 116-17, 118, 121.
Western Luminary, 38, 78, 95, 101, 109.
Westminster Confession of Faith, 15, 28, 32, 33, 34, 36, 47, 93, 109, 137, 160 n.
Westward movement, trials endured in, 18, 21; opportunities in, 93, 111.
Whisky, 43, 98-100, 143 n., 172 n., 173 n.
Williams, Loring S., 68.
Wilson, Hugh, 117.
Wilson, Joshua L., 43, 79, 181 n.
Witherspoon, John, 13, 142 n.
Witherspoon, T. S., 44.
Worcester, Samuel A., 70-71.
Wright, Alfred, 163 n.

Young, John C., 46, 57.

192

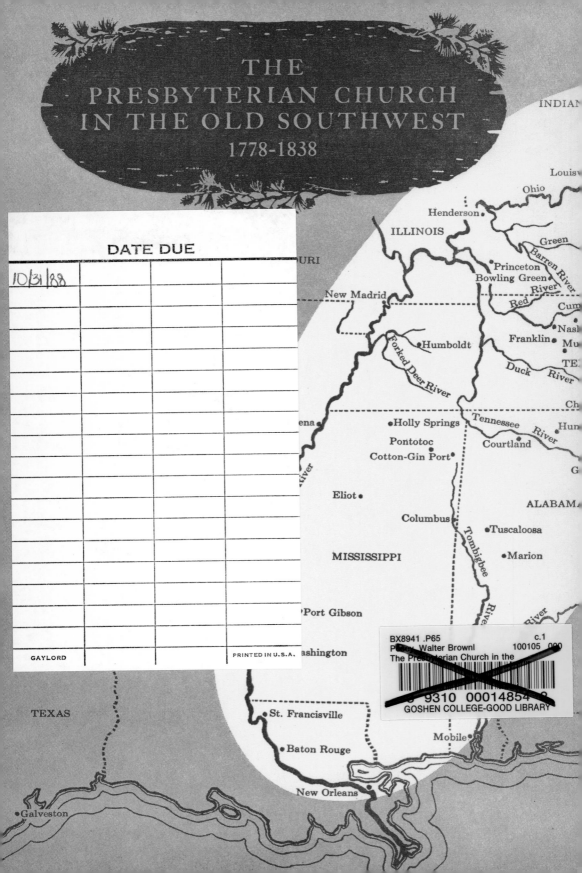

THE PRESBYTERIAN CHURCH IN THE OLD SOUTHWEST

1778-1838

INDIAN

Louis...

Ohio

Henderson

ILLINOIS

Green

Barren River

Princeton

Bowling Green

River

Red

Cum

...URI

Nash

Franklin   Mu

New Madrid

TE...

Duck   River

Humboldt

Forked Deer River

Ch...

...ena

Holly Springs

Tennessee   River

Hun

Pontotoc

Courtland

Cotton-Gin Port

G...

Eliot

ALABAMA

Columbus

Tuscaloosa

MISSISSIPPI

Tombigbee

Marion

...Port Gibson

River

River

...ashington

TEXAS

St. Francisville

Mobile

Baton Rouge

New Orleans

Galveston